T0270566

AN EMANCIPATION

of

THE MIND

ALSO BY MATTHEW STEWART

The 9.9 Percent

Nature's God

The Management Myth

The Courtier and the Heretic

Monturiol's Dream

The Truth about Everything

An EMANCIPATION
of
THE MIND

Radical Philosophy,
the War over Slavery, *and the*
Refounding *of* America

MATTHEW STEWART

W. W. NORTON & COMPANY
Independent Publishers Since 1923

For information about permission to reproduce selections from this book, write to
Permissions, W. W. Norton & Company, Inc., 500 Fifth Avenue, New York, NY 10110

For information about special discounts for bulk purchases, please contact W. W.
Norton Special Sales at specialsales@wwnorton.com or 800-233-4830

Manufacturing by Lakeside Book Company
Book design by Buckley Design
Production manager: Lauren Abbate

ISBN 978-1-324-00362-5

W. W. Norton & Company, Inc., 500 Fifth Avenue, New York, N.Y. 10110
www.wwnorton.com

W. W. Norton & Company Ltd., 15 Carlisle Street, London W1D 3BS

1 2 3 4 5 6 7 8 9 0

CONTENTS

ABOUT THIS BOOK

THE HUMANITIES TODAY are the unhappiest field of study. And one of their vulnerabilities, so easily exploited by the forces arrayed against them, is that the rewards they offer are often difficult to anticipate. You rarely know exactly where you are going until you get there or what unexpected encounter might spark the epiphany. This book is a case in point. The first of several steps on the journey that led to the pages that follow took place when I stumbled upon an unsettlingly familiar reference to a caterpillar.

For too long, I had no very plausible explanation for my decision to pursue graduate study in nineteenth-century German philosophy. Sure, there was something inspiring in the idealism of those old radicals and maybe something intoxicating in their ambition to liberate all humanity with their displays of philosophical virtuosity. I also had no trouble mustering the familiar platitudes about the greatness of great books— the urgent need to promote critical thinking, the imperative to educate a democratic citizenry, the importance of understanding our origins, and all that. But there was something quietly preposterous about devoting so much effort to parsing some old philosophical systems that few people have ever understood and that have long been rusting in the junkyard of the history of ideas. Eventually, I wrote it off as my "Teutonic episode" and moved on.

Then one day I happened to be leafing through some lectures that the great abolitionist Frederick Douglass delivered in the 1860s on the philosophy of photography.[1] I was trying to make sense of the haunting fact that the single largest "industry" in the American republic in the first century or so of its existence consisted in the enslavement, and the breeding for enslavement, of human beings. I was sure that Douglass would offer some perspective on the war over slavery. The detail that snagged my attention, however, was the caterpillar. Douglass refers to that insect to illustrate an argument that our consciousness, too, rarely extends beyond the leaf on which we happen to be feeding. The general point is to advance a surprisingly radical philosophical position according to which the world as we know it, with all its laws, morals, religions, and manners, begins and ends in the human mind, from which follows some bold insights into the struggle over slavery (and the nature of photography, for good measure). But never mind the general point—there will be plenty of time for that. I was pretty sure I knew where that caterpillar came from.

Ludwig Feuerbach (1804–1872) is remembered today, if at all, mainly by a doughty band of leftover Marxists who celebrate him as the "fiery brook" over which one must pass on the road from the reactionary idealism of G. W. F. Hegel (1770–1831) to the revolutionary materialism of Karl Marx (1818–1883). For at least fifteen minutes in the middle of the nineteenth century, however, Feuerbach was famous in his own right as the champion of a new kind of atheism. An intellectual very much of his heady, Germanic milieu, he was incandescent in his pronouncements on freedom and the common interests of humanity. In his own mind and in the opinion of his followers, he was the "philosopher of the future" whose humanism would light the way to a republican tomorrow—a tomorrow that dawned, then cruelly darkened, with the European revolutions of 1848. In the eyes of apologists for the established order, on the other hand, he was the most infamous infidel in an increasingly wicked age. The relevant fact for me, however, was that in one of his most influential books, Feuerbach describes the inherently conditional nature of consciousness with reference to the limited, leaf-centric consciousness of the caterpillar.

That Douglass admired Feuerbach I was able to confirm from the work of other scholars.[2] I could also see it with my own eyes in his last home, now the Frederick Douglass Museum in Washington, D.C., where a bust of the German philosopher glowers from the mantelpiece overlooking Douglass's writing desk. (Next to it sits a bust of David Friedrich Strauss—another German radical of the early nineteenth century, about whom more later.) That Douglass read Feuerbach closely—to a point where he effortlessly appropriated the philosopher's idiosyncratic metaphors—is what the caterpillar seemed to indicate. But what was a freethinking German insect-metaphor doing in the thick of the American struggle over slavery?

A CERTAIN KIND OF philosophical apparition seems to hover just outside the text of Abraham Lincoln's most famous writings. This ghost of philosophers past shows up most vividly in the address Lincoln delivered from the steps of the Capitol at the end of the rainy morning of his second inauguration—the last of his major speeches and the most intriguing. It steps out of the shadows in the most remarkable of the many remarkable sentences in that speech. Because that sentence supplies the axis on which much of the plot of this book turns, I quote it here in full. Referring to "the mighty scourge of war"—"scourge" being a whip of the punitive kind—Lincoln says:[3]

> Yet if God wills that it continue until all the wealth
> piled by the bond-man's two hundred and fifty years
> of unrequited toil shall be sunk, and until every drop
> of blood drawn with the lash shall be paid by another

drawn with the sword, as was said three thousand
years ago, so still it must be said "the judgments of the
Lord are true and righteous altogether."

This small collection of words packs more meaning than do many books. But there is also something strange about the way it combines a line from the Bible ("the judgments of the Lord are true and righteous altogether"; Psalm 19:9) with a bracing vision of natural justice ("every drop of blood"). The pieces began to fit together, however, after I discovered what Frederick Douglass had to say about Lincoln's Second Inaugural Address, and specifically about its most fascinating sentence.

Douglass first took in the speech from the soggy street on the eastern side of the Capitol. That evening he walked up Pennsylvania Avenue to the White House for the after-party. Once he got past the racist bouncers, Lincoln waved him over with warm familiarity. "I saw you in the crowd today, listening to my inaugural address; how did you like it?" the president asked. Douglass demurred, so Lincoln urged him on: "There is no man in the country whose opinion I value more than yours."[4] "Mr. President, that was a sacred effort," Douglass replied.

Douglass stakes out a complex range of views on Lincoln over his long career. In places, he hails the Great Emancipator as "the black man's President"; in other places, he drags the slow-moving, backward-looking "white man's President." But on the topic of this speech, Douglass is unequivocal.[5] In his third and final autobiography, published two decades after that second inauguration, he reproduces almost the entirety of Lincoln's address. Then he adds, "I know not how many times and before how many people I have quoted these solemn words of our martyred President. They struck me at the time, and have seemed to me ever since, to contain more vital substance than I have ever seen compressed in a space so narrow."[6]

In his commentaries on Lincoln's speech, Douglass often circles around that peculiar sentence about the mighty scourge of war. Just weeks after the assassination, he tells a group of mourners, "You remember with what solemn emphasis he expressed [himself] on the fourth of March"—and then recites that specific sentence in full. "Such a sentence I never heard from the lips of any man in his position before," he later says. In his subsequent writings and speeches, he reprises the same sentence so many times that on at least one occasion he slightly misquotes it, substituting "bondage" for "unrequited toil" and "wasted" for "sunk"—evidence that he was confident enough in its meaning that he would repeat it from memory without bothering to consult the original text.[7]

The source of his astonishment, Douglass makes clear, is the distinctive philosophical architecture that quietly sustains Lincoln's words. In the chosen sentence, says Douglass to his audience of mourners, Lincoln offers "a recognition of the operation of inevitable and universal laws as old as eternity. In this [war], he was willing to let justice have its course."[8] Elsewhere Douglass refers to the same "universal laws" as "the self-executing laws of nature." According to this line of thought, the "scourge of war" has come down on the nation in the way that a storm might cause rivers to overflow their banks. The lash and the sword, like the wealth amassed through slavery and the destruction wrought by war, describe a crime that entails its own punishment, as if the misdeed and its consequences were merely distinct aspects of a singular chain of events connected through physical causes and effects. The moral universe Lincoln inhabits in this speech, in Douglass's eyes, will be familiar to students of America's first generation of revolutionaries as one ruled only by "Nature's God."[9]

Douglass's insight into Lincoln's thought world was keen, or so I came to believe. And something in the encounter with

Lincoln reflects back on Douglass, illuminating the way he conceives of the great cause to which he dedicated the better part of his life and energy. In a memorable lecture of 1855, Douglass describes the nature and origins of America's anti-slavery movement in language that strangely anticipates his response to Lincoln's speech ten years later:[10]

> It is an error to speak of this venerable movement as
> a new thing under the sun. The causes producing it,
> and the particles composing it, like the great forces
> of the physical world, fire, steam, and lightning, have
> slumbered in the bosom of nature since the world
> began. . . . Whence are these elements? I trace them to
> nature and to nature's God.

Lincoln's Second Inaugural Address mattered so much to Douglass because Douglass grounded his own activism in the same philosophical vision he saw validated from the Capitol in that speech.

WAS NATURE'S GOD really present in the American struggle over slavery, somewhere in between the lines of Lincoln's address and Douglass's freethinking abolitionism? If so, how did it get there, and what was its role in the conflict?

It isn't surprising that an inquiry into the philosophical origins of America's second revolution should settle on the figure of Theodore Parker. As influential as he was paradoxical, Parker was an icy New Englander with a yen for incendiary political machinations; a Unitarian minister who achieved fame upon his "excommunication" from the Unitarian brotherhood; a universal reformer whose career ultimately came to be defined by his stand on the single issue of slavery; and the militant leader of a genuinely multiracial network of activists who nonetheless trafficked in racial stereotypes. Though typically relegated to the second rank in most accounts today, Parker played a dazzling role in the political, religious, and philosophical dimensions of the American struggle over slavery. Most relevant for this project, he was one of the principal vectors of German philosophy and scholarship in the new republic.

Among Parker's most ardent admirers were Frederick Douglass and Abraham Lincoln. He "had a voice for the slave when nearly all the pulpits of the land were dumb," Douglass writes in his final autobiography. "It was in his pulpit in Roxbury that I delivered my first anti-slavery speech. That its doors opened to me in that dark period was due to him."[11] In a visit to Parker's tomb in Florence, Italy, where the heretic preacher had succumbed to tuberculosis on the eve of the war, Douglass eulogized him as the champion of "the cause of human freedom . . . not only from physical chains but the chains of superstition . . . those which marred and wounded the human soul."[12]

Parker's influence on Lincoln may have been even more consequential. That Lincoln had access to Parker and his writings we know from William Herndon, his sometimes hapless but ever-loyal law partner, sidekick, and biographer. Idolizing Parker almost as much as he did his own boss, Herndon regularly plied Lincoln with copies of the renegade minister's printed speeches and books, and the future president "much admired and approved" of what he read.[13] Lincoln's close friend and fellow Illinoisian Jesse Fell, too, notes the affinity: "If . . . I was called upon to designate an author whose views most nearly represented Mr. Lincoln's . . . I would say that author was Theodore Parker."[14] But we don't need to rely on the judgments of third parties to gauge the significance of the connection. Some of the unforgettable phrases that Lincoln engraved in the American identity—"that government of the people, by the people, for the people shall not perish from the earth"; "a house divided against itself cannot stand"; and even fragments of that sentence from the Second Inaugural Address cited earlier—appear in some form in Parker's works well before making their way into Lincoln's speeches.

The bonds that connected Parker, Douglass, and Lincoln were made of more than a few shared abstractions and turns of phrase. None of the three could be confined to that category of what used to be called "men of ideas" and are now faintly praised as "public intellectuals." They were the kind of thinkers who regularly and enthusiastically converted ideas into action and then held on only to those ideas that make possible some useful change. In their activism, crucially, they interacted with one another in vital ways and, to an extent that is not sufficiently appreciated in the historical narratives, they pushed one another forward. With some astonishingly bold endeavors that converged around the catalyzing figure of John Brown, they together forged some of the critical links in the chain of events that set Lincoln on the path to the presidency, the nation on the path to war, and the Union on the path to victory. Their interconnected story of philosophy-in-action was of the kind that might one day serve as the basis of a movie about the war over slavery.

Maybe the most surprising aspect of the story is the capacity for intellectual growth that its three protagonists shared. Neither Douglass, Lincoln, nor Parker was the same thinker at the end as at the beginning of the struggle. None quite knew where he was going until after getting most of the way there. Their story belongs to a certain genre of philosophical narrative, and it happens to be one that Lincoln himself identifies in his annual message to Congress of December 1862.[15] "The dogmas of the quiet past are inadequate to the stormy present," he says, by way of preparing the nation for the Emancipation Proclamation of the following month. "As our case is new, so must we think anew, and act anew. We must disenthrall ourselves, and then we shall save our country."[16] The same journey toward a new consciousness of things—the kind of story in which caterpillars turn into butterflies, in a manner of speaking—is the moving element of the plot that connects Douglass, Parker, and Lincoln and that explains their impact on the course of the American struggle over slavery.

IT IS OUR GOOD FORTUNE to have outlived those hoary narratives according to which the American Civil War was a "brother against brother" struggle over a "lost cause." Sensible observers today will agree that Lincoln was right when he said, in his Second Inaugural Address, that slavery "was somehow the cause of the war." But how exactly did American slavery lead to war? Why did that war result in emancipation? And what meaning does the war over slavery have for us now, especially in view of the subsequent betrayals of its revolutionary ideals? The chain of events that links Douglass, Parker, and Lincoln invites a fresh perspective on these vital questions.

In the stories that Americans tell themselves today about slavery, many familiar culprits are rightly called to account. Yet one of the prime suspects typically gets a pass. Flip between the original sources and the tales later told, and the omission is blatant: Where did the religion go? In most of the histories, the American religion of the time either is set aside as a thin cover for material interests and prejudices already established or shows up on the side of the angels. But that is not the reality that Douglass, Lincoln, and Parker describe. American Christianity is the "bulwark of slavery,"[17] its "darkest aspect," and "the most difficult to attack," says Douglass.[18] Lincoln effectively agrees. Parker is harsher if anything. While believers could be found on all sides of the conflict, a certain, dominant variety of American religion, in both North and South, was a cornerstone of the slave system, as essential to its workings as the racism with which it colluded.[19] The fundamental aim of the slaveholding oligarchy in initiating the war was not merely to secede but to reorganize the entire Union around an ideology that today we would classify as a form of religious fascism. The fundamental aim of America's antislavery leaders was not only to end slavery but also to defeat this existential threat to democracy itself. Although the slaveholders' project failed, their ideology and the threat it represents live on in successor religious nationalist movements in America and around the world.

Many of the popular narratives today have rightly drawn attention to the grinding racial inequality around which the machinery of American slavery turned. Rather few devote similar attention to the economic inequality that also characterized the slave system. Most take for granted that slavery created wealth by extracting it from one race for the benefit of another. According to Douglass, Lincoln, and Parker, on the other hand, slavery did not create wealth but rather destroyed it, even as it concentrated what was left in ever fewer hands. Considered in the aggregate, it transferred wealth not merely from one race to another but from the many of all races to the few of one race. The resulting economic inequality was at least as consequential as the racial divide—and even to some extent the cause of it. The rise of a parasitic oligarchy, as rich, powerful, arrogant, reckless, and destructive as any aristocracy the world has seen, was the fundamental cause of the escalating disputes preceding the shooting war and of the war itself, or so they (correctly, I think) maintain. The defeat of this oligarchy, conversely, called upon an economic alliance that, however imperfectly and impermanently, united rather than divided races.

The underappreciation of inequality (broadly understood)

helps explain another curious omission in the favored narratives today. There were many heroes in the struggle for emancipation, and quite a few are still celebrated. The military leaders and their battles, for example, could hardly ask for more detailed coverage in the current literature. But whatever happened to the philosophers that Douglass admired and their ideas? The Enlightenment barely figures in most of our histories of the Civil War, and in some versions it is denounced as incurably racist, a merely white Enlightenment to be numbered among the enemies of freedom. Yet, for Douglass, Lincoln, and Parker, philosophy was an indispensable guide on the road to emancipation. They turned to reason because, as they understood it, reason is the great enemy of unreasonable distributions of wealth.[20] They counted the rise of proslavery religion and the deprecation of the Enlightenment among the most pernicious consequences of inequality. The profound philosophical meditations in Lincoln's addresses were not mere ornamentation supplied by some overeducated speechwriter for hire; they are the souvenirs of a very personal philosophical journey that shaped the way he understood and acted in the great conflict over which he presided. Like Douglass, he turned to philosophy not for the validation of dogmas but for the removal of those blinders that prevented a clear view of the struggle for freedom. Their story is about an emancipation of the mind as much as of the body.

That story of philosophical disenthrallment, as they also understood, was an essentially global one. In most of the prevailing narratives, the history of the American struggle over slavery is told in a thoroughly and unselfconsciously American way, as if the new republic inhabited a planet of its own.[21] In recent decades, historians have drawn attention to the global aspects of the trade in slaves and in the fruits of their labor. They have been less alert to the worldwide commerce in ideas. Yet Douglass, Parker, and Lincoln participated in an xx / About This Book

intellectual debate that spanned continents, and they knew it. The freethinking caterpillar that crawled into Douglass's lectures on photography was not there by accident; it is one trace of a global process whose outcome would have been vastly different had the United States indeed been as splendidly isolated as it sometimes imagines itself to be.

The global intellectual context of the American struggle over slavery invites us to think again about the place of the war over slavery in American history. Today the blame for slavery and the bloody conflict to which it gave rise is often laid entirely on America's founders. All you need to know about 1776, some interpreters seem to suggest, is that Thomas Jefferson was a racist slaveholder. The leaders of the antislavery cause, on the other hand, mostly had a very different take on the American founding. The rise of a Christian slave republic in North America, they understood, was the work of a counterrevolutionary movement that originated in the northern states after independence and consciously set itself against the ideals and achievements of the first American Revolution. It would not be the last such counterrevolutionary movement in American history, though it remains the only one to have initiated a major land war against the republic. Although that war took the form of a sectional conflict, it is best understood as a slave insurrection by proxy that evolved naturally into a revolutionary workers' war and ultimately into a fight for the rights of all humans against the rights of property. Notwithstanding their appreciation of the imperfections and mistakes of America's first generation of revolutionaries, Douglass, Lincoln, and Parker saw themselves to the last breath as champions of the American Revolution and Jefferson's Declaration of Independence—because that is what they were.

What bound these leaders of the antislavery cause to America's original founders, however, was not the commitment to preserve the Union but the promise to make the world anew. And, to an extent that remains underappreciated today, they kept that promise. The idea of America that we celebrate today—the one against which we constantly test an imperfect reality—dates not from 1776 or 1787 but from 1865. It is well and good that Washington and the rest of the crowd that populate most of our banknotes are the subject of so much interest today; it is not okay that they appear to rank above the many extraordinary individuals who created the republic as we now know it. The story of America's "refounders"—which is much more than just the story of Lincoln—needs to come first.

The tale this book recounts is therefore quite simple and maybe even old-fashioned. It features heroes and villains, and it tells of triumphs and disappointments—as I think any story about the American struggle over slavery must, so long as there are people who believe that tomorrow can be better than today. It takes for granted that ideas matter, and that they trace a visible arc through the disorder of human history. The plot starts with a radical philosophical vision that originated in early modern Europe and drew its initial strength from its encounters with the people and the circumstances of the New World. This radical vision achieved a limited practical expression in the first American Revolution and then again in successor revolutions, notably in France and Haiti. In the early American republic, its force dissipated under the growing pressure of a counterrevolutionary slaveholding oligarchy. The dream was nonetheless revived and reformulated in the cafés and classrooms of Germany and elsewhere in Europe in the context of the revolutions of 1848. Having suffered defeat there in the reactionary aftermath, it emigrated back across the ocean, often penniless but still burning with ambition, to ignite the refounding of the American republic in its second revolution.

AN EMANCIPATION
of
THE MIND

1

WE MUST DISENTHRALL OURSELVES

Henny's Fate

THE PEOPLE CAME FROM far away to be saved, in covered wagons and oxcarts, by foot, and on a pair of packed steamboats. In the middle of the wide, green field by the bay, they found an altar of wooden planks and an enclosed pen laid with straw where the fallen could kneel. Long rows of seats stretched off into the Maryland sunshine. Family tents ringed the open-air temple, in order of wealth, with the stateliest ones crowding the stage. By the afternoon of the second day, the air was thick with the groans of sinners giving birth to new hopes for life.

At the urging of the preachers and the shouting crowd, Thomas Auld rose clumsily from his seat and staggered into the pen. "Captain" Auld, as he was known, occupied a station of honor in the grassy temple, up in the first rows, closest to the wooden altar. He had no formal claim to the title, but he had once done some sailing on merchant vessels. With a successful shipbuilding business, a good marriage, and a clutch of enslaved humans to his name courtesy of his wife's family, he was counted an important man in the area. As far as the preachers were concerned, he was "a fish quite worth catching, on account of his money and standing," Frederick Douglass recalls.[1]

Frederick Augustus Washington Bailey—he later changed his name to "Douglass"—was fifteen years old at the time of the revival. He stood in the narrow, invisible space that was behind the preachers' stand and marked for colored people. His watchful eyes were locked on Captain Auld, alert for the signs of an interior transformation. He cherished the hope that a saving conversion would make his master "more kind and humane."

Frederick believed that he knew what it meant to be saved.[2] His own journey into the Methodist Church began from a place of genuine desperation. The trouble started when he learned how to read. After his master forbade his mistress from teaching him the alphabet, he took to tracing letters on the sides of boats and trading food with white street-friends for "that more valuable bread of knowledge."[3] Soon he seized a copy of *The Columbian Orator*, a compendium of inspiring speeches intended for pupils of rhetoric. In it he found a thrilling dialogue between a master and a slave, in which the slave argues his way to freedom. But the bread of knowledge had unexpected effects. It opened his eyes to "the horrible pit" but provided "no ladder upon which to get out."[4] It forced him to face the truth: "I AM A SLAVE FOR LIFE!"

The problem, he came to believe, was consciousness itself: "I have often wished myself a beast. I preferred the condition of the meanest reptile to my own. Anything, no matter what, to get rid of thinking! It was this everlasting thinking of my condition that tormented me. There was no getting rid of it." This was the dark moment when, with the help of an itinerant Methodist preacher, Frederick experienced "that change of heart that comes by 'casting all one's care' upon God."[5] Soon he was grasping for answers in the Bible, searching through "the filthy gutters of Baltimore" for "scattered pages from this holy book," which he washed, dried, and scanned closely for directions on the path to salvation.[6]

Captain Auld fell to his knees in the straw. His face turned red, his body shook, his hair flew into disarray. A lonely tear trickled halfway down his cheek, as if uncertain whether it should proceed or return to its source. In that indecisive teardrop, Frederick would later invest his doubts about the proceeding. But the crowd in that moment was utterly convinced. "Captain Auld has come through!" the people exulted.

Captain Auld returned home a new man. In the days and years after the great revival on the Maryland shore, he took to praying "morning, noon, and night." He invited so many holy men to dinner that the residence was soon known to all as "the preachers' home." He rose to become a class leader in the Methodist community and returned frequently to the revival tents to inspire others by his example.

He did not, however, become a kinder and more humane slave master. On the contrary, in Frederick's estimation, Auld proved "much worse after his conversion than before."[7] Before his salvation, Auld had "relied upon his own depravity to shield and sustain him in his savage barbarity; but after his conversion, he found religious sanction and support for his slaveholding cruelty."

Among the enslaved people in the Auld household was Frederick's cousin Henny. She was the girl with the mangled, useless hands. She had fallen into a fire as a child—a not uncommon experience among enslaved children—and now she was good mainly for carrying heavy loads on her back. Auld had always resented Henny. Her deformed hands made her all but useless. Where was the justice in feeding a slave who can't work?

One day after another, the Captain would find Henny guilty of some infraction or malfeasance. In his rage, he would strip off her shirt, tie her up, and tear into her flesh with a heavy cowskin lash. On some mornings, he would whip her before breakfast. He would leave her tied up for several hours, her blood dripping onto the kitchen floor, while he went to his store. Then he would return home to have his dinner, after which he would flay her again along the wounds opened in the morning. Even as he exulted in her screams of pain, the newly pious Auld took to reciting scripture:[8] "He that knoweth his master's will, and doeth it not, shall be beaten with many stripes."

The Captain eventually realized that Henny wouldn't go away unless he sent her away. He decided "to set her adrift to take care of herself." That is, he left her to starve and die.

It would be comforting to suppose that Captain Auld was a man of exceptionally bad character. But Frederick soon discovered to his dismay that, among religious slaveholders especially, he represented the norm. One of the preachers who dined at Auld's high holy table kept an enslaved woman's back "literally raw" for weeks at a time as a way of reminding her of the "master's authority." Another reverend diner boasted of whipping his slaves bloody every Monday morning "in advance of their deserving it." To be fair, there was one preacher in Auld's circle who saw in his religion a moral demand to seek emancipation for the enslaved. But he was an Englishman, and so his eccentricity seemed excusable. Of all slaveholders, Douglass insists, "religious slaveholders are the worst."[9] "The greatest calamity" that can befall a slave, apart from slavery itself, he says, is "being the slave of a religious master."

FIVE YEARS AFTER the slaveholders' revival on the Maryland shore, Frederick Douglass was a free man with a new last name. His first steps in his new life appeared to point in the direction of a career in ministry. He brought with him on his escape certain skills cultivated while preaching to fellow enslaved people in Maryland. He considered himself a Methodist; he did not see "how the northern churches could be responsible for the conduct of southern churches."[10] Upon attending a church service in New Bedford, Massachusetts, however, he experienced a keen disappointment. Seeing that the Black worshippers were relegated to the back row and hearing the minister speak to them with condescension and contempt, he vowed never to return. Next, he joined with a much more congenial Black Methodist congregation. But he abandoned that group, too, "when I found that it consented to the same spirit which held my brethren in chains."[11]

Soon enough, he found his spiritual home. While in Maryland, he had heard his enslavers pronounce the word "abolitionism" in horror and spite. He wasn't sure what the word meant, but he was eager to learn more. If the master class loathed it, he reasoned, it had to be a good thing. He scraped together an understanding through the glimpses of newspapers and stolen snatches of conversation. Enlightenment came when in his first days of freedom he invested the pennies earned as a free laborer in a subscription to William Lloyd Garrison's *The Liberator*. The abolitionist newspaper became "my meat and drink," he writes. "My soul was set all on fire."[12] Upon seeing at last in print that slaveholding is a sin, always and everywhere a sin, how could he not rejoice? Here at last was a "religion" that spoke truth. But what kind of religion was it?

At the age of twenty-three, Douglass attended an abolitionist convention on the island of Nantucket. Though he came alone and, he thought, anonymously, a participant recognized him and asked the flustered young fugitive to share his story. He was so nervous that he later remembered little of his speech. But the audience never forgot. The baritone voice, the imposing physical presence, the fierce wit, and the storytelling talent that would later make Douglass one of the most celebrated orators in a century stocked with outstanding speakers were already in evidence. What a preacher he might have made! He rocketed to the front of the movement with a performance that became a legend even before he sat down. William Lloyd Garrison leaped onto the stage at the end of the talk and thundered, "Have we been listening to the testimony of a piece of property or a man?"

Two years later, Douglass released his *Narrative of the Life of Frederick Douglass*, which included a preface by Garrison and an accompanying letter from fellow abolitionist Wendell Phillips. The book sold 6,000 copies in a flash and catapulted Douglass to national fame. It also revealed something extraordinary—and to many of his readers alarming—about its author's views on religion. Upon the publication of his *Narrative*, large segments of the public were horrified—not by the brutality of the slave system he described but by what they perceived to be his vicious attacks on their holy religion.

The connection between American Christianity and American slavery, Douglass explains in a blistering appendix to his first autobiography, runs far deeper than the hypocrisies of a few bad masters. "I assert most unhesitatingly that the religion of the south is . . . a justifier of the most appalling barbarity . . . a dark shelter under which the darkest, foulest, grossest, and most infernal deeds of slaveholders find the strongest protection," he writes. Then he underscores the rage all over again even as he extends it to the entire nation: "I hate the corrupt, slave-holding, woman-whipping, cradle-robbing, partial and hypocritical Christianity of this land. . . . I am filled with unutterable loathing when I contemplate the religious pomp and show . . . that everywhere surrounds me." American Christianity and slavery are more than merely coresidents of the same country, he makes clear; they operate as partners, each advancing the interests and passions of the other: "Revivals of religion and revivals in the slave-trade go hand in hand. . . . The bitter cries of the heart-broken slave are drowned in the religious shouts of his master."

Americans today are pretty sure that slavery is a bad thing and that religion mostly means well. So they take for granted that the motivations of those who opposed slavery were religious while the religion of those who supported slavery was merely an insincere and hypocritical cover for material interest. Historians, with some notable exceptions, have by and large abetted them in these comforting assumptions. They are quick to associate slavery with acceptable bogeymen such as Western thought, capitalism, and racism, yet they remain strangely silent when the subject turns to the more consequential support slavery found in the religion of its time. "If we try to assign a role to scientific and religious beliefs in the politics of slavery," one popular writer blithely concludes, "we find that nothing like a pattern emerges."[13]

But Frederick Douglass saw a pattern. He did not say that bad slaveholders could be found in equal numbers on both sides of religious belief, or that religious revivals and emancipation go hand in hand, or that religion was just one among many thin excuses that enslavers deployed to their advantage. He said the opposite: that religious slaveholders are "the worst"; that revivals and slavery somehow reinforced each other; that American Christianity was the "bulwark of slavery." He also learned early that this is the hardest aspect of the slave system to discuss in American society.

On the Transient and the Permanent

ON A CHILLY BOSTON AFTERNOON in May 1841, Theodore Parker delivered the sermon that divided his life in two.[14] He had intended only to distinguish the "transient" from the "permanent" in Christianity.[15] But he succeeded mainly in placing himself beyond the pale of right belief, at least in the eyes of his communicants. Just thirty years old, obscure but desperately ambitious, the young Unitarian minister was "disgraced in the eyes of good men as an infidel clergyman," or so said Andrews Norton, Harvard's huffy guardian of Unitarian orthodoxy—who some years previously had unloaded a similar fusillade against Ralph Waldo Emerson.[16]

It all came as something of a surprise. The journey that brought Parker to the crisis began well within the conventions of his time and place. As a child, he stunned the elders by reciting hundreds of lines of Latin poetry and performing other precocious feats of scholarship. From the beginning, he was the kind of student that teachers always say they want. In a single, eighteen-month stretch, the young scholar consumed 270 books in five languages, if his notebooks are to be believed. And that isn't counting the one hundred or so titles checked out from libraries. He won a place at Harvard, but his family couldn't afford to pay for board, so he took his degree from home, pursuing his studies in between barnyard chores. In the first years of his career, he gave every indication that he would deploy his intellectual gifts not to set the world on fire but to add prodigiously to the fireproofing. The Ten Commandments, he inveighs in his student papers, were etched in clay "by God's own finger."[17]

He was also, in the eyes of most of his contemporaries, a thoroughly American figure, of the earthy, New England variety. One of the first things people learned about Parker—one of the first things he told them—is that he was born to a family of American heroes. Over his writing desk hung the firearm with which his grandfather, Captain John Parker, fired "the shot heard 'round the world" at the Battle of Lexington. But his American pedigree had not translated into American money—hence the distance-learning plan at Harvard. Even after his erudition brought him celebrity, the insufferable Brahmins who ruled Boston's highest social circles still thought he carried himself "more like a ploughman than a priest."[18]

Surely the most important part of the backstory of Parker's break with civilized society, however, has to do with the mountain of books that the young minister-scholar so avidly climbed. An excess of reading is rarely good for the orthodox mind, and indeed Theodore's dogged studies appeared to lead him step by step away from the religion of his fellow New Englanders. In letters and diaries, he begins to express contempt for the religion of the established churches—"idol-worshipping" he calls it. He feels something closer to disgust for the religion of the revival camps. He walks away from one of Lyman Beecher's howling tents appalled by the "dark theology" of the revival religion and the "malignant" demon-deity it claims to worship. He decries the "killing letter" of biblical literalism and resolves to set off on his own search for truth. He has every expectation of finding that truth in books, and the books in which he expects to find it turn out to be written mostly in German.[19]

For the unconventional minds of New England, the encounter with German thought was like opening a giant bay window by the sea. A generation of freedom-loving Boston thinkers jumped out that window and sailed to Germany, in their own minds if not in person, and they tossed many Puritan heirlooms overboard along the way. William Emerson, writing to brother Ralph from Germany, describes how his faith evaporated in face of "rapid advances in theology" in Germany, which he takes to be "the results of so many centuries of struggle against ignorance and superstition."[20] The historian George Bancroft returned from Germany sporting a magnificent beard, spouting grand claims about truth and history, and, unforgivably in the eyes of Harvard faculty, kissing acquaintances on both cheeks, continental style. His pupil and companion on the grand tour, Frederic Henry Hedge, the eventual founder of the Transcendental Club, translated and promoted so many Teutonic tomes that he came to be known as "Germanicus Hedge."[21] Up in Vermont, James Marsh became an authority on both the philosopher G. W. F. Hegel (1770–1831) and his bewildering English admirer, Samuel Taylor Coleridge. Much of the real teaching fell to actual Germans, such as the popular émigré and freethinker Karl Follen, who took up a post at Harvard. Meanwhile, Parker's ally George Ripley translated Victor Cousins, the French popularizer of Hegelianism, whose works made it into the offices of young lawyers as far afield as Springfield, Illinois.

To more conventional minds, on the other hand, German thought represented a vulnerable exposure to invading elements. George Edward Ellis, editor of the *Christian Examiner*, the Unitarians' flagship journal, and Parker's stolid classmate at Harvard, warned that Germany was a place of "reckless spirit" and "the mother of all things new and strange."[22] Many of the learned and the comfortable took German thought to be tantamount to atheism or, worse, "that horrible system of pantheism, which owns Spinosa as its originator and Strauss as its modern teacher."[23]

David Friedrich Strauss (1808–1874) was the central figure in this unsettling wave of Germanic radicalism, at least as far as America's religiously oriented intellectuals were concerned. As a twenty-eight-year-old *wunderkind* of German biblical scholarship, Strauss rocked the theological universe with the publication of *Das Leben Jesu, Kritisch Bearbeitet* (*The Life of Jesus, Critically Examined*) in 1836. Parker first laid eyes on Strauss's tome one year after its publication, when his mentor at Harvard, Reverend Henry Walker, took to quietly passing around copies. The reverend might as well have been handing out live rattlesnakes, or so many thought. In his lengthy work, Strauss sets out to show that Jesus was surely a man, not a god, and mostly a question mark. He further maintains that the Gospels consist mainly of myths that are drawn from the minds of early Christians and adapted to the limited understandings of the common people. Stripped of fables about miracles and other improbable events, says Strauss, the essence of Christianity is a simple and true system of morals that answers to reason. True religion, therefore, has no need for the Bible or any other supernatural validation because it is accessible to the individual through experience.[24]

The souvenirs of Parker's first journeys through continental radicalism are all present in the career-destroying sermon of 1841. The "transient" to which Parker refers in his sermon ultimately comes to include the actual words of the Holy Scriptures; the Christian ecclesiastical organizations of the past millennia; and possibly Jesus himself—a genius for sure, but one who might very well be superseded by other, better Jesuses in the future. "If it could be proved . . . that the Gospels were fabrications . . . that Jesus of Nazareth never lived, still Christianity would stand firm, and fear no evil," he says—seemingly oblivious to the conflagration that the brazen counterfactuals would ignite in the minds of the orthodox. He blithely pours fuel on the fire with comparisons between the Gospel stories about Jesus and salacious ancient fables about Hercules and Neptune.

The "permanent," in Parker's version of Christianity, amounts to nothing more than an "absolute, pure morality," an "eternal truth recognized by all religions," expressed in some way by Jesus but by no means grounded in his mere personal authority. Parker is undoubtedly laying the foundations of a modern religion, one that might preserve some sense of spiritual inspiration without ever falling back on revealed authorities or contradicting natural science. He calls it "absolute religion," and he means by that a religion synonymous with individual moral experience—a religion of which every creed in every temple throughout time and space is merely an imperfect and ephemeral representation.

A few more years would pass before Parker could bring himself to admit the impact of his Germanic explorations, and, even then, he continued to distance himself from the unacceptable extreme and hedged in acknowledging his debts. But the more educated of his listeners did not have to work hard to know who or what was to blame for the anticonversion. It was right there in the title of Parker's sermon. Strauss himself had already published a pamphlet under the very same title: "On the Transient and the Permanent in Christianity."[25] In letters to his theological mentors, Parker seems more forthcoming about the source behind his heretical program. "Is not Strauss right?" he asks Dr. Convers Francis. "Do not all the miracles [in the Gospels] belong to the mythical part? The resurrection—is that not also a myth?"[26] (Parker goes on to say that Strauss "goes too far." Then, in a double-backtrack move that would prove to be a distinguishing feature of his theological meditations, he adds: "but pray tell me where is far enough.")

The blowback started within hours on that chilly Boston afternoon. Three ministers who attended the sermon— a Baptist, a Methodist, and a Congregationalist—published a formal protest in which they accused Parker of promulgating gross impieties and an insidious form of deism. A fourth minister proposed that Parker should receive the same treatment as Abner Kneeland, the "cantankerous and inflexible heretic" of Boston who in 1838 was convicted of blasphemy and imprisoned for sixty days.[27] Soon the Boston air was thick with pamphlets and counter-pamphlets decrying the corruption of the city's spiritual life and the imminent demise of its sacred religion. From his exalted station in Cambridge, Andrews Norton singled out Parker as a representative of "the latest form of infidelity," which "takes the Christian name" yet strikes "at the root of faith" and is "founded on the boldest assumptions of blank atheism."[28] Even Parker's sympathizers were bewildered: "He has with justice annihilated the Transient, but where is the Permanent?" asked one.[29]

"I am the most unpopular man in Massachusetts, and am probably more hated than any person in the state who is not connected with politics," Parker would later say. But "I can stand alone." In his own mind, Parker was no more likely to retreat than his grandfather would have been to lay down that flintlock at Lexington. He plunged back into the libraries and bookstores, burned candles through the night, tested the limits of his fragile health, and doubled down on his defiant bid for intellectual martyrdom. "He turned up his nose at their murmuring and stammering, / And cared (shall I say) not a d— for their damning," James Russell Lowell records.[30] It all came out in a series of lectures gathered into a book in 1843: *Discourse of Matters Pertaining to Religion*. As far as the defenders of orthodoxy were concerned, the book was even worse than the sermon. It was "bad, sarcastic, arrogant—contemptuous of what the wise and good call sacred," they said.[31] He had to go.

Formally speaking, there was no church hierarchy from which Parker could be properly ejected. That was just not how the Unitarians operated. The closest thing was the Boston Association of Ministers, a group of which Parker had been a loyal, if somewhat aloof, member from the start of his ministerial career. The case of Theodore Parker now presented the brotherhood with a vexing predicament. How does one excommunicate a Unitarian?

They decided to invite him to tea. In January 1843, twenty of the city's holiest men gathered in the parlor of a Boston townhouse.[32] After a polite interval of cookies and conversation, they put down their cups and turned to face the wayward prelate. Reverend Frothingham denounced Parker's creed as "vehemently deistical, in the worst sense" and "subversive of Christianity." One after another, the preachers followed suit, blasting Parker for his theological deviations and his open disrespect for the brotherhood. Even as teacups trembled and cookies crumbled, the accused valiantly fired back with his own slings and arrows—until the stinging moment when ministers, in order to be cruel, decided to be kind.

An old colleague stood up to say that he would always remember Theodore as a sincere man of the highest moral character. One after another, the assembled ministers offered wistful words of praise, as if to bless him with a living eulogy. It was just too much. Looking into the faces of his former mentors, Parker burst into tears and fled the house.

In the weeks after his melodramatic and somewhat ambiguous separation from the brotherhood, Parker fell ill—a sign of bad things to come. He never formally withdrew from the association. But he never returned either. He was going to fight—also a sign of things to come.

In those first years of saving the world, curiously Parker had remarkably little to say on the subject of slavery—even by the ostrich-like standards of his time. Stray references to "docile negroes" and fiery "Anglo-Saxon blood" hinted at racialist views that he never entirely relinquished.[33] Parker himself later noted that in 1835, when the abolitionist leader William Lloyd Garrison was nearly killed by a mob, "I was so lost in Hebrew, and Grecian, and German metaphysics I barely noticed."[34]

Yet in the years after Parker's sermon from hell, much that seemed permanent in his career proved transient. He soon found himself traveling in a direction opposite to that from which he appeared to have been sent into the world. He emerged as if from a slingshot on a collision course with the most powerful economic and political institution of his time. In the narrative about the struggle over slavery that Americans still prefer to tell themselves, a band of heroes turned to abolitionism after they found religion. In Parker's case, things happened the other way around. He turned to abolitionism after he lost his religion.

A Flame Confined

THE CELEBRATED *philosophe* Denis Diderot ghost-wrote all the liveliest sections in *A History of the Two Indies*, the anticolonial blockbuster that went out under Abbe Guillaume-Thomas Raynal's name in 1780. In a particularly memorable passage, Diderot fantasizes that one day a "great soul in a body of ebony" will arise as "the avenger of nations" and lead the enslaved populations of the world in violent revolution against their imperial oppressors.[35]

At least one such great soul evidently got the message. In August 1791, an unnamed rebel commander and his fellow enslaved people ransacked a plantation in the Caribbean colony of Saint-Domingue (now Haiti). As the horrified owner discovered upon his return to the wreckage, the mysterious slave leader had both a keen sense of humor and a deep appreciation of the Enlightenment. All the books in the library had been scattered save Raynal's *History*, which had been thoughtfully left open on the writing desk at the page where Diderot warns of the "terrible reprisals" that would befall those colonists that did not emancipate their slaves before the avenger arrived.[36]

Among the kind of people who read Raynal, it was understood that the revolution in Haiti was a consequence of the

French Revolution, and that the French Revolution was the invitation to a future first glimpsed in the American Revolution. As Karl Marx (1818–1883) later writes in a letter to President Lincoln, America was where "the first impulse was given for the European revolutions of the eighteenth century."[37] The deep philosophical affinity between the European and American revolutionaries is easy to see in Diderot and Raynal's thought, the genealogy of which could be traced back through Diderot's most prominent intellectual ally, the Franco-German *philosophe* Paul Henri Thiry, Baron d'Holbach (1723–1789), and from thence to Baruch Spinoza (1632–1677) and the other figures of the Radical Enlightenment that figured so significantly in the American Revolution.[38] Diderot filled long sections of Raynal's *History* with reflections on the American experiment, some of them lifted almost verbatim from Thomas Paine's revolutionary pamphlets.

Toussaint L'Ouverture, the inimitable leader of the Haitian Revolution and the man who by all appearances fulfilled Raynal's prophecy, faced down the forces of empire and established the world's first genuinely multiracial republic. He died in a French prison in 1803, but the extraordinary success of the revolution he initiated was the subject of animated coverage in the European press. The *Edinburgh Review* and *Minerva*, among other learned periodicals of the time, reported extensively on events in Haiti in the first years of the nineteenth century. Over in Jena and Berlin, Hegel likely read the news reports from the Caribbean and possibly found in them some inspiration for his musings about dialectics between masters and slaves.[39] For a certain variety of educated Europeans, Haiti was proof that the American dream yet lived—and that it was bolder than anything hitherto imagined.

Perhaps Germany's novelists captured best the thrilling, transgressive spirit that seemed to beckon from across the ocean.[40] The writer Heinrich von Kleist (1777–1811) penned

The Engagement in Santo Domingo, a torrid novella about a tragic, interracial romance set in the Haitian Revolution. The internationally acclaimed novelist Clara Mundt (1814–1873), writing under the nom de plume Luise Mühlbach, set her version of the story in Suriname. In *Aphra Behn*, the eponymous white heroine falls madly, unapologetically in love with the Black rebel leader Oronooko. Aphra declares, "I want to have the right to live according to my own free will. I do not want to ask: Is that proper?"[41]

Among those swept up in the wonder was one of Clara Mundt's friends, a consummately educated and wildly liberated young woman named Ottilie Assing (1819–1884).[42] She knew all about Diderot, Raynal, L'Ouverture, and Spinoza. She thrilled over the pages of Kleist's throbbing "engagement in Santo Domingo." In *Aphra Behn*, Ottilie Assing found her own philosophy of life compressed into a single line. She was the kind of person who rarely asked herself: "Is that proper?" Around the time that she was reading her friend's novel, at any rate, she would have had to answer that question in the negative.

OTTILIE ASSING REBELLED in everything except the commitment to learning in which she was reared from birth. Possibly her father was to blame. He was born at the crest of the Enlightenment and lived out his intellectual life in thrall to Moses Mendelssohn (1729–1786), Gotthold Ephraim Lessing (1729–1781), and the other philosophical heroes of that promising age. More likely, it was her mother. She was the family powerhouse; she wrote poetry and novels, mostly in the high romantic style involving people marrying outside their station. Ottilie's uncle on her mother's side, Karl Varnhagen von Ense (1785–1858), was a fading intellectual luminary and diplomat, erstwhile editor of a poetry journal, and correspondent of the world-famous naturalist and liberal champion Alexander von Humboldt (1769–1859). Aunt Rahel Levine Varnhagen (1771–1833) presided over Berlin's most celebrated literary salon, around which swarmed the likes of Goethe, Hegel, and Heine.

Ottilie and her sister, Ludmilla, grew up in a household where David Friedrich Strauss's latest work counted as good material for dinner-table conversation, and where no friend was ever disinvited for having unusual opinions or indulging in sexual behaviors at odds with the prevailing orthodoxies. Private tutors schooled the girls in English, Latin, and Italian; mother handled the French herself. The one lesson that appeared to stick was that women are equal to everything. Clara Mundt later mused about her friend that if one thought of Ottilie as a man in a woman's body, her behavior suddenly seemed understandable and even admirable.[43]

The household also lived with an open secret, always present, rarely broached. Her father tried to leave his Jewish identity behind by converting to Lutheranism and changing his name from Assur to Assing. But no one in Hamburg let Ottilie forget that she was "half-Jewish," and she did not.

Her parents' deaths just as she approached adulthood set Ottilie free even as they burdened her with her impossible sister, Ludmilla. Equal and opposite in every way, the siblings were unable to enter the same room without combusting and, at the same time, incapable of separating from one another for the rest of their lives. No one in the world understood the other better; no one wanted more to annihilate the other. Ottilie wasn't quite sure what to do with her new freedom except perhaps move with her fratricidal alter ego into her uncle's house in Berlin and become the light around which the intellectual moths of Germany might circle. This turned out to be the first in a series of extravagant failures.

She stabbed herself three times in the chest, so deep that her survival would later be judged a miracle—and then she turned up bleeding in the living room of Clara, the author. Was she trying to write herself into a tragic novella? Brilliant, energetic, and complicated beyond measure, Assing was a gifted mind trapped in a maddening time and place.

Upon returning to Hamburg, sans sister, she became an expert in forbidden love. Possibly she had fallen earlier, while still a teenager, for the actor who became her lover. How could she not love a hero of the stage whose plays mostly featured heroic martyrs engaged in tragic struggles against superstition? By the time she moved in with him in her mid-twenties, he was already married with children. That didn't stop Ottilie from assuming command of the household and even of taking care of the pet dog. The wife, luckily, seemed to like the new arrangement. It was a militantly unconventional ménage, but then again, in the radical circles where Assing moved, the failure to take a lover from the other side of the marital tracks could be interpreted as an indicator of weak artistic potential.

OTTILIE ASSING WAS undoubtedly a creature of her time, or at least of the most interesting part of it. The catastrophic denouement of the French Revolution in the first decades of the nineteenth century came as a colossal disappointment for the heirs of the Enlightenment. Across Europe the reaction triumphed, and the hoped-for rule of the people yielded to the rule of the oligarchs and their priestly allies. And yet, somehow, the iron fist failed to reach very far into the cafés and classrooms. The educated people were denied the freedom of speech, but they spoke anyway. They were ordered not to associate, but they associated anyway. The triumph of the reaction did not put out the brush fires of revolutionary idealism; rather, it dispersed the embers into not-so-secret printing houses, lecture halls, and taverns. The fires of revolution, confined to political irrelevance, now burned in a wistful, almost nostalgic way.

The utopian socialist Étienne Cabet (1788–1856) dreamed up a workers' paradise he called "New Icaria"; his fellow traveler Charles Fourier (1772–1837) talked of turning the oceans into lemonade. The ideas became more extreme even as their impact withered, and so they acquired a degree of unreality. Unhappy people from the middle and lower ranks of viciously stratified societies wanted to know what was happening in faraway places such as America. The dangerous fact of the matter was that the aspirations of the people were far ahead of the political systems under which they were governed.

The political turmoil had a way of destabilizing personal relations, too. The energies once devoted to changing the world were invested in leading exotically curated private lives. The best revenge is to be the way they don't want you to be, or so the would-be revolutionaries consoled themselves; the personal is the political. But it was thin comfort for lives lived under the shadow of grand purposes unfulfilled. This was the story of Ottilie Assing in her first decade of adulthood. She could shake the steely bars of the cage; she just couldn't find a way out.

There was a telling contrast in this respect between Europe and America, where the political system remained formally democratic even as the ruling culture moved in an increasingly reactionary direction. Long after many Americans had shed their revolutionary ideals in the genocidal rush to expel natives from their expanding slave territories across North America, European radicals might raise a drink or two in honor of Thomas Paine in their smoky cafés. In Germany they even went to the trouble of publishing new translations of Paine's work in the 1840s. In counterrevolutionary America, on the other hand, the once-celebrated author of *The Rights of Man* faded into an object of contempt. The mere association with the name of the erstwhile hero of the revolution was often sufficient in polite society to condemn any person or cause. "It took a brave man before the Civil War to confess that he had read the *Age of Reason*," Mark Twain would later observe.[44]

ASSING WAS SPIRALING, and she knew it. Her actor-lover was dying of a mysterious disease, "Christ-like" in the purity of his suffering.[45] Caring for him on his deathbed converted Assing from garden-variety freethought to militant atheism. Where others tried to speak of the mysterious ways of God or fate, she saw only more injustice against which to hurl the rage. At the same time, her rather bourgeois contempt for the bourgeoisie was starting to cause problems. In columns posted in the local press, she turned her pen into a scalpel and eviscerated the many hypocrisies of the good people of Hamburg. Friends smiled politely, but the list of enemies was growing. The one-woman cultural revolution was careening toward its natural end when, to compound the indignity, she lost her savings. Though she denied the rumors for years to come, she had in fact turned most of the pennies of the modest inheritance that had funded her freedom over to her dying lover in the name of art. Ottilie Assing rejected all religion, but at bottom she was a believer.

She bought some brushes and briefly tried on a career as a painter, but that fell flat with a stash of unconvincing landscapes and snickers from her sister. Then, over at the aptly titled *Morning Paper for Educated Readers*, a friendly newspaper editor, somehow alert to her talents, assigned her a story. The topic would be emigration. She went down to the Hamburg docks, inspected belowdecks, and there discovered more injustice. The shivering masses from all over central Europe were huddled in steerage, yearning for a breath of fresh air. In later reporting, she describes one ninety-six-day voyage in which 38 of 286 passengers died en route to the land of the free.[46]

How bad must things be in Germany, she wondered on behalf of her educated readers, if so many were willing to endure so much just to escape? How brightly must that dream shine on the other side of the ocean? The more she thought about it, the more it all began to make sense. In the eyes of the people she would leave behind, it would surely look like a desperate flight from failure. In her own eyes, on the other hand, it was a chance to reinvent herself, perhaps to wreak herself on the world in a lasting way. Ottilie Assing, it turns out, wasn't just a believer; she believed in America.

Billy Finds a Hero

THE FOUNDERS OF the College of Illinois in Jacksonville cherished the wish that their new institution would become the Yale of the West. But they placed rather few of those hopes on their student William Herndon. Billy, as everyone called him, was a child of the Kentucky frontier. He was the favorite son of Archer Herndon, a hard-driving, Jacksonian Democrat who rose all the way from tavern keeper to political boss in the backroom of the tavern. Within weeks of his arrival at school, Billy had earned a reputation as the kind of student who laughs like a horse, drinks like a hog, and babbles like a creek after a rainstorm. The historian Carl Sandburg, surveying the variety of interests that moved him in later life, describes Herndon as "extraordinarily picturesque" and "often lovable."[47] By his own lights, he was, in those early years, an "undisciplined, uneducated, wild man."[48] Something changed for Billy, however, on the day that the news came up from down river about the murder of Elijah Parish Lovejoy.

In the fall of 1837, in the ambitious town of Alton, Illinois, a printing press arrived on a river steamer. The press belonged to Elijah Parish Lovejoy, and he intended to use it to spread his abolitionist message across the new state and beyond. A minister and graduate of the Princeton Theological Seminary, but hardly a paragon of its official, slavery-friendly creed, Lovejoy had taken up journalism five years previously while residing just over the state border in St. Louis, Missouri. Starting not far from the political center, his political views marched step by step toward the abolitionist extreme. First, he joined the popular, church-based colonization movement and advocated shipping America's enslaved and free Black population off to Africa. Then, he argued for emancipation within the District of Columbia. By the time his press made it to Alton, he was calling for immediate and universal abolition. He was a hated man, at least among the proslavery Democrats who dominated much of society in the lower Midwest. Vigilante mobs had already seized three of his printing presses and tossed them into the Mississippi River.

On November 6, 1837, a drunken, proslavery mob gathered outside the grocer's warehouse in Alton where Lovejoy's press had been temporarily stored. The newspaperman and his supporters stayed inside to guard their truth machine. Fueled with liberal doses of whiskey, the mob was working itself up to do something. They decided to torch the warehouse. Then they fired shots through the windows. Lovejoy's men returned fire, killing one of the attackers. During a lull in the shooting, Lovejoy opened the door to the warehouse. Five bullets slammed into his body. Within minutes he was dead, and a martyr to the abolitionist cause was born.

The news of Lovejoy's murder radiated across the nation in a way that his own words never had. It hit "like the shock of an earthquake throughout the continent," said John Quincy Adams in Boston.[49] Over in Hudson, Ohio, the tremors prompted a thirty-seven-year-old tanner named John Brown to stand up at a community dinner and take a vow. "Here, before God, in the presence of these witnesses, from this time, I consecrate my life to the destruction of slavery," he said—and in his case, it turns out, he really meant it.[50] In Springfield, Illinois, a young lawyer named Abraham Lincoln soon referred to the incident in a grand speech on the future of democracy in America: "Whenever the vicious portion of the population shall be permitted to gather in the hundreds and thousands, and burn churches, ravage and rob provision stores, throw printing presses into rivers, shoot editors, and hang and burn obnoxious persons at pleasure and with impunity, depend upon it, this government cannot last."[51]

The news struck with notable force upriver, in the college town of Jacksonville, Illinois. On the day the news broke, the faculty, students, and many townsfolk—quite a few of whom were proslavery people—spilled onto the campus for what promised to be a loud and possibly dangerous event. At the urging of his fellow students, Billy somehow found his way to the podium, or so the story goes.[52] Standing before the crowd, to his own surprise, he hotly denounced Lovejoy's murder and took a brave stand for "abolitionism pure and simple," to cite his later words. The students, at least, were thrilled. They bundled him off the stage, hoisted him on their shoulders, and paraded him across campus. "I hope to live to see the day when I can make slavery feel my influence. That shall be *the one* object of my life," he wrote to his friend Theodore Parker in later life.[53] "I intended to sow seeds which should never die."

Though Billy had always hated slavery, he would later say, the act of declaring himself in such a public way appears to have made him his own man, in a manner of speaking. It also changed his approach to his studies. Though his academic performance remained unspectacular, he developed a thirst for the literature of the Enlightenment—a thirst that ultimately led him to amass one of the finest private libraries in Illinois. In his case—unlike those of Theodore Parker or Frederick Douglass, for example—the denunciation of slavery and the embrace of radical philosophy happened simultaneously.

Archer Herndon was not amused. His political views were not subtle—the enemy was ever and always "abolition federal silk-stocking ruffle-shirt Whigs"—and his parenting techniques were hardly more delicate. Seeing that his son was becoming "a damned abolitionist pup" and suspecting that the College of Illinois was permeated with the woke ideology of its day, or what he called "the virus of abolitionism," he yanked Billy out of school after only one year and formally disinherited him. "But it was too late," Herndon later writes. "My soul had absorbed too much of what my father believed was rank poison."[54] For good measure, Billy joined the party his father detested, the Whigs. The once-favored son was now clearly in search of a new source of authority.

He landed in Springfield, Illinois, where he at first seemed to pursue a career in "ruin, drink, and women," or so the locals sneered. Then he took a job in Joshua Speed's general store and met Speed's roommate in the apartment upstairs, a gangly lawyer nine years his senior named Abraham. A sense of order at last entered Billy's life. He joined a debating society called the Young Men's Lyceum, found a wife, had children, and took to studying fourteen hours a day, after work, for his law degree. In 1843, when Lincoln at last offered him the opportunity to become his junior law partner, he broke down in tears. "I thought I was in Heaven," he later writes. "I was a drunkard until he took me."[55]

They were an odd pair. One was phlegmatic and reserved, the other ebullient and unstable.[56] Both could move a crowd, but while Abe did so with eloquent conviction, Billy relied more on verbal combustion and common-denominator humor. Lincoln always knew that Herndon would be the last man to desert him, just as he was always the last man at Herndon's side. One of the very few occasions on which the financially lackadaisical Lincoln was known to care about collecting a debt he was owed was on the day he needed to raise bail to spring Billy out of jail after an unbalanced night on the town had ended in broken glass and hard feelings. Bloodied, bleary, and incoherent, Billy stumbled into the street, certain only that he was no good and that Abe would rescue him anyway.

It is possible that Abe and Billy bonded over shared anti-slavery sentiments. Lincoln would later say that he could not recall a time when he was not opposed to slavery. It is certain that they bonded over a shared philosophical sensibility. The aspect of their friendship that perhaps mattered most, and yet has escaped the attention it deserves, was their common interest in a certain kind of reading. "When I met a young man of my profession who had high hopes—who was pure—who had an idea of the perfection of purposes who was really religious in God's view of actual religion, I gave him a list of books and made him buy them," Herndon writes to Parker, with Lincoln in mind. "You know probably what I recommended and whose books."[57] The bookshelf in Lincoln's office, curated by Herndon, ultimately included such spine-stiffening authors as John Stuart Mill, the Hegelian popularizer Victor Cousins, Ludwig Feuerbach, David Friedrich Strauss, and, of course, Theodore Parker.

Educating Abraham

HERNDON WAS PLANTING SEEDS in a mind that had already proved itself receptive, and he knew as much. Lincoln's path to freedom began with books. He, too, broke with an unyielding father and looked for answers in the written word. Among the first of the books to come his way, curiously, was *The Columbian Orator*, the same one that had inspired the young Frederick Bailey with its dialogues between masters and slaves. Shakespeare and Robert Burns, the Scottish scoffer, were not far behind. Later in life, Lincoln became a more sporadic reader, dipping into books strategically, pondering them deeply, and finishing them rarely. He had few scholarly pretensions. Yet his writing was of a literary quality that can only be acquired through careful attention to the written word.

At a low moment in his political career, when he was hoping to reinvent himself as a public lecturer, he quietly underscored the vital importance of his early reading. The human mind comes into the world in the thrall of superstition, unaware of its capacity for freedom, he explains in one lecture. "To emancipate the mind from this false and under estimate [*sic*] of itself, is the great task which printing came into the world to perform."[58] Not many years would pass before Lincoln would tell Congress and the nation that "we must disenthrall ourselves"—as nobody else will do it for us.

According to Herndon's report, Lincoln had disenthralled himself of superstitious belief even before he landed in Springfield. At the age of twenty-two, when he moved to New Salem, Illinois, Lincoln immediately fell in with an "exceedingly liberal" crowd, Herndon reports. Copies of Thomas Paine's *The Age of Reason* and of Constantin François de Chasseboeuf, Comte de Volney's (1757–1820) *Ruins, or Meditations on the Revolutions of Empires*, "passed from hand to hand," and many gleeful evenings were spent demolishing the established religion.[59]

Lincoln probably read Volney's *Ruins* in the translation started by Thomas Jefferson and finished by his fellow founder Joel Barlow. In that work, Volney offers a simplified version of the pantheistic philosophy descended from the Radical Enlightenment. Most of Volney's contemporaries identified him (correctly) as a kind of atheist. All things are part of an interconnected whole answering to the laws of reason and nature, Volney explains, "a fatality of causes and effects, whose chain extends from the smallest atom to the greatest of heavenly bodies."[60] The idea of "free will" is a misconception, for all activity of the mind and body answers to motives: "Self-preservation, the desire of happiness, and an aversion to pain, are the essential and primary powers that nature creatively imposed upon man."[61] The individual soul is just a temporary fiction that emerges from and returns to an ocean of existence that ebbs and flows and operates entirely according to the laws of nature. Within this thoroughly natural universe, Volney concludes, "God" reduces to just a word for "the force in things, the moving principle, the soul of the world."[62] The philosophical vision here is borrowed quite directly from the *Système de la nature* of d'Holbach, who cribbed much of it from the Anglo-Irish iconoclast John Toland (1670–1722), who relied above all on the work of Spinoza.

Also worthy of note is that Volney kicked off the great anthropological debate about the role of Black Africans in the creation of human civilization. On his travels to Egypt, Volney had toured the extraordinary ruins and noted well what he took to be the African features of the Sphinx. "A people now forgotten discovered, while others were yet barbarians, the elements of the arts and sciences," he marvels in *Ruins*. "A race of men now rejected from society for their *sable skin* and *frizzled hair*, founded on the study of the laws of nature, those civil and religious systems which still govern the universe."[63] Such antiracist musings added greatly to Volney's infamy in some quarters—surely the white man created civilization, the critics ranted in response—even as they likely added to the frisson in New Salem.

Paine, of course, was a hero of the American Revolution who later made himself quite unpopular with his slashing religious skepticism. In *The Age of Reason*, he announces that "of all the systems of religion that were ever invented, there is none more derogatory to the Almighty, more unedifying to man, more repugnant to reason, and more contradictory to itself than this thing called Christianity." Less well appreciated, even today, is that Paine's deism is largely a gloss on the same, essentially atheistic tradition of rationalist philosophy on which Volney draws.

The young Lincoln was every bit as radical as his sources, according to Herndon's report; he studied Paine and Volney intensively and "assimilated them into his being."[64] In a conversation recorded by Herndon, Lincoln emphatically embraces the "fatalism" for which Volney was famous: "There are no accidents in my philosophy. Every effect must have its cause. The past is the cause of the present, and the present will be the cause of the future. All these are links in the endless chain stretching from the finite to the infinite."[65] Lincoln adds that "there is no freedom of the will" and that "there was no conscious action of man that was not motivated by some motive, first, last, and always."[66] In sum, Herndon concludes, the early Lincoln "was an elevated pantheist, doubting the immortality of the soul as the Christian world understand that term. He believed that the soul lost its identity and was immortal as a force."[67] In such a universe there is no room for a personal God.

Lincoln's attachment to Paine shows up at unexpected moments in his life. At a busy point in his legal career, for example, Lincoln somehow found the time to study a six-volume edition of Euclid. Paine, as it happens, singles out Euclid's work as the "one ancient book that authoritatively challenges universal consent and belief."[68] In his first notable speech, delivered at the Young Men's Lyceum shortly after Lovejoy's murder, Lincoln quietly pays homage to the author of *The Age of Reason* when he argues that, in the face of threats to American democracy, "reason—cold, calculating, unimpassioned reason—must form all the materials of our future support and defense."[69]

In the free-spirited taverns of New Salem, Lincoln counted as a radical. He would open up chapters of the Bible only to rip the contents to shreds. He "was enthusiastic in his infidelity," one of Herndon's informants records; so much so, that sometimes he appeared to reject all belief in a god: "He went far that way, and shocked me."[70] The late-night philosophizing, says Herndon, prompted Lincoln to write "an extended essay—called by many, a book" intended "to prove that the Bible . . . was not God's revelation, and that Jesus Christ was not the son of God."[71] It was, blatantly, Paine and Volney redux, and it evidently became the subject of animated discussion among the friendly infidels of New Salem. But then one of the young heretics, strangely aware of the existential threat to

Lincoln's future political career, grabbed the manuscript and thrust it into the fire, or so the story has it. The great man's "political future was secure," Herndon intones, "but his infidelity and skeptical views were not diminished."[72]

Given the extraordinary (and continuing) efforts to reinvent Lincoln as a Bible-believing Christian, it is worth stressing that the available evidence amply confirms Herndon's assessment concerning his persistent infidelity. Lincoln's first law partner, John T. Stuart (1807–1885), recalls that Lincoln was "an avowed and open infidel, and sometimes bordered on atheism."[73] Colonel Ward Hill Lamon (1828–1893), who was introduced to Lincoln by Stuart and became Lincoln's law partner and friend and his bodyguard at the White House, agrees that Lincoln in his youth was known as an "infidel." "Never in all [the] time" that he knew Lincoln, Lamon adds, "did he let fall from his lips or his pen an expression which remotely implied the slightest faith in Jesus as the son of God and the Savior of men." David Davis (1815–1886), another ally from Illinois and Lincoln's campaign manager in 1860 and the executor of his estate, arrives at the same conclusion: "He had no faith in the Christian sense of the term." Upon hearing stories that the president supposedly experienced certain epiphanies during the war and especially upon the death of his son, Lincoln's friend and private secretary during his presidency, the German-born John G. Nicolay (1832–1901), flatly declared: "Mr. Lincoln did not, to my knowledge, in any way change his religious ideas, opinions, or beliefs from the time he left Springfield to the day of his death."

Lincoln's close, lifelong friend Jesse Fell (1808–1887), elaborating on the subject in a long letter written after Lincoln's death, concludes that, on central Christian doctrines such as the divinity of Jesus, the infallibility of written revelation, the innate depravity of man, the performance of miracles, future rewards and punishments, and "many other subjects,"

Lincoln "held opinions utterly at variance with what are usually taught in the Church" and that "in the estimation of most believers, would place him outside the Christian pale." In 1854, Fell reports, "he asked me to erase the word God from a speech and read it to him for criticism, because my language indicated a personal God, whereas he insisted that no such personality ever existed."

THE MOST INTERESTING insight we have into Lincoln's infidelity, however, comes from his own pen, and it establishes the pattern for everything that follows in his religious career. In Lincoln's 1846 campaign for Congress, his opponent, a well-known evangelical preacher named Peter Cartwright, sought political advantage by spreading the word that Lincoln was an unbeliever. The charge was accurate, of course, but Lincoln knew he had to defend himself. So, he sat down at his law desk and composed a handbill.[74]

"That I am not a member of any Christian Church is true," Lincoln announces in that publication. It is a remarkable concession and politically costly. It is also accurate: he had not been, and never would be, a member of any Christian congregation. "He was never a technical Christian," his widow later writes.

He then goes on to characterize the charge that has "got into circulation" as "in substance that I am an open scoffer at Christianity."[75] But this is a misdirection. The charge from Cartwright was that Lincoln was an unbeliever, not that he was an open scoffer at it.

Having reframed the charge as a matter of his public performances rather than his private beliefs, Lincoln moves to deny that he has "spoken with intentional disrespect" of religion in general or Christianity in particular. He adds for emphasis that he himself would never vote for "an *open* enemy of, and *scoffer* at, religion," for no man has "the right to insult the feelings, and injure the morals, of the community in which he may live" [emphasis added]. In a letter to a newspaper editor accompanying the handbill, he swears that "Cartwright never heard me utter a word in any way indicating my opinions in religious matters, in his life."[76] All of which proves nothing about Lincoln's actual beliefs other than that he believed—or wished it to be believed—that he had succeeded in keeping his mouth shut.

Lincoln goes on to cede even more territory in this curious handbill. "It is true that in early life I was inclined to believe in what I understand is called the 'Doctrine of Necessity'—that is, that the human mind is impelled to action, or held in rest by, some power, over which the mind has no control," he writes. The confession is strangely gratuitous in its detail. Why not simply say that he toyed with some unnamed bad beliefs as a young man before seeing the light? Herndon's records make clear that Lincoln had indeed embraced a form of necessitarianism, and not just when he was young. Lincoln attempts to mitigate the confession with the same dodge about the alleged openness of his infidelity. He never "publicly" maintained this "Doctrine of Necessity" and has since stopped arguing for it, he writes. Which of course does little to address the matter of his belief—or the fact he continued to believe in the doctrine for the rest of his life.

Lincoln's next move is even more subtle. "I have always understood this same opinion to be held by several of the Christian denominations," he writes. This is partially true—but mostly Pinocchios. Calvinism does involve a doctrine of predestination that looks like Lincoln's "Doctrine of Necessity"—provided one stands at a distance and puts on fuzzy glasses. Calvinist determinism follows from the absolute will of God, who knows exactly what he wants and orders it to happen at every instant, and it specifically involves God's

choices regarding the fate of individual souls. Lincoln's necessitarianism, on the other hand, arises from the laws of nature,
not the will of God, and it involves doubts about the very existence of the soul as anything other than an emergent and temporary mode of nature. Lincoln's necessitarianism, in short,
is un-Calvinist, heretical, and derived from Enlightenment
sources such as Volney's *Ruins*.

From Lincoln's strange handbill, we learn that Lincoln
was an infidel, at least in his own mind. We also learn, most
important, that he understood very well the political peril of
any candid admission of nonbelief. And we can gather that
he was oddly determined not to say anything that was downright false. His insistence that he is not and never would be a
"scoffer" was surely his best shot at taming public fears about
his religion without risking the hit to his credibility that might
follow from a hypocritical profession of faith.

In retrospect, the Cartwright handbill marks a decisive
change, not in Lincoln's beliefs but in his willingness to share
them. The reckless infidel of the New Salem tavern has disap-
peared; a far more circumspect and reserved character has
taken his place. The new Lincoln is not going to go the way of
Lovejoy or Paine. Although many steps remained to be taken,
the journey from youthful infidelity to the leadership of America's antislavery movement had begun.

2

SOMEHOW THE CAUSE OF THE WAR

Ghost Ships

"YOU KNOW WHAT IS a swine-driver?" Frederick Douglass thundered at a meeting of the Rochester Ladies' Anti-Slavery Society on July 5, 1852. "I will show you a man-driver. You will see one of these human flesh-jobbers, armed with a pistol, whip, and bowie knife, driving a company of a hundred men, women, and children from the Potomac to the slave-market in New Orleans."[1] Douglass knew firsthand about the pain that these forced marches trailed in their wake. Frederick had an older brother named Perry, four years his senior. Though the boys grew up on different plantations, separated by slavery, they snatched some opportunities to play together. Perry would lift young Frederick on his shoulders and protect him from the bigger boys. Then one day Perry was gone. Only forty years later did Douglass learn that slavery had sent Perry first to a plantation nearby, and much later to Texas. In 1867, the brothers enjoyed a bittersweet reunion in New York.

The grim columns of enslaved humans that trudged across the nation's expanding road network had not always been a feature of American slavery. In earlier centuries, American enslavers relied on a supply of African captives hauled across the ocean in the blood-stained hulls of wooden slave ships. By the time Frederick was born, however, that old system was a distant memory. A new logic of slavery reigned in the United States, and its most visible manifestation was these shackled processions that traversed the American landscape like a land-born fleet of spectral slave ships. In the end, 1 million Americans were forcibly transferred from the breeding states of the Upper South to the new states and territories to the south and west—far more than the number of captives unloaded on American docks in the Atlantic slave trade.[2] Most were young adults and children, ripped away from the only family they knew, never to be seen or heard from again.

In the prevailing narratives of American history, an often-unexamined assumption is that slavery was the same thing in 1860 as it was in 1776 and even in 1619. Yet slavery on the eve of America's second revolution was not a legacy institution left over from some earlier age, nor was it the inevitable product of timeless prejudices. Slavery had evolved. The new slavery was grander in scope, more calculated in its cruelty, and far more deeply integrated in the political economy of the new republic than anything that its original creators could have imagined. The new ghost ships that plied the country roads could not be excused as a crime perpetrated on the inhabitants of another continent; they were a kind of horror that the new nation, with its immense efficiency and creativity, had learned to inflict on its own children.

In the decades immediately after the American Revolution, the slaveholding elite of the South commandeered a counter-revolutionary movement—one that began with northern elites, set itself against the ideals of the first American Revolution, and continued in different forms through the present. This counterrevolution passed through a critical inflection point around the time that young Frederick Douglass lost his older brother and certainly not later than the year that Theodore Parker delivered his exploding sermon. It eventually became the basis for a comprehensive, alternative vision for the republic as it entered modernity. America's slaveholders resolved for war against American democracy not to defend the past but to claim the future. It is not possible to explain the crisis the antislavery leaders confronted—even in its philosophical and religious dimensions—without understanding something of the colossal transformation in the economic and political fundamentals of American slavery during the rise of the counter-revolutionary slave republic.[3]

THE INTENTIONS OF America's founders can be the subject of endless debate, but their predictions about slavery are much easier to establish. Frederick Douglass writes that the founders of the republic "regarded slavery as an expiring and doomed system, destined to speedily disappear,"[4] and Theodore Parker agrees.[5] Senator William Seward of New York, who later served in the Lincoln administration, echoes the sentiment: "Our forefathers . . . regarded the existence of the servile system in so many states with shame and sorrow." Lincoln himself adds that Americans can prove that slavery is "a vast moral evil" simply by consulting "the writings of those who gave us the blessings of liberty." From the beginning of the republic, Lincoln concludes, this evil was thought to be "in the course of ultimate extinction."[6]

A survey of the founders shows that Lincoln and his fellow antislavery leaders were largely correct. Gouverneur Morris of New York, the author of the preamble of the Constitution, was not staking out a controversial position but summarizing common wisdom when he described slavery as "a nefarious institution" that would have to be eliminated soon.[7] Southern elites, too, had a generally dour view on the institution and its future. Virginia slaveholder James Madison insisted on keeping any explicit mention of slavery out of the Constitution, in anticipation of a future in which the mention of the practice would be considered shameful. George Washington signaled his view on the future of the institution by providing in his will for the emancipation of all 317 of his slaves—a step he evidently could not bring himself to take while still alive.

The tangled and, no doubt, self-serving view of many of America's founders on the eventual fate of slavery received its most famous expression in the first, unapproved draft of the Declaration of Independence, in which Thomas Jefferson—another Virginia slaveholder—rails against the "CHRISTIAN KING" of England, perhaps too histrionically, for having foisted upon hapless American settlers an institution that even infidel powers found abhorrent. Somehow—and to be sure, there were heavy doses of self-induced blindness and hypocrisy packed into that "somehow"—this barbaric relic of the age of superstition[8] would have to be left behind in the march of human progress.

The Constitution of 1787 notoriously failed to supply that "somehow." With its thin euphemisms ("person bound to service," "all other persons"), the first American Constitution provided plenty of ammunition to those who wished to see in it a defense of slavery. But it also supplied principles and specifics in support of an antislavery interpretation. The most telling of these specifics, for many people at the time, was the clause that prohibited Congress from banning the slave trade until 1808. As James Wilson pointed out, the text here acknowledges that Congress has the power (and presumably the inclination) to cut off what all at the time took to be the lifeblood of the slave system.[9] Some proslavery leaders saw the danger—and then couched their opposition to the Constitution in the gloomy language about slavery that prevailed at the time. "Slavery is detested," said Patrick Henry at the Virginia State Convention, standing in opposition to the federal Constitution. "We feel its fatal effects—we deplore it with all the feeling of humanity." Then comes the catch: "As much as I deplore slavery, I see that prudence forbids its abolition." [10]

With the benefit of hindsight, the fatal flaw in that first Constitution from an antislavery perspective had less to do with its specific pronouncements on slavery than with the political system to which it gave rise. That political system, with its ill-defined judiciary, divided and unrepresentative legislature, isolated executive, and unresolved claims of state sovereignty, ultimately proved unable to resolve the defining crisis of the new republic. As slavery began to consume the republic from within, the Constitution yielded a politics incapable of eliminating the problem short of a civil war. Consequently, the first American constitutional system was a catastrophic failure. (And the chief failing of the second system, which emerged after the Civil War, is that it disguised its revolutionary features as amendments; by refusing to use its new powers to transform fully the states and the society that had sponsored rebellion, it surrendered in peace much of what it had gained in war.)

Events in the northern states of the Union after the revolution at first suggested that the founders were largely correct in their forecast for slavery. In fits and starts, through a combination of court cases and state laws, all the northern states banned slavery and emancipated their enslaved populations by the early decades of the nineteenth century (though pockets of enslavement remained in New Jersey almost up to the war). The Northwest Ordinance of 1787 further extended the ban on slavery to all parts north of the Ohio River.

The course of events in the southern states of the Union, however, soon falsified the founders' projections for the future of slavery. New technology, in the form of the invention of the cotton gin in 1793, coupled with the breeding of higher-yield varieties of cotton, rescued slavery from its crumbling economic prospects and had the further consequence of aligning the southern slave interests around a single crop: "King Cotton." In between its two revolutions, the American republic increased its cotton production a hundredfold, from a mere 20 million pounds per year to 2 billion pounds per year.[11] By the 1840s, cotton accounted for about half of all American exports in dollar value, and American cotton captured about two-thirds of the global market. In 1850, two-thirds of America's enslaved population lived on cotton plantations. In those regions where cotton cultivation was not viable, with few exceptions, slavery also proved not viable.[12] (A similar kind of concentration, not coincidentally, occurred in the other two major slaveholding nations in the Western Hemisphere—in Cuba, with sugar, and in Brazil, with coffee.)

The founders' assumption that the African slave trade was the essential precondition of the slave system was also soon refuted on the ground. By the time Congress banned the slave trade in 1808, at the first constitutionally permissible moment, southern elites had discovered that the "natural increase" of the domestic slave population was more than enough to sustain the practice. Between 1776 and 1860, the population of enslaved persons in the United States multiplied from something over half a million to nearly 4 million, and all but a minuscule fraction of those alive in 1860 were born in the United States and its territories.

The new slavery received a further, critical boost with what one may call the financialization of the business of human enslavement. Energetic bankers and traders, with the assistance of friendly regulators and state governments, created highly liquid markets in "human capital," and these markets allowed enslavers to leverage the value of their property to amass still more property. By the time the shooting war started, mortgages on slave property rested at the bottom of one of the largest piles of credit in the global financial system.

The classification of enslaved people as a species of capital had the further benefit for enslavers of identifying the defense of slavery with the defense of property rights. In a nation that saw itself as having been born in a struggle against an empire that trampled on its citizens' property rights, this was a powerful rhetorical tool.[13]

This financialization, combined with the new agricultural technology, the rapid expansion of slave territory, the rising premium for enslaved women of reproductive age, and the growing efficacy of the nationalized systems for controlling the enslaved population, resulted in a substantial appreciation in the price of enslaved people. At an average of roughly $1,000 per person, the total capital value of America's enslaved population in 1860 was estimated as high as $4 billion, or roughly 75 percent of annual GDP.[14] On paper, at least, the slave "industry" was worth more than the railroad industry, the banking industry, the mining sector, or any other single sector of the American economy. If slavery today represented a comparable proportion of GDP, its capitalization would exceed the combined total of that of the energy sector, the communications sector, and the entire industrial sector, from aerospace to construction to transportation.

This paper capital, to be clear, was not of the kind that corresponds to productive investment in anything of real value. It was wealth in name only. It amounted to a stash of licenses enforced at public expense to expropriate the product of other people's labor.[15] The value of slave "capital" was a measure not of the system's economic productivity but of its ability to prevent enslaved people from either receiving fair compensation for or absconding with the fruits of their own efforts. A writer of the time captures something of the unintended irony of calling it capital in the first place: "It is fearful to think that the capital of a nation, and its almost sole means of support, and worth, as it is rated, $4,000,000,000, is on *legs,* and may some morning turn up missing."[16]

The most obvious feature of the new slavery was its regional character. Even as the northern states abandoned slavery, the proportion of the population in slavery increased in the South, from under 40 percent to 45 percent in Georgia and as high as 57 percent in South Carolina. Step by step, the South evolved from a society that practiced slavery into a slave society. And yet this regional character was in some sense misleading. As King Cotton grew in power, it sought to remake the nation— and even the rest of the world—in its image.[17]

The extraordinary success of American enslavers in converting coerced labor into cheap cotton elevated the American South into a significant player in the global economy. A symbiosis emerged between the enslavers and the emerging industrialists of the world. The "lords of the loom" and the "lords of the lash," as the abolitionists put it, worked together to keep wages artificially low and raw materials artificially abundant, and both sought state and social support for their unstable oligopolies. The factories of New England and old England alike were scarcely conceivable without the produce of enslaved people in the American South. Karl Marx[18] offers a characteristically sharp summary of the globalization process: "Without slavery you have no cotton; without cotton, you have no industry. It is slavery that has given the colonies their value; it is the colonies that have created world trade, and it is world trade that is the pre-condition of large-scale industry."[19] America's planters sought to lead the world by example, too. Collaborating with elites in Cuba, South America, and Asia, they worked to internationalize the plantation system, often by enslaving local peoples rather than importing them, and envisioning a global anti-abolitionist alliance.[20] In 1860, southern elites chose war over Lincoln because, in their estimation, the Union needed King Cotton more than it needed the Union.

To those who benefited (or thought they benefited) from the arrangement, the founders' view that slavery was a necessary evil limping toward an inglorious end no longer seemed credible or even safe. The new dispensation on slavery announced itself to the world in the celebrated speech that John Calhoun delivered on the Senate floor in 1837. Explicitly taking aim at America's misguided founders, Calhoun announced that slavery is "a positive good"—good for the slave, good for the master, good for the nation.[21]

The change in attitudes toward slavery—and toward the founders themselves—is distinctly visible across the generations of leading southern families. George Mason, a Virginia slaveholder and the author of the Virginia Declaration of Rights, which inspired both the Declaration of Independence and the Bill of Rights, confided to private manuscripts that slavery is a "slow poison, which is daily contaminating the minds and morals of our people."[22] With eerie prescience, he issued a dire forecast in the language of the deistic Enlightenment: "As nations can not be rewarded or punished in the next world, they must be in this. . . . By an inevitable chain of causes and effects, providence punishes national sins by national calamities."[23] When his grandson, US senator James Murray Mason—a gopher for John Calhoun and a militant advocate for the Fugitive Slave Act—discovered the elder Mason's writings in the attic one day, he was horrified. Having inherited none of George's broody erudition, James was, in the estimation of the German immigrant and later US senator, Carl Schurz, "a sluggish intellect, spurred into activity by an overweening self-conceit."[24] He turned the papers over to the historian George Bancroft, but with the proviso that none of his grandfather's deviant thoughts and gloomy prognostications on the peculiar institution be published, lest they fall into "profane or depraved hands."[25]

The New Slavery

TWO ATTRIBUTES OF the new slavery would prove decisive for the fate of the American republic, and the first and most important was the extreme concentration of (paper) wealth that it produced. In the most widely accepted narratives today, it is taken for granted that the only kind of inequality that mattered in the slave system was racial inequality. In the eyes of the more acute contemporaries, on the other hand, the economic inequality to which slavery gave rise was at least as grievous and ultimately more consequential. "The influence of slavery in creating property for the whites out of robbery of the blacks was hardly more marked than its influence in concentrating the property of the whites in the hands of a comparatively few of their number," notes Charles Spahr, one of the first economic analysts to study the distribution of wealth in the United States.[26] "The rebellion of 1861 was a rebellion of the richer classes in America against the rule of the middle classes."

The extreme rise in economic inequality was a direct consequence of the business model of the new slavery. The financialization of the slave system effectively turned so-called investments in plantations into a device for placing immense, publicly subsidized bets on the cotton market. For would-be members of the planter class, the business plan for glory was to buy the slaves when the price of human capital was relatively low and then sell the cotton when the price was high. The credit system made it possible to leverage these gambles enormously. When the bets went bad—and, by virtue of the odds in all such markets, the silent majority was destined to go bad—the would-be planters retreated into whiskey and bankruptcy. The history of the Old South is littered with the untold stories of erstwhile enslavers who stumbled into a financial ditch on the road to riches. Even among those enslavers who survived the slings and arrows of the marketplace, the financial anxieties were immense and yielded a clinical level of stress-induced behaviors. When the bets came through, on the other hand, the winnings were extraordinary and the sense of accomplishment grand. Wade Hampton of South Carolina (1754–1835) was among the first to grasp the logic of this winner-take-all system, and he rapidly built up a fortune that made him the wealthiest planter in America. Naturally, there followed a Wade Hampton II, a Wade Hampton III, and a clan that dominated South Carolina politics up to the twentieth century.

By 1860, two-thirds of all estates in the entire nation worth more than $100,000 were in the hands of southern white men, even while the northern states had twice the total population and more than double the economic product—and even while the median southern white person was substantially poorer than the median northerner.[27] In a list of the richest Americans at the time, 70 percent of the names are slaveholding southern white planters—even while less than 25 percent of the nation's white population lived in the South. The North had twice as many farms as the South, but the South had seven times as many mega farms of 500 acres or more. Between 1830 and 1860, even as the ratio of the enslaved population to the free population rose, the proportion of free southern households owning slaves declined precipitously from 36 to 25 percent. The concentration of slave ownership among the part of the population that held slaves, moreover, was extreme. The bottom 70 percent of slaveholders could claim only a tenth of the enslaved population. The top tenth of the enslavers held about half of the enslaved, and the bulk of that fraction was in the hands of a top 1 or 2 percent of interconnected families that often owned multiple plantations in more than one state. At the end of the war, according to the Radical Republican congressional leader Thaddeus Stevens, the richest 70,000 individuals in the South—something less than the top 1 percent of the regional population—owned 394 million acres, or 85 percent of all private land. W. E. B. Du Bois narrowed the ranks of privilege still further. Of the 390,000 households that held title in other humans, he estimated, only about "8,000 really ruled the South."

In brief, the control over the southern economy—and by extension over national political life—rested in the hands of the top 0.1 percent of an extremely skewed distribution of wealth. The new oligarchy rapidly acquired the habits of mind and body that have characterized aristocracies since the Bronze Age. It was a clique notorious for its arrogance, recklessness, violent tendencies, fatuous "honor" codes, gender fetishes, thinly disguised polygamy, and sexual aggression.[28]

The second decisive attribute of the new slavery was its resolute commitment to expansionism. For proslavery leaders, taking slavery into new states, territories, and even continents was just as important as—indeed, it was the same thing as—protecting slavery within their own states. To perceptive contemporaries, the expansionist logic of the new slavery was its most salient—and dangerous—aspect. In an issue of 1859, *The Economist* of London concludes that it is a matter of economic law that slavery is doomed to extinction wherever it cannot expand.[29] Karl Marx makes the same point: "Were it to relinquish its plans of conquest, the Southern Confederacy would relinquish its capacity to live and the purpose of secession."[30] The English political philosopher John Stuart Mill agrees: "The day when slavery can no longer extend itself, is the day of its doom. The slave-owners know this, and it is the cause of their fury."[31]

Proslavery theorists perceived the same expansionary imperative, though for them it glowed with desire. They indulged fantasies of a slave empire extending across the North American continent, down through Cuba, Central America, and maybe tomorrow the entire Western Hemisphere. Where direct conquest was not feasible, they worked to form an international power bloc with other slaveholding republics, notably in Brazil and the Caribbean, whom they regarded as their natural allies in a global war against abolitionism, socialism, and secular liberalism in all its forms.[32]

Fear was a motivating cause of the expansionary drive—as it was of almost everything the slaveholding oligarchy did—a fear rooted in the knowledge that the enslaved population did not wish to be enslaved.[33] No specter haunted the slaveholders more than "the terror of Santo Domingo," as they referred to the Haitian Revolution. Denmark Vesey's attempted revolt in 1822 and Nat Turner's bloody uprising of 1831 further stoked the fears of slave rebellion. Proslavery theorists became convinced that one should never allow the slave population to outnumber the free population within any state or region. Senator Robert Toombs of Georgia draws the critical conclusion: "without a great increase in Slave territory, either the slaves must be permitted to flee from the whites, or the whites must flee from the slaves."[34]

The expansionary drive also drew some of its energy from a competition internal to the population of enslavers. As the plantation owners in the older states consolidated their grip on their local landscapes, the sons of the same enslavers, along with other, ambitious white people in the vicinity, realized that they had no future in their home territories. To the frustrated, would-be enslavers of the old dominions, the next slave territory over smelled of opportunity. The breeders of enslaved people, one could say, overproduced their own breed of enslavers, who were then compelled to seek markets to the south and west where they might export themselves along with their growing "capital" stock.

The expansionist logic was also, to some degree, the response to an ecological predicament that also followed from the inner dynamic of the slave system itself and its inegalitarian tendency. In an 1851 book on American agriculture, Royal Society member James F. W. Johnston reports that Virginia had exhausted its soil through slave-plantation agriculture. As historian Walter Johnson explains, "Cotton mono-cropping stripped the land of vegetation [and] leached out its fertility."[35] The planters could have rotated the land away from their favored cash crop, of course, but the source of the cash was not the land itself but the publicly subsidized enslaved labor that worked upon it, and no crop could compete with cotton in monetizing that labor. Their only realistic hope of joining the oligarchy was to place more and bigger bets on cotton. Land in the South was cheap because the disguised subsidies for enslaved labor had the inevitable effect of devaluing every other factor of production, including land.

In the final analysis, all the forces driving the expansionary imperative—demographic, ecological, and financial—were fundamentally consequences of the winner-take-all logic of the new slavery. Extreme inequality, as in so many other contexts throughout history, generated a profound instability that could only be resolved through aggression. The rise of the new aristocracy and the resulting expansionism were the driving force of American politics during the first nine decades of the

American republic. For the families that found themselves at the top of the slaveholding oligarchy, the only viable political alternative to personal calamity was to wrest control of the nation from a democratic people and invest it with the lords of property.

Slaves are only as valuable as one's ability to recapture them, the oligarchs reasoned, and that ability depends on one's control of a political system that will enforce one's property claims.[36] The slaveholders (like their ideological heirs today) talked a good game about "limited government," but when it came to enforcing the claims to the species of property they favored, they demanded public subsidies and government without limits. As Lincoln and Douglass among many others pointed out, the great complaint of southern slaveholders throughout the 1850s was not that their states' rights were being denied but that the states' rights of the northern states were being asserted in defiance of federal law concerning the rendition of fugitives.

Up until the election of 1860, the slaveholding interests were spectacularly successful in securing the requisite degree of control over both federal and state governments. In the state governments of the South, the oligarchs had little trouble pushing the common people out and capturing the legislative and executive branches of government for themselves.[37] In the effort to dominate the national political system, the slaveholders were able to count on the antidemocratic aspects of the US Constitution: the overrepresentation of small states in the Senate and the Electoral College; the growing power of an unelected judiciary; and the absence of meaningful checks on the corruption of state governments. To maintain control in the future, however, proslavery strategists grasped that it would be essential to continue to add (eminently corruptible) slave states to the Union at least as rapidly as free states were added. The American republic's push to the west—and with it the program of ethnic cleansing and genocide aimed at native populations—was in significant measure the consequence of American slaveholders' efforts to secure a controlling interest in the federal government.

The Birth of a
New Aristocracy

THE FLEET OF GHOST SHIPS that Frederick Douglass saw crossing the American countryside was the crowning economic
achievement of the new American slavery. Through the miracle
of the free market, the United States had re-created a domestic
version of the old international slave trade, complete with an
internal division of labor. The states of the Upper South, having accumulated more enslaved children than could be used
in their overtilled fields, retooled themselves as producers and
exporters of individuals marked from birth for enslavement,
while the newer slave states to the south and west converted
that human livestock into piles of cotton. "The chief pecuniary
resource in the Border States," the abolitionist Moncure Conway bluntly observes, was "the breeding of slaves."[38]

The most obvious cultural achievement of the new slavery
was to entrench the racism on which American slavery had
always relied. Under the expansionary regime, the indispensable key to the profitability of the slave system for its overlords,
especially in the upper states of the Old South, lay in the enslavers' political control over the wombs of enslaved women. To

claim title to the offspring of the enslaved was to claim police powers over the future streams of income in the expanding territory of the slave republic. Race thus became doubly important even as it went national in scope. It was a means not just of marking out certain individuals for lives of coerced labor but also of monetizing the value of their indefinite—and ultimately even more lucrative—posterity. It was on this account that the legal status of free Blacks in the South deteriorated markedly in the antebellum period, with new and harsh penalties for educating free Blacks, for example, passing into law. It was for the same reason that enslaving the Irish—a prospect that some proslavery ideologues seriously entertained—proved unworkable. Lacking the superficial traits that might visibly distinguish them from their unenslaved cousins, their children could blend back into the general population too easily.

The other, obvious cultural achievement of the new slavery was to diminish the legacy of the Enlightenment that the new republic inherited from its first generation of revolutionaries and replace it with a certain variety of religion. If human beings are equal in nature and reason, then their systematic subordination can only happen by appeal to something unreasonable and supernatural. The slaveholding oligarchy understood this inference as a practical matter long before the antislavery side grasped it in theory. The new religion that swept America in the first half of the nineteenth century, together with the growing attacks on the same Enlightenment that had figured in the founding of the republic, had their roots in this fact. Inequality was, as it always has been in human history, the enemy of reason.

Within a span of three or perhaps four generations, in brief, through the often-unremarked advances of a counterrevolutionary movement, the new slavery had brought forth on the American continent an oligarchy that was as wealthy and powerful relative to its subordinate free and enslaved populations as any ancient aristocracy. This oligarchy, moreover, had a clear vision for the future, as radical as it was ambitious. It dreamed of one nation, united under God and Bible, dedicated to the proposition that all people are *not* created equal and consecrated to the protection of property in man. The rise of this oligarchy—even more than the establishment of a racialized caste system that sustained its economic power—was the driving force of American history in the first half of the nineteenth century. It was the root cause of that racialized caste system, of the new religion, of the attack on the Enlightenment, and of the suppression of speech—just as it was the root cause of the war over slavery. The so-called Civil War was at bottom the continuation of an earlier, ongoing war of property against humanity.

The categorical, forward-looking aspect of proslavery vision is perhaps most visible in the least-appreciated aspect of the Constitution of the Confederacy; namely, that it offers every state of the Old Union the opportunity to join the new Confederacy. As Karl Marx accurately observes at the outset of the war, the goal of the Confederacy "is supplanting the hitherto existing democracy by the unrestricted oligarchy of 300,000 slaveholders."[39] Should the Confederates succeed, he says, "what would in fact take place would not be a dissolution of the Union, but a *reorganization* of it, a *reorganization on the basis of slavery*, under the recognized control of the slaveholding oligarchy."[40] In an 1864 letter to Abraham Lincoln, Marx asserts without fear of contradiction that the war began when "an oligarchy of 300,000 slaveholders dared to inscribe for the first time in the annals of the world, 'slavery' on the banner of Armed Revolt."[41]

Theodore Parker was aware of the threat from the slaveholding oligarchy well before Marx—and even before either side took up arms in earnest. In an 1854 lecture, he sums up the rise of the American slave republic this way:[42] "In fifteen States of America, three hundred thousand proprietors own thirteen hundred millions of money invested in men. In virtue thereof they control the legislation of their own States . . . they keep the poor white man from political power, from comfort, from the natural means of education and religion; they destroy his self-respect, and leave him nothing but his body; from the poorest of the poor, they take away his body itself. Next, they control the legislation of America; they make the President, they appoint the Supreme Court, they control the Senate, the Representatives; they determine the domestic and foreign policy of the nation. Finally, they affect the laws of all the other sixteen States." In sum: "the consolidated property of one-eightieth part of the population controls all the rest."

In his Second Inaugural Address, Lincoln points a finger directly at this oligarchy. "All knew that this interest [in slavery] was somehow the cause of the war. To strengthen, perpetuate, and extend this interest [in slavery] was the object for which the insurgents would rend the Union," he says. Yet there is a significant subtlety in Lincoln's "somehow." He does not say—for it would not be true—that all participants fought explicitly over slavery. The North, he acknowledges, entered the war with the stated goal of preserving the Union only. The South could and did appeal to any number of grievances. What Lincoln says with his "somehow" is that the many issues and motives that divided the nation were at bottom rooted in the fact of slavery—whether the participants did or (as was often the case) did not understand this consciously. Slavery, he came to think, is a kind of ongoing war—a war of the enslavers against the enslaved, of white against Black, of an oligarchy against humanity—and the armed conflict known as the Civil War was a continuation of this war by other means.

Abolitionists had long been saying as much. The Black abolitionist John Rock anticipates the logic of Lincoln's "somehow" in a spirited talk delivered in Boston in 1862: "The present war is an effort to nationalize, perpetuate, and extend slavery in this country. In short, slavery is the cause of the war: I might say, is the war itself."

3

BOTH
READ THE
SAME BIBLE

The Slaveholder's Sermon

AT THE PEAK of his career as an itinerant abolitionist speaker, Frederick Douglass was a familiar enough figure on the circuit that the old-timers showed up demanding to hear all the greatest hits. According to Elizabeth Cady Stanton, one of the favorites came to be known as "the Slaveholder's Sermon." Someone in the crowd would shout out, "Douglass, give us the sermon!" And Douglass, if he judged the time was right, would deliver.

He would stride across the stage, "grand in his physical proportions, majestic in his wrath," Stanton recalls, and "with keen wit and satire" that "completely magnetized" his audience, he would take on the high-pitched voice and campy mannerisms of a southern Methodist preacher. To the white people in the stalls, he would offer assurances in a voice shrill with sanctimony that the Bible guarantees their right—even their duty—to hold slaves. Gesturing toward the Black people in the audience, who were often relegated to the balcony, he would say that their "gnarly hands" were made for work in the fields, while the delicate bodies of their masters were better suited for the task of thinking. But not to worry! It was all part of the plan. "You too my friends have souls of infinite value—souls that will live in endless happiness or misery in eternity. Oh, labor diligently to make your calling and election sure. Oh, receive into your souls these words of the holy apostle—'Servants be obedient to your masters.'"[1]

Douglass had an exceptional (and today underappreciated) gift for humor—the transcriptions of his speeches are regularly punctuated with brackets recording the laughter of his audiences—and the crowds roared with delight at the pitch-perfect impersonations of priestly hypocrisy. But Douglass specialized in the kind of humor that sparkles over seething rage, the kind that people turn to when reason alone proves insufficient to move the target. That was the joke in the Slaveholder's Sermon. To get the joke, of course, you had to know, as his audiences did, something about the state of religion in America at the time.

FREDERICK DOUGLASS IS a big name today, and his deeds and writings are rightly studied in intimate detail. But in the years of the Slaveholder's Sermon, he was the troll. Literate Americans would have known much less about him than about the individuals he was satirizing. They would have been far more likely to have followed the career and studied the works of, for example, James Henley Thornwell (1812–1862), the great champion of Presbyterianism in South Carolina.

Orphaned along with his brother at a young age, James Henley Thornwell rose from modest beginnings as the son of an overseer on a slave plantation to become a proud slaveholder in his own right. He graduated from the Harvard Divinity School at nineteen and then married Nancy Witherspoon, the great-niece of Princeton founder and enslaver John Witherspoon, but he always preferred life in the South. He became the president of South Carolina College (later the University of South Carolina), the leading theologian of the Southern

Presbyterian Church, and "the most learned of the learned" in Boston historian George Bancroft's estimation.[2] Perhaps his finest hour was when he served as a theological adviser of sorts to President Jefferson Davis and the Congress of the Confederate States of America.

Perhaps owing to his grief-stricken childhood, Thornwell identified with the enslaved people in a certain way. He insisted on seeing them as brothers, at least in his own mind. It was for this very reason, as he explained it, that he loathed the abolitionists so much. How dare they threaten to take slaves away from their happy station in the households of their benevolent masters? He was the prince of the proslavery theology, both by natural disposition and in virtue of his dominance of the Southern Presbyterian Church. The Presbyterians, in both their southern and northern branches, were counted at the time as the most assertive of America's ecclesiastical hierarchies.

Thornwell's many pamphlets and published sermons swayed a national audience in his time. It is a shame that they are so little read today. It's not that they have any great merit as exercises in wisdom or theology. It's that one can hardly understand the point of Douglass's "sermon" absent an appreciation of the seriousness, the depth, and the breadth of the vision that men like Thornwell offered on the future of Christian America.

A Christian Nation Awakes

ACCORDING TO THE story that many Americans like to believe, America's God landed on Plymouth Rock around 1620 and kept His name and distinctive personality down to the present. Yet the American religious landscape has always been a scene of change, and no change in American religious history has been as far-reaching as the transformation that took place over the same decades that the proslavery counterrevolution was remaking the American political world. These parallel upheavals in religious life and the political economy of the American slave republic were hardly unconnected.[3] Indeed, one was the spiritual face of the other.

The extraordinary dimensions of the American religious transformation in the first nine decades of the new republic are easily visible in the basic statistics on the nation's evolving church networks.[4] Between 1770 and 1860, the Methodists exploded across the American countryside, rising from a mere 20 churches to an astonishing 19,883. The Baptists mushroomed from 150 to 12,150 churches over the same period, and the hardline Presbyterians climbed from 500 to 6,406. At the same time, the older, established denominations that set the religious tone in the colonial period—the

Congregationalists and Anglican-Episcopalians—plummeted to minority status. Their numbers remained roughly static at little more than 2,000 churches each through the period, even as the national population boomed.

In the southern states, the evangelical surge was both larger and more intense. By 1850, Methodists and Baptists had carved pews enough in the southern landscape to seat 74 percent of the population. The comparable figure in the North was 44 percent.[5] In the northern states, immigration added still further to the religious landscape. While the variety of the northern churches stretched out along a spectrum that extended all the way to a small irreligious extreme overseen by the likes of Theodore Parker, southern religion came in only a handful of colors, all starkly similar. There were no Theodore Parkers in the South (or at any rate none that were not forced to flee for safety in short order).[6]

In most of its many iterations, the new American religion insisted on the absolute, prior necessity of opening one's eyes to that "horrible pit" of one's own utter worthlessness. The crime was always personal; the atonement usually involved absolute submission. Consequently, the dominant theology gravitated around a deity conceived as an extraordinarily willful being, beneficent beyond reason and cruel beyond imagining. Certain that such a deity's commands must be as unalterable as they are unconditional, it naturally inclined toward the conviction that the truth could be read directly from a single, unchanging, written source. Though the proliferating sects contradicted one another promiscuously in their interpretations of the Bible, they were as one in their conviction that the Good Book contains the indisputable answer to every question worth asking. The harsh theology and the biblical literalism reinforced the other, central feature of the emerging American religion; namely, its totalizing character with respect to social and political life. The value of everything was to be measured in terms of its conformity with religion. And everyone had to have some. The most unacceptable category of belief was nonbelief.

The popular face of the new religion was that of charismatic preachers such as Lyman Beecher, Charles Grandison Finney, Lorenzo Dow, and a gaggle of less well-remembered names who should be classed as religious entrepreneurs, if not hucksters. Masters of campground theatrics, these energetic revivalists dispensed with elaborate robes and hierarchical pretensions and instead made use of folksy props, shouting fits, bad jokes, and the blunt language of ordinary people. Their religion was individualistic, egalitarian, and fragmented in ways that would hardly have been conceivable before the American Revolution. Their theology was informal to the point of heresy, for, as Finney often repeated, it was far more important to bring a man to Jesus than to worry about what sort of doctrinal baggage was needed to get him there. The looseness in the outer garments, however, should not be confused for a looseness within. The message only grew starker as the talk grew hipper: be saved or be damned.

In the prevailing narratives today, the popular aspect of the new American religion is often taken as evidence of its democratic character.[7] But this is to confuse its demotic tools with democratic intent. The tools of the new religion indeed made use of the language and passions of ordinary people. But the intent—at least among those in a position to lead rather than follow the movement—was something different. As the counterrevolution progressed, it would become clear that the aim was not to advance democracy but to tame and suppress it.

In any survey of the complex trajectory of religion in America, the one fact of which any historian may be certain is that Thomas Jefferson and his fellow enlightened founders were as wrong about the future of religion in the new republic as they were about the future of slavery. Along with Thomas Paine,

George Washington, Ethan Allen, and many of the leaders of America's first generation of revolutionaries, Jefferson predicted that the old and hard forms of religion would soften in the new democracy and a liberal, enlightened creed would sweep the land. Everyone born in his time, Jefferson suggested, would die a Unitarian. Paine and Allen thought they might all become deists.[8] Ironically, the fear and loathing of deism itself came close to becoming the defining feature of the new American religion. Of course, it may also have been the case that the founders were correct in their reasoning but wrong in their premise. Possibly an increasingly democratic republic would have become increasingly liberal in religion. The error was to have supposed falsely that the American republic, in the throes of its first counterrevolution, was becoming increasingly democratic.

IN THE IMMEDIATE aftermath of the storming of the Bastille in 1789, most Americans exulted in the impending triumph of a revolution that they rightly saw as the sequel to their own. "From that bright spark which first illumed these lands / See Europe kindling, as the blaze expands," writes Philip Freneau, the famed "poet of the American Revolution," in a lyrical paean to the French Revolution penned in 1790.[9] "This ball of liberty . . . will roll around the globe," says his friend and political ally Thomas Jefferson as late as 1795. "It is our glory that we first put it into motion."[10] Across the new republic, democratic clubs bloomed, where high-spirited men (and a few women) from all walks raised toasts to Thomas Paine, to the revolution in France, and to the power of the people around the world. Shays's Rebellion of 1786–1787 in western Massachusetts and the Whiskey Rebellion of 1791–1794 in western Pennsylvania, both of which featured settlers saddled with intolerable debt and tax burdens, indicated that even the American people might rise up in revolutions of their own against the established order.

Two overlapping classes of Americans found these developments particularly alarming: men with property to defend and men in clerical robes. Both were plentiful and powerful in New England. It would be hard to overstate the degree of fear and loathing with which the high and the holy in the North regarded the popular rebellions at home and abroad. When the French Revolution descended into terror and dictatorship, the privileged classes felt the grim satisfaction of seeing their worst fears confirmed. Conservative leaders began to suggest that the root of the trouble lay in the very idea of democracy. A Boston Federalist cleric named David Osgood, aghast at the "monstrously disorderly" behavior during Pennsylvania's Whiskey Rebellion, captured the spirit of the reaction when he inveighed that the "great body of people" should be "content to move in their sphere and not meddle with things too high for them."[11] The writer of *The Ecclesiastical History of Essex County* in Massachusetts speaks of the revolutionary years as "the darkest period in the whole history of these churches" and asserts that the American Revolution itself "opened a flood gate of iniquity."[12] From the beginning, the counterrevolution claimed to speak for true religion against the horrors of both the new irreligion and the American democracy. Incessantly and invariably, they slammed the emerging class of rebellious nonbelievers with an epithet that has since gone out of fashion: infidels.

The counterrevolutionary impulse quickly settled its fury on familiar bogeymen. Ethan Allen, the outsized hero of Fort Ticonderoga, put a target on his back when he self-published his freethinking *Oracles of Reason* in 1787. Here was the proof that infidelity and democracy were made for each other like whiskey and the hand flask. (The clerics' vituperations may explain Lincoln's fondness for humorous anecdotes about old Ethan.)[13] The Comte de Volney, whose atheism was compounded by his Frenchness, also became persona non grata. Ultimately, it was Thomas Paine who made for the perfect representative of the terrorist infidel. Notwithstanding his vital role in precipitating American independence, Paine let his true colors fly in his vehemently anti-Christian *Age of Reason*, which had to be smuggled in from France, where its author had gotten mixed up with the worst of the Jacobins.

Jedidiah Morse, a founder of the Andover Theological Seminary and father of the telegraph inventor, was a typical representative of this first phase of the counterrevolution. He couldn't make up his mind which was worse: the "deplorable" Thomas Paine or the proliferating democratic clubs, which he saw as "the greatest danger which, at present, threatens the peace and liberties of our country." When Volney visited the United States in person in 1797, at Jefferson's warm invitation, Morse spoke for many powerful clerics in New England in naming the French philosopher as one of the "agents of Satan."[14]

Alexander Hamilton delighted over the political capital to be made out of this kind of hate. In the campaign against Jefferson, he sneered that "irreligion, no longer confined to the closets of concealed sophists, nor to the haunts of wealthy riot, has more or less displayed its hideous form among all classes. A league at length has been cemented between the apostles and disciples of irreligion and of anarchy."[15] In what could be read as a first iteration of the culture wars, Hamilton declared that American voters in 1800 faced an apocalyptic choice: Federalism along with its true religion—or "Jefferson and NO GOD."

Perhaps the most representative figure in the formative years of the counterrevolutionary movement was Timothy Dwight (a.k.a. "the Pope of the Federalists"), the president of Yale and the grandson of the famous revivalist Jonathan Edwards. During the War of Independence, Dwight's calls for liberty and equality were as loud as those of any other patriotic preacher. In the aftermath of the American Revolution, however, he realized his mistake. He soon denounced America's godless founders and condemned the Constitution of the United States. "Government since the days of [John] Locke, has been extensively supposed to be founded in the social compact. No opinion is more groundless than this," he inveighs in one of many sermons on the topic to his pupils at Yale.[16] "The foundation of government," he countered, "is undoubtedly the will of God." In the heat of his reaction to the French Revolution and the early American rebellions, he drilled his students on the conviction that democracy in America had led inexorably to "the triumph of infidelity" and that terror was just around the corner. America needed religion, and fast, he intoned, if it was to avoid slouching toward Gomorrah.

When Dwight and his allies such as Princeton's Stanhope Smith surveyed the religious landscape during the revolutionary period, they mostly experienced dread and terror, and their feelings had some basis in fact. By most accounts, church attendance around the years of the first American Revolution was at a historic low, and infidel philosophy was at a high. As prelates of exalted station in the nation's most influential churches and schools, however, Dwight and friends were in a position to do something about the rot. They sat near the beating heart of the nation's financial system and thus were poised to pump old money along with their hard theology into the nation's religious infrastructure. Soon enough, the shiny seminaries and divinity schools of Harvard, Yale, Princeton, and Andover spawned an army of young, privileged clergymen that fanned out across the American countryside. Even in the South, the churches took in most of their manpower from these theological hothouses of the North. James Henley Thornwell, the Harvard graduate who married Princeton royalty and went on to rule the Southern Presbyterian Church, was no outlier.

Dwight and his fellow theologians were never able to gain full control of the doctrine—the revival tents were far too unruly for that—yet their fundamental message came through loud and clear. The lodestar of the new religion, its ultimate purpose and principal effect, was obedience. It promoted individualism in its variety of expression, yet its deepest impulse was to police conformity. It was democratic in its spectacle yet profoundly hostile to democracy in its aims. It was innovative in rhetoric but reactionary in its effects. It captured the spirit of the counterrevolution in an imperfect yet decisive way. Although the religion of the reaction was conceived in the North, it proved to be nothing if not adaptable. As the paper value of the property held in humans grew to eclipse all other forms of property in the new republic, the creed of the counterrevolution had little trouble meeting the needs of its new masters.

CHRISTIANITY AND SLAVERY arrived almost simultaneously on American shores, and for the first century or more they coexisted as they had for the preceding 1,600 years in Europe.[17] Timothy Dwight's celebrated grandfather, Jonathan Edwards (1703–1758), for example, was a slaveholder, and he never thought it worth the trouble to defend the practice. Indeed, he took care to exercise his right to inspect in person his purchases of human beings at dockside, as they were disembarked from the ships that had relocated them from Africa. George Whitefield (1714–1770), the most famous revivalist of the First Great Awakening, went fishing for souls in the southern colonies and came back with title to a plantation. Convinced that "hot countries cannot be cultivated without negroes," Whitefield explained, "I should think myself highly favored if I could purchase a good number of [African slaves], in order to make their lives comfortable, and lay a foundation for breeding up their posterity in the nurture and admonition of the Lord."[18] Unhappy that Georgia had abolished slavery in 1735, Whitefield was instrumental in the successful effort to legalize it all over again in the colony in 1751.

Nonetheless, dissenting voices on the question of slavery began to speak up. In 1700, the Massachusetts jurist Samuel Sewall—otherwise famous for his role in the judicial murder of several women in the Salem witch trials—penned America's first antislavery manifesto. It was titled *The Selling of Joseph*, and it weighed in at three pages. The Quakers produced the first serious abolitionist movement in the Americas, just as they did in other parts of the British Empire, and by the 1750s the Pennsylvania Quakers had effectively proscribed slave trading at least among themselves. Though these early gestures toward abolitionism were surely sincere and religiously motivated, they were neither representative of general religious opinion nor remotely effective. Sewall reported that his screed met with "frowns and hard words."[19]

Antislavery sentiments in America appeared to reach a first peak in the years around the War of Independence.[20] In 1776, the theologian Samuel Hopkins, a former slaveholder and pupil of Jonathan Edwards, issued an antislavery tract. In 1789, the Virginia Baptists urged "our brethren to make use of every measure to extirpate this horrid evil from the land," and in 1791 the Presbyterians produced a similar resolution. The Methodists especially stood out in their opposition to the slave trade. Methodist leader John Wesley detested slavery, and in 1780 his tiny but mushrooming sect of followers resolved in conference "that slavery is contrary to the laws of God, man, and nature, hurtful to society; [and] contrary to the dictates of conscience and pure religion."

The abolitionist impulses in America drew strength from the movement in Britain, for antislavery was an international phenomenon from the start. In 1785, William Wilberforce, a member of Parliament, converted to evangelical Christianity, and two years later he began a campaign to end the slave trade, which culminated successfully in the Slave-Trade Act of 1807. He continued to fight for a complete end to slavery, and the efforts resulted in the 1833 Slavery Abolition Act, in which Parliament, at taxpayer expense, abolished slavery in most parts of the British Empire. Though the terminal decline in the Caribbean sugar business was likely the driving cause of the event—and the debt incurred by financial reparations to slaveholders was still being paid off by British taxpayers into the twenty-first century—the successful abolition of slavery in Britain with strong support from the evangelical movement there served as inspiration to reformers around the world and as a grave warning to slaveholders that abolitionism was to be taken seriously.

While the British churches (in part) fired up hopes among abolitionists and struck fear in slaveholders, their American counterparts marched swiftly in the opposite direction. By the time the revivalists showed up on the shores of the Chesapeake Bay to save the likes of Captain Auld in the early 1830s, it was clear that the American evangelicals' early pronouncements against slavery were all bark and no bite. Pretty soon, the churches stopped barking, too. In the face of the growing power and resolve of slavery in the new republic, the nation's major denominational groups shelved their earlier declarations and, in many cases, forbade even discussing the topic. Maintaining peace within congregations that included both proslavery and antislavery members was a far more pressing concern than securing justice for the enslaved.

As Christianity spread (or was imposed) upon the enslaved population, there, too, a gradual accommodation took hold amid many messy particulars. The slave-preacher Nat Turner's Southampton Insurrection, which took place in Virginia in the year preceding Frederick's revival experience with

Captain Auld, at first appeared to confirm the fears of those who worried that sharing religion with the enslaved would be sure to motivate demands for emancipation. But the extreme reaction to Turner's rebellion—a reaction that harvested about three times as many deaths as the rebellion itself[21]— provided the template for the churching of the enslaved population. Slaveholders figured out that the answer was not to deprive the enslaved of religion but to ensure that they were supplied with the right religion and the right preachers, which is to say, a proslavery religion.[22] In hundreds of steps, coordinated only by the roughly discernible logic of the road on which they found themselves, America's churches transformed themselves from bystanders to sometimes-reluctant enablers of the slave system. It was a surprisingly short step from there to what would become in effect the great commission of the American church (or most of it); namely, the active defense and promotion of the American slave republic as the divine work of God himself.

IT CAN'T BE KNOWN whether American Christianity and American slavery would have taken that crucial, final step in their evolving partnership had it not been for the sudden, shocking emergence in the 1830s of a new breed of abolitionists. What was new in the new abolitionists was not their idea that slavery should be proscribed or the suggestion that it contradicted the laws of God and nature. All of that had been said before. It was the categorical denunciations of slaveholders as the worst kind of evil, the nonnegotiable commitment to immediate abolition, and the apparent determination to deliver this message as loudly as possible across every cotton field in every state of the Union. This wasn't abolition as mere moral posturing or virtue signaling; it was a dagger aimed at the heart of the existing national order.

Among the first wave of new abolitionists was David Walker (1796–1830) of Boston. A Black man born to a free mother (and hence free himself), Walker decried the injustices of the slave system and called the nation's churches to account for their complicity in the sin.[23] William Lloyd Garrison, who is generally credited with birthing the revival of American abolitionism with the launch of *The Liberator* in 1831, fired off his opening salvos on the same, religious lines. Slaveholding, Garrison announced, is "a sin—always, everywhere, and only a sin."[24] His first instinct was therefore to lay siege to the nation's churches. He and his fellow abolitionists imagined that the solution was simply a matter of opening eyes and calling forth repentance. How could any true Christian not see sin as sin? Theodore Dwight Weld, the son and grandson of Congregationalist ministers who became a disciple of the evangelist Charles Grandison Finney, launched his abolitionist career on the same, religious premises, and so did the wealthy, Massachusetts-born, New York–based businessmen Arthur and Lewis Tappan, who bankrolled much of the early abolitionist movement.

"I will be heard!" William Lloyd Garrison shouted from the first pages of *The Liberator*. And indeed, he was. The new generation of abolitionists delivered their harangues at the doorways of the nation's churches, and they stuffed the nation's post offices with mailers denouncing the sin of slavery. They were the first to grasp, if often imperfectly, that slavery in the new republic was now *the* national issue. Their activism was rooted in an awareness that the counterrevolution had already triumphed—that the United States was no longer a republic with slaves but a slave republic. What was novel in abolitionism—its national scope and its utterly transformative intent—was what was novel in American slavery. What was not so new was the religious language in which it framed its arguments. In making it all about religion, the abolitionists got what they asked for—and more. The world might never have discovered what

American Christianity teaches about slavery had the abolitionists not placed the matter so pointedly before the public.

THE COUNTERREVOLUTION, at first caught sleeping, was soon armed and ready for theological combat. A phalanx of divines rushed out into the nation's presses and pulpits, among them the wealthiest and most powerful names in the ecclesiastical hierarchies in both the North and the South. They were prepared to fight the question of slavery down to the last letter of the Holy Scriptures. The abolitionists had not merely pricked the nation's conscience. They had awoken a sleeping giant.

The Presbyterians of the South sent in the formidable trio of James Henley Thornwell of South Carolina, Frederick A. Ross of Alabama, and Robert Lewis Dabney of Virginia. The Presbyterians of the North could count on Charles Hodge at Princeton and his protégés in the most powerful priestly network in the nation. The Baptists called on Thornton Stringfellow in Richmond, Richard Furman of South Carolina, and Francis Wayland at Brown University in Rhode Island. The Methodist contingent included Wilbur Fisk at Wesleyan College (later Wesleyan University) in Connecticut and Albert Taylor Bledsoe of Kentucky. The Episcopalians were represented by James Warley Miles of South Carolina and Bishop John Henry Hopkins of Vermont. The Congregationalists had their champions in Moses Stuart at Andover Theological Seminary and Nathan Lord at Dartmouth College.

All sides could also draw on reinforcements from overseas— from Britain, her West Indian colonies, France, Germany, Italy, the Vatican, and Latin America—for the debate over the theology of slavery, though centered in the United States, was a global event. All knew that there was always only one sure path to victory. The people everywhere demanded to know: What does the Bible say?

The Battle of the Bible

THE BIBLE SAYS nothing at all about the merits of chattel slavery in North America. This was the slender truth at the root of the tangles over the revealed theology of slavery. The scriptures were assembled in a time when slavery, like winter, was universally regarded as a fact of life. Consequently, the Bible, in all its versions, features many masters and many slaves, some good and some bad, but it no more condemns slavery as such than it does the changing of the seasons.

Among the bad masters in the Old Testament (as American Christians referred to the text) was Pharaoh of Egypt, the enslaver of the Hebrews. Among the good masters, on the other hand, was Abraham, "the father of all believers" and the proud enslaver of many Egyptians. Among the bad slaves in the Old Testament who learned what it meant to be a good slave was Hagar, the human property of Abraham's wife, Sarah. After having had sex (likely forced) with Abraham (who was eighty-six years old at the time) and then taking physical abuse from Sarah (who had loaned her to Abraham for sex in the first place), Hagar ran away to a spring in the wilderness. There she encountered an angel of the Lord. This would have been the ideal "opportunity" for God "of teaching the world how much he abhorred slavery," the Virginia Baptist Thornton Stringfellow sneers.[25] Yet the angel of the Lord told Hagar in no uncertain terms: "Return to your mistress and submit to her authority."[26]

True, there were glimmers of redemption for the enslaved to be found in the pages of the Bible. Among those biblical figures involved in the liberation of slaves, the most inspiring by far was Moses. The glorious story of the Israelites' escape to freedom across the parting seas was like gold to the anti-slavery camp. Given that the chosen people, upon getting clear of Egypt, promptly enslaved the Canaanites, however, the proslavery debaters were surely correct in pointing out that ending slavery per se was hardly part of God's plan. Pharaoh's mistake was not to have practiced slavery, but to have enslaved the wrong people.

Unsurprisingly, given that it came from a people who practiced forms of slavery, the Old Testament confines itself to offering guidance on the proper management of the institution. For example, it advises that a master "who beats their male or female slave with a rod must be punished if the slave dies as a direct result; but they are not to be punished if the slave recovers after a day or two, since the slave is their property."[27] It also insists you must give your slaves time off on the Sabbath, along with your donkeys.[28] And that among the properties of your neighbor that you should not covet, aside from his wife and donkeys, are his slaves.[29] And that selling your daughter into slavery is permissible, but you must be prepared to take her back "if she does not please her master."[30] It further recommends that you may keep slaves for life and bequeath them to your children, but that you should really make an effort to take slaves mostly (though not exclusively) from foreign tribes.[31] All of this helpful counsel on the management of slavery, moreover, is written entirely from the perspective of the enslavers and prospective enslavers.

As far as America's proslavery clerics were concerned, there really wasn't much more to say about the God's attitude toward slavery in the Old Testament. "The Southern Master, by divine authority, may today consider his slaves part of his social and religious family, just as Abraham did," concludes Frederick Ross.[32]

It isn't hard to read, in between the lines, that the reality-based members of the abolitionist community agreed with that analysis. In a curious poem titled "The Tyrants' Jubilee,"[33] Douglass offers a mocking summary of the proslavery reading of the Old Testament to this point. The tone of the poem surely matches that of the "Slaveholder's Sermon" he delivered to laughing audiences across the northern states. "Our slavery is God's Holy Institution," he writes, mimicking the voice of a group of jubilant slaveholders celebrating the suppression of a recent slave revolt:

Infidels oppose us and impiously condemn
The Father of the Faithful, Holy Abraham;
The Bible doth sanction it [slavery], that is quite plain;
It doth both our rights and our duties explain

The antislavery camp, to be sure, did not surrender the letter of the Old Testament without a fight. One line of attack, advanced by evangelical abolitionists such as Theodore Dwight Weld and George B. Cheever, is to argue that "slave" in the Bible (*ebed* in Hebrew) doesn't mean "slave." Unfortunately, notwithstanding subtle evolutions in practices over the time frame recorded in the Bible, "slave" basically means slave. A related strategy, mooted by David Walker and Henry Ward Beecher, is to suggest that slavery in ancient times was a kinder, gentler thing than slavery in America.[34] But ancient slavery was not a walk in the park—just ask Hagar— and proslavery theorists easily turned the argument around, loudly proclaiming that American slaves really had it good. Another collection of strategies involves seizing on passages that appear to ameliorate or limit slavery, such as a section in Leviticus that recommends holding a Jubilee every fifty years in which all debts are canceled and all slaves emancipated. But the Jubilee's freedom-after-fifty program, for what it was worth, appears to be limited to Hebrew slaves only, and there is little evidence that it was ever implemented in any systematic way.

Abolitionists, including Douglass, also invested a great deal of rhetorical capital in a line from Exodus (echoed in 1 Timothy) that makes "man-stealing" punishable by death. It sounds righteous enough—except for the fact "man-stealing" isn't slavery. It's kidnapping. Indeed, as the proslavery Presbyterian Frederick Ross points out,[35] the relevant passage in Exodus goes on to say that "man-stealing" remains a capital crime whether or not it additionally involves the act of selling the victim on to someone else as a slave—thus implying not only that slavery is distinct from man-stealing, but also that slavery as such is not the thing that makes "man-stealing" a capital crime.

For the proslavery side, in the final analysis, it isn't the word of God but the silence of the Old Testament that makes antislavery literalism an obviously losing position. Kidnapping, murder, bearing false witness, adultery, certain kinds of substance abuse, sodomy, wearing inappropriate garments under certain conditions—all are explicitly proscribed in the Bible, and the corresponding punishments are typically spelled out in excruciating detail. If slavery is the gravest sin imaginable, then wouldn't you think that the Bible would just say so? "Polygamy and divorce are at once and forever condemned, but not a syllable is breathed against slavery," the proslaveryBaptist Richard Fuller says in his epistolary debate with the (tepidly) antislavery Baptist Francis Wayland.[36]

With the Old Testament looking like a lost cause, the anti-slavery Christians pinned their hopes on the New Testament and the spiritual revolution that it is said to have inspired. They drew courage from the fact the differences between the two Testaments prove that some of the rules of life are subject to change. Moses permits divorce, for example, but Jesus bans it. Therefore, it was hoped, the rules on slavery may be open to change, too. But in the case of slavery, unlike marriage, there is little evidence of any change in attitudes. The slender, piercing fact running through the debate is that the Christian gospel, too, emerged from a slave society and coexisted with slavery for 1,800 years before the antislavery writers allegedly uncovered its true meaning. The New Testament, just like the Old, features masters and slaves—with the difference here that the (partial) taboo on enslaving fellow religionists appears to have been lifted. There are Christian masters, in good standing with the church, and they own Christian slaves, in equally good standing.

The clearest message on the subject in the New Testament is that slavery per se is fundamentally irrelevant to personal salvation. "Were you a slave when called?" Paul asks the Corinthians. "Do not be concerned about it."[37] In Galatians he adds: "There is neither Jew nor Gentile, neither slave nor free man, neither male nor female, for you are all one in Christ Jesus."[38] Although modern readers like to see in such claims a demand for equality, Paul's point is quite simply that inequality in this world is irrelevant because the only equality that matters is the one to be secured in another world.

Inequality in this world is not only compatible with equality in a future world, according to this line of thought, but may indeed be a useful part of the preparation for it. Should you happen to find yourself enslaved in this world, Paul therefore emphasizes, the thing to do is to be as good a slave as possible. The relevant passages, recited millions of times in the

American South across the pews and over the rows of cotton bushes, are as pellucid as anything in scripture ever is:

> Slaves, obey your earthly masters with respect and fear, and with sincerity of heart, just as you would obey Christ. Obey them not only to win their favor when their eye is on you, but as slaves of Christ, doing the will of God from your heart.[39]

> Slaves, obey your earthly masters in everything; and do it, not only when their eye is on you and to curry their favor, but with sincerity of heart and reverence for the Lord.[40]

The distilled version of the message offered to America's Black population was plainer still. At a revival camp in South Carolina, David Walker reports, "our Reverend gentleman told us (coloured people) that slaves must be obedient to their masters . . . or be whipped."[41]

In the antebellum theological debates, the master-slave relationship in the New Testament that drew the most attention was that of Philemon and Onesimus—a Christian master and his Christian slave. From a brief and somewhat opaque letter from Paul to Philemon, we gather that Onesimus has run away, come to Paul, and converted to Christianity. Paul has now decided to return Onesimus to Philemon. There is much ambiguity in this very brief letter as to whether Paul is sending the slave back with encouragement that he be freed or just sending him back with a friendly letter of reference. What isn't in much doubt is that Paul recognizes that Philemon owns Onesimus, that Philemon has the right to dispose of his property as he sees fit, and that his ownership of property in another human being by no means excludes him from the Christian community.

The case of Onesimus proves decisively that "slaves should not be taken nor detained from their masters without their master's consent," writes the Episcopal bishop of Vermont, citing the work of a respected Scottish Presbyterian.[42] The Massachusetts theologian Moses Stuart emphatically agrees that the letter on Onesimus proves that enslavers may continue in their practice "without violating the Christian faith or church."[43]

Frederick Douglass, once again finding the scriptural text of little use, turns to scalding sarcasm in his "Tyrants' Jubilee":

To servants the Bible says, "Your masters obey";
No word is said in favor of running away;
If anything be said on that subject at all,
It's the case of the fugitive sent back by Paul!

As far as James Henley Thornwell and his proslavery allies were concerned, the utility of biblical literalism in resolving the question of slavery was so decisive that it supplied convincing additional proof, if ever it was needed, that "the only rule of judgment is the written word of God." For "if men had drawn their conclusions upon this subject only from the Bible, it would no more have entered into any human head to denounce slavery as a sin than to denounce monarchy, aristocracy, or poverty."[44]

Faced with the pile of textual evidence on the Bible's malign indifference to slavery, antislavery advocates now faced a dilemma. Should they continue a hopeless duel over the literal meanings of the text? Or should they deploy alternative interpretative strategies that would subordinate the letter of the text to the spirit—a spirit that, they did not doubt for a moment, favored justice for the enslaved? The antislavery writers fled in droves to figurative methodologies of interpretation, where they have since been joined by the vast majority of those who identify with biblical religions. The histories related in scripture, the antislavery writers and their successors aver, serve to illuminate certain moral principles, and this "interior spirit" is incompatible with slavery. "The whole Bible is opposed to slavery," writes the leading Presbyterian abolitionist John Rankin; "Beams of love and mercy emanate from every page."[45]

The first and foremost beam of love, by all accounts, is the Golden Rule. "Do unto others what you would have them do unto you," the Gospel according to Matthew tells us.[46] Thus, the Bible teaches us that all people deserve to be treated as moral equals, and slavery violates this teaching, or so the characters of *Uncle Tom's Cabin* along with many abolitionists stridently presume. But the proslavery theologians had little trouble deflecting the argument from the Golden Rule. As Frederick Ross, John Henry Hopkins, and James Henley Thornwell all note, the Golden Rule does not require that a king should treat his subject as if the subject were king, nor that a husband should treat a wife as if she were a husband.[47] Masters adhere to the Golden Rule insofar as they treat slaves as they would wish to be treated if they were slaves, just as husbands obey the same rule when they treat a wife as she should be treated. Elijah Heddings, a Methodist bishop from New York, takes the logic all the way to the opposite side. Because the institution of slavery itself depends on the ability of every master to treat his slave with the same benevolent concern that he would expect were he the slave, the bishop maintains, "the right to hold a slave is founded on this rule, 'whatsoever ye would that men do to you, do ye even so unto them.' "[48]

Further weakening the argument from the Golden Rule is the fact, noted by Ross and Hopkins, that the rule in question is hardly unique to the Christian religion. Douglass himself routinely appeals to the Golden Rule—and then adds that

Confucius "had the Golden Rule in substance five hundred years before the coming of Christ" and favored "notions of justice that are not to be confused with any of our own 'Cursed be Canaan' religion."[49]

Where the Golden Rule falters, the antislavery writers turn to the biblical teaching concerning the unity of the human race. Douglass himself frequently cites Paul in Acts: "From one man He made all the nations."[50] The belief in the common descent of man, known formally as the theory of monogenesis, deals a deathblow to slavery, or so it is often assumed today. Except that it doesn't. The common origin of man, the proslavery side pointed out, comes with the understanding that Adam's descendants were subsequently divided into distinct groups that were expected to play very distinct, collaborative roles in God's providential design for Earth's inhabitants. Indeed, Paul himself, immediately after declaring that God made all "nations" from one man, adds: "And he marked out their appointed times in history and the boundaries of their lands."

Surely the most important instance in which God divided the progeny of Adam into distinct nations was the case of Noah and his three sons. Shem, the favorite son, became the ancestor of the Hebrews and of the surrounding tribes in Mesopotamia. Japheth, the firstborn, spread his seed to the regions to the north and west of Israel, the future land of the gentiles. And then came Ham, who was a descendant of Adam just as surely as Noah's other two sons, and who populated points south of Israel.[51] Before departing, Ham made the mistake of seeing Noah naked and hungover, which, for reasons that are not entirely clear, caused enormous offense. So Noah, perhaps with unsteady aim, landed a curse on Ham's son, Canaan, according to which his offspring would become the slaves of the offspring of Ham's brothers. When Shem's descendants the Hebrews finally got clear of Egypt, they promptly received divine instructions to enslave all those accursed Canaanites whom they did not first murder.

Jefferson Davis summarizes the biblical wisdom well at an optimistic moment preceding the war over slavery: "the Creator, speaking through the inspired lips of Noah, declared the destiny of all three races of men. Around and about us is the remarkable fulfillment of that prophecy."[52] One of the best things about slavery, adds Davis, is "that it dignifies and exalts every white man by the presence of a lower race" and is therefore "essential to the preservation of the higher orders of republican civilization."[53] South Carolina's James Henley Thornwell is equally exultant about the opportunity slavery affords to better all the races: "We cannot but accept it as a gracious Providence, that [the Africans] have been brought in such numbers to our shores, and redeemed from the bondage of barbarism and sin."[54]

Douglass, with his usual acuity, mimes the rhetoric in "The Tyrants' Jubilee":

Our slaves were in Africa—poor fallen creatures;
They could know nothing of our pure gospel preachers,
But were heathenish mortals as ever man saw—
They were strangers alike to Religion and Law

The widespread embrace of monogenesis did not of course stop more secular-minded proslavery theorists from endorsing the pseudoscientific theory of polygenesis, or multiple human origins—any line of defense was welcome. Science proves, they argued without the benefit of any credible science, that "the African" arose separately from the white man and is fit for servitude only. Douglass himself saw early the threat from racist "pretenders to science" and he attacks it directly in an important lecture of 1854, where he cites, among others, Lincoln's old favorite, Volney, on the legacy of Black Africans in

Egypt.[55] The right answer to pseudoscience, Douglass insists, is more science, not less.

Polygenesis was in any case a dish for educated audiences, and it mattered much more in popular racial politics after the war than before. In the antebellum world, the severest critics of polygenesis were the proslavery theologians. For them, the brotherhood of man was a cornerstone of the defense of slavery, whose divine purpose was to require brothers to play their appointed roles. In a sermon delivered just a few days after "the public calamity and distress" of Lincoln's election, Thornwell takes time to insist that "no Christian man . . . can give any countenance to speculations which trace the negro to any other parent but Adam." Polygenesis, says Thornwell, is the "offspring of infidelity" and one of the "assaults of infidel science upon the records of our faith." It finds its "warmest advocates among the opponents of slavery."[56]

In modern times, the argument that the Bible uniquely promotes a message about the dignity of man—a message associated with the passage in Genesis that describes man as "the image of God"—is thought to provide an additional support to the antislavery interpretation. But this argument made little headway in the battle of the Bible. Part of the problem is that the doctrines of America's popular religion rely for their emotional punch not on the dignity of the human being but on her depravity. Indeed, proslavery theologians regularly prescribe slavery as the proper remedy for the gross immorality of humans beginning with Eve. Part of the problem, too, is that the genocidal warfare, the murderous family relationships, and the contemptuous acts of a wrathful deity that occupy much of scripture do not always appear to imbue human existence with the highest dignity. But the core difficulty has to do with what "dignity" means in a biblical context, and it is evident in the very passage in Genesis most often cited in its favor.

The most obvious attribute of the God of Genesis is that he dominates. He is a creator and a patriarch, the master of everything, and all of creation exists to serve him. Not only is there nothing wrong with slavery in this picture of the world; there seems to be something very right with it. The Hebrew people are the happy "slaves" of Yahweh,[57] just as the followers of Jesus call themselves, as Paul does, "the slaves of Christ."[58] And when Jesus returns to set up his kingdom, should he find that some of his subordinates have been denying his authority in his absence, he will "cut them in pieces," as any self-respecting master might when confronted with disobedient slaves.[59] What makes man "the image of God" is that man, too, is a master, at least when he is kicking down rather than kissing up. Immediately after making man in his own image, God grants man "dominion" over all the animals of the earth (and arguably over women, too).

The salient message connected with the doctrine of "the image of God," then, is that there is a rightful order of authority in the world, established by God, revealed in the scriptures, and vouchsafed to humans through the mediation of priests and pulpits—and that the sacred duty of the individual is to serve her master within this providential chain of command. Read in this way—as countless representatives of the Christian religion read it for well over one millennium—the underlying principle is not one of universal equality but of universal inequality. "Dignity" is simply the reflected measure of the gap between species and among individuals in the great chain of being. Paul himself gets to the bottom line fast: "the powers that be are ordained of God."[60] Frederick Ross slaps that line on the title page of his 1857 tome, *Slavery Ordained of God*. James Henley Thornwell, too, invokes it to explain why slaves really should stay in their place: "God assigns to every man, by a wise and holy decree, the precise place he is to occupy in the great moral school of humanity. . . . For God is in history."[61]

The real danger that the antislavery camp courted in embracing the putative spirit of the Bible over the letter, however, is not that the spirit might favor the other side, but that the appeal to the new method of interpretation invited disastrous doubts about their own commitment to the authority of the Bible. If the principles allegedly vouchsafed by the Bible are anathema to slavery, the proslavery writers repeatedly pointed out, then one still needs some ground on which to explain how those principles may be elicited from a text whose characters and narrators neither state them explicitly nor apply them in the slave societies in which they live. The figurative interpreter is in effect compelled to claim access to a standard of judgment to which the Bible and its prophets do not have access. Leonard Bacon, a moderate Congregationalist minister, put his finger on the problem when he lamented that the proslavery aspects of the Bible "cannot be got rid of without resorting to methods of interpretation which will get rid of everything."[62]

It was a hopelessly heretical predicament. To appeal to principles is to seek reasons for what is right. But to appeal to the authority of the Bible is to suppose that what is right can be established in advance of knowing the reasons. Had the scriptures spoken directly on the evil of slavery, the difference might have been overlooked. Yet the Bible remains stubbornly silent, and so the antislavery theorists are forced to concede that, for them, the principles come first, and the word of God matters only insofar as it confirms what they could better deduce from reason.

But in that case, why care at all about what the Bible has to say? In America's Bible-besotted slave republic, the only wrong answer was to say that the Bible does not have the answers. The fatal problem for the antislavery side, in the final analysis, was written not in the Bible but in the assumptions built into the question with which the debate began.

Under the comforting dogmas of relativism, it is customary today to suppose that everybody gets the Bible they want. The text itself, we like to think, is innocent of the uses to which it is put. But the reality was very different. The battle of the Bible was a rout.[63] No one at the time seriously doubted the outcome. Though the cries of the defeated abolitionists lingered in the nation's presses for some time, the fighting was over well before the shooting war began.

A Christian
Nation Redeemed

ON THE EVE OF SECESSION, James Henley Thornwell took to his perch in South Carolina and painted a vision of the authentic nature and glorious future of the American republic, at least as he saw it. In a widely circulated sermon on "National Sins"— and then again more boldly in a memorial on the "Relation of the State to Christ" prepared for the Confederate government—he explains where America has gone wrong. He then articulates the foundations of a new, modern, Christian slave republic that, in his fond hope, will one day redeem not just the southern states but the entirety of the Union.[64]

Our greatest national sin, says Thornwell, is that "we have deified the people": "The tendency to sink our institutions in pure democracy is growing." The atonement will come, he avows, once we accept that "civil government is an institute of Heaven" and that "it connects itself directly with the government of God" or "the Supreme Jehovah." As Thornwell knew, the original republic, founded by heirs of the Enlightenment as a self-consciously secular republic, famously left "God" out of its Constitution. "A foundation was thus laid for the worst of all possible forms of government—democratic absolutism," he sternly informed the Confederate legislature. Happily, the Constitution of the Confederate States of America explicitly invoked the "favor and guidance of Almighty God" in its preamble.

"We long to see, what the world has never yet beheld, a truly Christian Republic, and we humbly hope that God has reserved it for the people of these Confederate States to realize the grand and glorious idea," Thornwell gushed. The new, Christian republic, moreover, would dispense with the conceit that individuals have unalienable rights. It would take as its point of departure that no society prospers without an order of rank, and that the best society is the one that cultivates benevolent Christian masters and grateful Christian slaves.[65] A fellow South Carolinian summed up the counterrevolutionary program with admirable precision: "The lie which has been written, by Northern construction, upon the margins of our noble Declaration of Independence, must soon be erased. That greater truth, that 'all men are not born free and equal,' written by the finger of God in lines so plain upon the world's history, and so indelibly stamped upon the organization of the negro, must be inscribed boldly upon our banner."[66]

Thornwell's counterrevolutionary political vision of a Christian nation rising out of the ashes of the old republic united the denominations of the South in a way that little else could (apart from the loathing of abolitionists). The Episcopal bishop of Georgia declares that God himself had called upon "the heroic race" of southern white Christian men "to drive away the infidel and rationalist principles sweeping the land."[67] "We are working out a great thought of God" and exhibiting "the supremest effort of humanity" in creating a slave society "sanctified by the divine spirit of Christianity," adds a leading Episcopalian of South Carolina.[68] In a speech delivered in the boisterous week after Georgia seceded from the Union, the Baptist reverend Ebenezer W. Warren declares that "both Christianity and slavery are from heaven; both are blessings to humanity; both are to be perpetuated to the end of time."[69] Proslavery Christian nationalism even helped heal the divide between Protestants and Catholics in the South. Thornwell was as viscerally anti-Catholic as the typical Presbyterian preacher of the time, and yet he bonded with Catholic bishop Patrick N. Lynch of South Carolina, the son of Irish immigrants and proud owner of one hundred human beings, over the divinely ordained future of the slave republic.

Of course, no one outdid Thornwell's fellow Presbyterians in their fervor for the new order. In Richmond, the Presbyterians took it as self-evident truth that slavery is "the most blessed and beautiful form of social government known."[70] In conference in 1862, the Southern Presbyterian Church happily announced: "We hesitate not to affirm that it is the peculiar mission of the southern church to conserve the institution of slavery, and to make it a blessing for master and slave."[71]

The Christian nationalist vision that emerged from the battle of the Bible was future minded, not backward looking. It was self-consciously illiberal and authoritarian in a way that clearly anticipates the fascist and neo-fascist movements of the twentieth and twenty-first centuries. It cast aside as mere illusion the liberal ideal of individual freedom; among a depraved species in a haunted world, it averred, no such freedom is possible without inviting catastrophe. It promoted instead a collectivist and paternalist ideal in which every person—slaves included—would have their place in the great chain of being, and each would possess the dignity to which they were entitled, not as individuals but in virtue of their group identities. Not just enslaved people but women—enslaved or free, they were mothers all—would know their place, which is one reason why the slavery debate tended to divide the political world along almost the same lines as the women's movement. To be sure, the proslavery version of fascism lacked the mass mobilization and the leader cults of its early twentieth-century successors. On the other hand, proslavery fascism was ahead of its immediate successors in its deployment of popular religion and church hierarchies, and in this respect it arguably anticipated the overtly theocratic fascist movements of the early twenty-first century.

IT WOULD BE A serious mistake to suppose, as many modern readers do, that proslavery Christian nationalism originated in the South or was confined there. Proslavery theologians had to change hardly a single word of the counterrevolutionary theology they had imbibed from their teachers in the North. Thornwell's denunciations of America's godless democracy and his call for a Christian nation could have been—indeed they arguably were—lifted from the sermons of Timothy Dwight. Thornwell was far from the only graduate of the elite northern seminaries to take up the cause. Three out of every five clerics who published proslavery material were trained at Harvard, Yale, Princeton, Andover, and other divinity schools north of the Mason-Dixon line.[72] As far as the theology of the propertied classes was concerned, it appeared not to matter much whether that property happened to be in human beings or in, for example, mortgage deeds held against backcountry farmers.

Contrary to popular assumption today, the leaders of the established churches of the North lined up overwhelmingly on the side of slavery in the battle of the Bible. On the central doctrine that slavery is "of Divine Appointment, established by the law of Christ," Douglass observed with scorn, "the teachings of the Northern pulpit differed little from that of the South,"[73] and Parker emphatically agreed with the sentiment.[74] As in the South, proslavery theology unified the squabbling northern denominations in a way that little else could. Charles Hodge, the iron-fisted ruler of Princeton Theological Seminary and the nation's foremost Presbyterian theologian; Wilbur Fisk, the Methodist president of Wesleyan College in Connecticut;[75] Moses Stuart, the esteemed Bible scholar at Andover Theological Seminary;[76] Nathan Lord, president of Dartmouth College;[77] Nathaniel W. Taylor, the founder of Yale's Divinity School and Timothy Dwight's "spiritual and theological child";[78] and John Henry Hopkins, the Episcopal bishop of Vermont[79]—these and many other leading lights of the northern ecclesiastical establishments were as one in their conviction that the Bible positively approves of slavery.

Between 1837 and 1845, the Presbyterians, the Methodists, and the Baptists in succession divided into northern and southern branches, and these administrative schisms were sometimes then and are more often now represented as proof that the northern religion had at long last taken up the slave's cause. "Grosser fraud and falsehood was never told," the abolitionists said at the time; the motive behind the sectional division of the churches "was one, not of principle, but of policy." The purpose was to end the debate rather than to end the practice of slavery. Not one of the major denominations of the North endorsed abolition before the war broke out, and most continued to welcome border-state slaveholders into their communion throughout the period.[80]

In the North as in the South, support for proslavery theology even helped bridge the (sometimes bloody) divide between Catholics and Protestants. "The Catholic Clergy are on the side of slavery," observes Theodore Parker with typical Protestant disdain. "It is an institution thoroughly congenial to them."[81] The American Catholic bishops John Hughes and John England did confirm that the pope was avowedly opposed to the slave trade, but, they hastened to add, the Holy Father had nothing against "domestic slavery," which he viewed as consistent with both natural law and the Gospel.[82] Catholic leaders were always far more concerned to contain the nativist backlash against the Irish than to advance the rights of the enslaved.

Even the rabbis appeared to fall into line. Isaac Leeser of Philadelphia and Isaac Wise, a progressively oriented leader in New York who moved to Cincinnati and eventually became "the foremost rabbi in America," issued opinions in support of proslavery theology. Slavery was bad, they allowed, but abolitionism was far worse—and theologically preposterous. M. J. Raphall of Brooklyn was so certain that the Bible permits slavery that he declared himself mystified "how this question can at all arise in the mind of a man that has received a religious education."[83]

There were exceptions, to be sure, and they fell into two broad groups: a select number of free Black churches, and a collection of dissenting individuals and church groups that split from their parent denominations over the issue of slavery. As remarkable as these church-based champions of the antislavery reading of the Bible were, they represented the splinters, not the hard frame of northern religious opinion. Douglass, looking back from the war, accurately observes that in antebellum America, "a few heterodox, and still fewer orthodox ministers, filling humble pulpits and living upon small salaries, have espoused the cause of the slave; but the ministers of high standing—the $5,000 divines—were almost to a man on the side of slavery."[84] Theodore Parker saw the same reality. Yes, there were antislavery preachers, he acknowledges, but "seldom an eminent voice in an eminent place, then to be met with obloquy and shame."[85]

Black abolitionists were particularly keen observers of the American churches' complicity in slavery. In 1858, a Colored Citizens Convention resolved that "the hostile position of the American church and clergy" and "their complicity with the Southern church" was to blame for "perpetuating the horrible system of American slavery."[86] David Walker, William Wells Brown, and Harriet Jacobs offer the same grim assessment of the outcome of the battle of the Bible. Black churches, on the other hand, provided some of the most reliable support among church groups for the abolitionist cause. Even so, Black churches were far from immune to the same pressures that turned their white counterparts into safe havens for proslavery belief. In the pages of Frederick Douglass's newspaper, the *North Star*, the Black abolitionist William C. Nell criticizes the Black churches for siding with slaveholders.[87]

In the end, the triumph of the proslavery church in the battle of the Bible was so resounding that it proved to be one of America's gifts to the world. "The antislavery sentiment of England is exposed to no influence more dangerous than that exerted by American proslavery divines who visit that country," Douglass writes.[88] In the glow of its success at home, the new, proslavery theology of America sought out and found a warm welcome in the powerful churches of Europe, the Caribbean, and Brazil.

4

WELCOME INFIDELITY!

Infidelity Ascendant

STEPHEN SYMONS FOSTER (1809–1881) was a large man, but he was no match for the anti-abolitionist crowd that gathered at the First Parish Unitarian Church in Portland, Maine, on one fine Sunday in 1842. Foster had come with fellow abolitionist William Murray Spear to make the case against slavery, but the crowd didn't want to hear it. They tore Foster's coat in half and pummeled him almost to death. An auxiliary unit from the local women's antislavery group at last dragged him from the mêlée and helped him escape through a back window. Spear, meanwhile, took a bloody beating out in front of the church. In the following year, Foster published *The Brotherhood of Thieves*, in which he lays out a searing case that America's churches, in the North as well as the South, are "the bulwark of slavery." In 1844, he showed up at an antislavery convention wearing a spiked iron collar on his neck and carrying iron manacles in his hands brought by a fugitive from New Orleans. "Behold the emblems of the American church and clergy!" he said.[1]

By the time that Foster made his shackled entrance, the abolitionists who had gathered around William Lloyd Garrison had long known that the churches were a lost cause. Already

in 1837, Garrison's ally Elizur Wright announced at an abolitionist conference that "the most effective opposition we have
met has been from the professed ministers of Christ." In a text
written long after the war, Wright repeats the same assessment: "The pulpit everywhere—with a very few exceptions—
either justified slavery from the scriptures or denounced
abolitionism as a pestilential sin."[2] Garrison's man in Ohio,
Samuel Brooke, asserted that the "votaries" of proslavery religion "control all the large churches of our land" and "have
established a tyranny over the mind which, if not broke, will
sweep away everything dear to man."[3] Henry C. Wright and
Garrison himself echoed the sentiment, and Frederick Douglass spoke for all: "The church is beyond all question the chief
refuge of slavery. It has made itself the bulwark of American
slavery, and the shield of American slaveholders."[4]

In the early iterations of their counterattacks on the church
of slavery triumphant, the abolitionists went out of their way
to declare that their quarrel was with the churches, not with
the religion of Jesus itself. Douglass, like many others, insisted
that he remained true to the "peaceable" religion of Christ.[5]
But as the battle wore on, it became clear enough that the
quarrel was with the Bible, too. In 1845, Garrison took the
attack directly to the scriptures. "To say that everything contained within the lids of the Bible is divinely inspired . . . is
to give utterance to a bold fiction. To say that everything in
the Bible is to be believed, simply because it is found in that
volume, is equally absurd and pernicious," he announces in
The Liberator.

It was an understandable move; it would prove fateful, too.
The abolitionists were willing to try on any religion or none,
as long as it spoke the truth about slavery. Surveying the theological battlefield in the aftermath of the proslavery triumph,
a decade after his initiation in the abolitionist movement,
Frederick Douglass would synthesize the logic in a single

exasperated cry: "Welcome infidelity! Welcome atheism! Welcome anything! In preference to the gospel as preached by those divines!"[6]

JUST AS THE ABOLITIONISTS began to abandon the battle of the Bible in favor of outright infidelity, a new and powerful ally emerged on the scene in Boston, and he appeared to have just the kind of irreligion that the abolitionists craved.

In 1845, Theodore Parker returned from his dream vacation in Europe. He had left under the cloud of theological suspicions and personal health concerns that had accompanied his traumatic "excommunication." In Europe, he spent "a whole year of leisure," he later says. "It was the first and last I ever had." Parker's idea of "leisure" was of the kind that would leave most people begging for a rest. He came not to see Europe but to conquer it. He "carried the towns by storm, he harried the countryside, he swept through the galleries and museums, ransacked the libraries, and despoiled the universities," his first biographer writes.[7] By his own later account, that year of "leisure" provided him "the opportunity to review my scheme of philosophy and theology, to compare my own system with that of eminent men, as well living as dead, in all parts of Europe."[8] Something happened on that journey of the mind—of that we can be certain. Upon his return to Boston, Parker was a minister on fire.

Casting off his clerical robes, he threw himself into establishing his own, independent ministry. Except that it wasn't properly speaking a ministry. It was more like a lecture series and discussion forum on topics of interest to spiritual seekers and social activists. It took up residence in an old music hall in downtown Boston, and Parker presided over it dressed in ordinary street clothes. In typical New England style, he opted to keep pretentions out of the title and called it simply "the 28th

Congregational Society of Boston." But few could doubt the boldness of the ambition lurking behind the pedestrian name.

Much of Parker's process of intellectual growth took place in the context of what is typically labeled the transcendentalist movement. The historiography of this movement today typically emphasizes its esoteric, spiritual, individualistic, and provincial dimensions. Sometimes it gives the impression that the whole affair resulted from unmediated encounters between solitary geniuses and untouched nature. But Parker's intellectual trajectory moved in a very different direction. His transcendentalism—which is to say, the transcendentalism that changed American history, as opposed to the one that later served to flatter the self-image of the nation's educated classes—was radical, of partially alien origin, and, as would later become apparent, intensely political.

The 28th Congregational Society soon became a phenomenon. Thousands of Bostonians joined, and they filled the music hall to capacity. The orthodox never stopped hating him, but the heterodox could now see in one another's faces that they accounted for an appreciable fraction of the population of the city. Religious infidelity was always socially problematic; but Parker's presence, and especially his reputation for fearsome scholarship, made it morally and intellectually respectable.

It would be easy to underestimate the impact that Parker had on his contemporaries, for his influence operated as much by personal example as through elaborate argument. A thin, nervous man with cold blue eyes, he wasn't prepossessing in any physical sense. He was the kind of person who performed best when his fellow humans were one step removed, where they might behold his actions from a distance. Yet, on that stage, his intense, introverted personality made him all the more convincing as the misunderstood hero fighting against prejudice on behalf of truth. A growing number of Bostonians saw in him a paragon of the moral courage they wished to find in themselves. Whether intentionally or not, he was now competing not with his fellow ministers but with the likes of Ralph Waldo Emerson for the role of rogue spiritual leader on behalf of those educated people who hankered for something more adventurous than their Puritan predecessors might have considered acceptable.

Elizabeth Cady Stanton (1815–1902), who visited Boston during the "fierce conflict" that followed Parker's sermon on the transient and the permanent, remembered his presence well. "The repose and simplicity of his manner and language while hurling such thunderbolts of denunciation and defiance at the old theologies, carried his audience along with him, quite unmindful of the havoc he was making of time-honored creeds and opinions," she recalled. The thunderbolts struck Stanton herself, galvanizing the future author of *The Women's Bible* to push past her own crisis of faith and pursue a career as a freethinker and advocate for women's rights. More than forty years later, wishing to acknowledge that "we who have known and loved Theodore Parker . . . are indebted to him in a measure for the religious liberty we enjoy," she advocated erecting a monument in his honor.[9]

Stanton's fellow traveler Caroline Healey Dall (1822–1912) was only nineteen years old when she heard Parker speak. She, too, experienced that strange combination of dread and ecstasy as she watched the heroic minister do battle with the religion in which she was reared. To the scandal of friends and family, Dall soon declared herself a "humanitarian" and—what amounted to the same thing—a disciple of Parker.[10]

Parker's brand of pious infidelity energized activists of every type and cause; he was too ambitious to settle for a job as a single-issue reformer. He took on prison reform, labor reform, education reform, women's rights, temperance, and every cause in which he could hurl his intellectual grenades against the established systems of oppression. "His character was cast in a mold too large to be pressed into a form or reform less broad than humanity," says Douglass.[11] And yet, in retrospect, every step that Parker took in the direction of universal reform would prove to be a step in the direction of antislavery.

Parker first committed his antislavery views to print in 1843—appropriately enough, in a warm eulogy for the influential German émigré and freethinker Karl Follen.[12] Soon he was inviting antislavery speakers to join him in his pulpit. In 1844, he reached out to leading abolitionists, exchanging letters with the Garrisonian minister Samuel May. Upon Parker's return from Europe in 1845, the Mexican War forced his hand, as it did many others. Here was a nefarious war that had no justification except to expand the institution of slavery across the North American continent, or so Parker and the abolitionists agreed. Parker seems to have realized that he hated the war in the same way, and for the same reasons, that he hated slavery. He had long been saying that "the Christianity of America enslaves men to the Bible."[13] Now he began to suggest that the Bible enslaves men to one another.

In his writing of the time, he no longer judges slavery by theology but rather theology by slavery. "If the Bible defends slavery," he declaims, "it is not so much the better for slavery, but so much the worse for the Bible." When he needs a definition of atheism, he reaches for slavery: "Those who say, 'slavery is a Christian institution' are the genuine atheists."[14] When he needs a definition of true religion, he turns to antislavery: the "infidels from Germany do not range on the slaveholder's side."[15]

If heresy led Parker to abolitionism, his newfound abolitionism in turn slammed the door on any hope of a return to orthodoxy. In letters to friends, he now explicitly embraces the same heresies with which he was earlier charged.[16] "I say there is no evidence—internal or external—to show that the

Bible or Jesus had any thing miraculous in their origin or nature," he tells Samuel Chase.[17]

EVEN AS PARKER was speeding in the direction of antislavery, the abolitionists were hurtling in the direction of Parker. In the pages of *The Liberator*, favorable references to the renegade preacher pop up with increasing frequency. Having experienced so much trauma at the hands of prelates, the writers seem surprised at first to find themselves offering kind words to a minister. A glance at his long list of enemies, however, convinces them that, most unusually, he is a minister worthy of moral respect. Why else would he have found so many adversaries among the same theologians who spend their days apologizing for slavery and assailing abolitionism as pestilential sin?

Buoyed by Parker's example, the abolitionists resumed their attack on the established theology with renewed vigor. In 1851, Daniel Foster contributed a piece to *The Liberator* under the title: "The Bible Not an Inspired Book."[18] By 1858, Henry C. Wright felt free to dedicate a whole book to *The Errors of the Bible*.[19] The Bible, viewed as a source of infallible truth, he concludes, "has ever been an enemy to human progress in knowledge and goodness."[20] Garrison himself ultimately came to the conclusion that "all reforms are anti-Bible."[21]

The intellectual trajectory of the heretical tip of the spear of the abolitionist movement is perhaps best illustrated in the story of Moncure Conway.[22] The scion of a leading slaveholding family in northern Virginia, Conway began his idiosyncratic journey as a Methodist minister in the nation's capital. He abandoned both his native region and his ministry upon discovering how deeply both were implicated in slavery. He turned for help first to the writings of Ralph Waldo Emerson, and then to his great idol, Theodore Parker. The Methodists soon hounded him out of Washington, D.C. He moved out to Ohio, where he thought he might find a more congenial congregation on which to exercise his antislavery theology. In Cincinnati, Conway kept company with Peter H. Clark, a Black educator who held high the memory of Thomas Paine. Clark's "views of God," reports a local paper, come not from "revelations of the Scriptures, but from the book of nature."[23] Conway's journey eventually led him to a full-throated embrace of the legacy of Thomas Paine and the leadership of a humanist society in London.

Parker's emerging role as the irreligious spiritual leader of the antislavery cause put him in a unique position to bridge the divides within an increasingly fractured abolitionist movement. As the centrifugal forces of the moment pushed the abolitionists into warring extremes, he was among the few who remained on speaking terms with just about everybody in the movement. No one could have known it at the time, but Parker's spiritual engagement with all parties across the abolitionist spectrum would ultimately put him in a position to bring many of them together around the plot that would set that nation on the path to war. In no case was this mediating role more consequential that in that of Gerrit Smith.

A wealthy New York landowner who favored a more politically pragmatic and engaged form of abolitionism, Smith had a complicated religious past, involving multiple conversion experiences and denominational shifts. As his abolitionism progressed, however, he found himself in a new spiritual place, and he took the trouble to publish his views in some discourses on the "religion of reason." "Why . . . is it that slavery is able to make so plausible and effective defense of itself?" Smith asks. "It is because its defenders have been allowed to take it out of the jurisdiction of reason, and submit its claims to the Bible." His conclusion: "Reason must sit in judgment upon the Bible."[24] Smith tried to adulterate his newfound Enlightenment creed with some pious nods in the direction of holy inspirations, but the guardians of Presbyterian orthodoxy were far from swayed. They hit back hard at such "wicked aberrations." "Mr. Gerrit Smith," the prelates declaimed, having found himself in "bad company" of "unbelievers, pseudo-reformers, champions of fanaticism, has fallen into the ranks of infidelity."[25] They might as well have slapped him on a "wanted" poster next to Theodore Parker, for Smith's heresies amounted to paraphrases of the discourses that his friend and political ally was delivering over at the music hall in Boston.

The rapidly shifting politico-theological terrain had a decisive impact on the career of Frederick Douglass, too. In 1847, Douglass resolved to leave behind the moral suasion school associated with William Lloyd Garrison in Massachusetts and join with Gerrit Smith and his circle of politically minded abolitionists in New York. Douglass had hopes of establishing his own newspaper and, perhaps in a certain sense, after several years of service as a lieutenant in the movement, of gaining full control over his career. The break with Garrison had a strong personal element and eventually brought forth the scalding outbursts and vinegar memories of a family psychodrama. It probably wasn't necessary for Garrison and his allies to spread unfounded rumors about an alleged extramarital affair between Douglass and his white, female deputy at the time, Julia Griffiths (1811–1895). But the split also emerged out of growing differences over both the tactics and the philosophy of the abolition movement.

On the tactical side, Douglass had had enough of occupying the moral high ground with a purity clique; he felt a need to dirty his hands with political action. The way to confront the power of the slaveholding oligarchy was to produce an equal or greater opposing power. On the philosophical side, the differences could be summed up in a name: Theodore Parker. If

American religion would not defeat slavery, both Douglass and Parker believed, then America needed a new religion.

The defiance of the abolitionists in the face of the overwhelming theological firepower lined up against their cause may seem inspiring. But that hardly means it was successful. The reality, as Douglass intuited, is that the abolitionists were a despised, marginal sect in a country that had made up its mind. They had been crushed in the battle of the Bible, and their flight to infidelity served only to prove the point, not to change the facts on the ground. Indeed, as Douglass also understood, the turn to infidelity made things worse. It was politically toxic. Douglass and the pragmatic allies who gathered around Gerrit Smith made efforts to distance themselves from the most heretical of the Garrisonian infidels, such as Stephen Foster and Parker Pillsbury, because they knew they would never win an election with such overt iconoclasts in tow. But Douglass also understood that they wouldn't win without them either. They would still be tarred, with reason, as infidels themselves. At some level, he sensed, abolitionism was entering a dead end.

The Infidels' Predicament

IF THE TURN TO INFIDELITY was intellectually unavoidable, it soon proved to be politically disastrous. The first consequence of infidelity was to fracture the abolitionist movement itself. The evangelical wing of the movement could not abide their fellow abolitionists' scathing counterattacks on the churches. Still less could they tolerate the unholy assaults on the Bible. The last straw was the growing association between abolitionism and the ungodly struggles for women's rights and workers' rights. Surely it was no coincidence that women filled the rank and file of the antislavery societies and that the nation's leading abolitionists—Douglass, Foster, Maria Stewart, Sojourner Truth, Lucretia Mott, and Lucy Stone among them—were its most outspoken feminists. For those committed to supporting the existing hierarchies of status and property, gender equality posed a threat at least as ominous as that of racial equality—a threat that could only be met with urgent appeals to the theology and science of gender difference.

In the face of such outrages, the church-based wing of the movement therefore broke away in search of a form of abolitionism consistent with its belief in the literal truth of the scriptures, the subordination of women, and the sanctity of

property. In the end, it committed itself to a form of abolitionism that stood little chance of abolishing anything.

In 1840, Arthur and Lewis Tappan, the devoutly pious mer-
chants who funded much of the early abolitionist effort, abandoned the Garrisonians to form the American and Foreign
Anti-Slavery Society. They simply concluded that they could
no longer work with their irreligious comrades. Later, as the
foreign elements washed ashore, the schism in the abolition
movement widened into a chasm. When Karl Marx's old drink-
ing buddy Karl Heinzen showed up in New York and began to
publish a newspaper valiantly promoting the abolitionist cause,
Arthur Tappan naturally thought to pay a visit. According to
Heinzen, however, "when I told [Tappan] I was a decided atheist, the pious man replied that I could not be a true abolitionist.
He left me with a sad face."[26]

Once separated from the radical core of the movement, the
evangelical contingent fell into some of its worst habits before
dwindling to irrelevance. For the minority of the evangelicals
that did care about the slavery issue, abolition was typically
only one of many items to be considered on the path to saving
the soul of the nation. As the issue attracted controversy, it
inevitably slipped down the list, yielding to other, ostensibly
more urgent causes, such as work-free Sundays and alcohol-
free lives (the Tappan brothers' other pet causes). Charles
Grandison Finney, often celebrated today as an example of
the Jesus-driven abolitionist, was a case in point. Funded by
the Tappan brothers and eventually placed with their money
at the head of Oberlin College in Ohio, he detested slavery and
infidel abolitionism in equal measure, both of which got in the
way of organizing revivals to save souls.[27] But he also didn't
think that the issue needed much of his attention. "We look
in vain in his sermons for any formal discussion of slavery,"
writes his biographer. "His references to it . . . were frequent
and forcible, indeed, but they were casual, and were brought

in as illustrations, rather than as his main proposition."[28] In 1857, in the midst of a financial crash that left many Americans clutching their Bibles, Finney showed up in Boston and won thousands of converts. But his only real concern, as Theodore Parker observes in an acid critique, was "to remove unbelief in ecclesiastical doctrines." He had nothing to say about slavery or any of the other ills of the age; he was simply exploiting the anxieties of an economic crisis with the promise that "a moment's belief in the ecclesiastical theology . . . will admit a pirate, a kidnapper, a deceitful politician . . . , a hypocritical priest . . . to heaven."[29]

Further hobbling the evangelical wing of the abolitionist movement was the fact that from its beginnings in the eighteenth century, it identified the African slave trade, rather than slavery itself, as the chief moral problem to be solved. That is, it proposed to put Black Americans (free and enslaved) on boats and ship them to Africa. According to this line of putatively antislavery thought, slavery was a dark blot on white, Christian America, and it was best dealt with through some form of stain removal.[30] The evangelical plans for a "Benevolent Empire," purged of slavery, remained at bottom part of an ethno-nationalist project in support of a nation that its proponents imagined to be both spiritually and racially pure, and the real effect of the plans was not to move any number of Black Americans to Africa but to reinforce the caste system on which slavery depended. "All the Emigration and Colonisation Societies that have been formed, have been auxiliaries of the Slave Power, and established for this purpose," the formidable abolitionist John Rock correctly observed.[31]

By far the most influential of the evangelical abolitionists was Harriett Beecher Stowe, the daughter of revivalist superstar Lyman Beecher and the author of *Uncle Tom's Cabin*. Stowe's novel drew on evidence of the evils of slavery that the Tappan brothers' protégé Theodore Dwight Weld (1803–1895), with the help of Sarah Moore Grimke (1792–1873) and Angelina Emily Grimke (1805–1879), had collated, along with that provided by fugitives such as Frederick Douglass. It performed an invaluable service for the abolitionist cause by packaging the many narratives and reports of actual witnesses and victims of enslavement into a compulsively readable work of literature, as Douglass and others acknowledged at the time. But the price of the packaging was that the work had to be framed within the racialized assumptions of evangelical abolitionism and its constituency. In *Uncle Tom's Cabin*, the presumption of Black inferiority makes Uncle Tom a better object of Christian pity and thus a perfect vehicle for the redemption of white America. The final solution, Stowe makes clear in her last chapter, is to thank America's enslaved Black population for playing Jesus by shipping it off to Africa.

Meanwhile, Theodore Dwight Weld, the great white hope of the early evangelical movement, retreated from antislavery activism along with his wife, Angelina, and her sister, Sarah Grimke. Daughters of a South Carolina slaveholding clan, the Grimke sisters converted to Quakerism in the 1830s and made their mark as abolitionist speakers. By the 1850s, however, Sarah had become a militant vegetarian, Angelina was preoccupied with apocalyptic cults and "spirit manifestations," and Theodore was devoting his energy to idiosyncratic, New Age–style mind-body healing projects.[32] White evangelical abolitionism always had this vice, that it was more concerned about the redemption of white souls than the emancipation of Black bodies. As one scholar has suggested, many evangelicals thought slavery was a sin for the same reason that beating your dog is a sin: because it reflects badly on the master, not because the slave is an equal.[33]

As an organized political movement, evangelical abolitionism faded from national life in the aftermath of the split with the infidels, even while many church groups across the country soldiered on as supporters of abolition and as valuable stations on the underground railroad. By 1855, the Tappan brothers' society stopped holding annual meetings and became largely inactive. On the eve of the war over slavery, Douglass offered a damning assessment of the state of what he called the "Church Anti-Slavery Society." "It has little more than a *paper* life. . . . It is for the salvation of the church rather more than for the destruction of slavery. . . . It has no press, no agents, no auxiliaries. . . . [It is] not much more than dead," he writes.[34]

To be sure, the good work continued, in individual churches and in splinter denominations scattered around the country, some of them associated with the small liberal arts colleges that survive to the present like the odd blueberry stain on a red midwestern tablecloth. But the static presence of these islands of evangelical abolitionism served mainly to convince observers of the political scene that they posed no threat to the system. Indeed, by joining the chorus of religious denunciations directed at their estranged partners in the abolitionist movement, they could even be accepted as a positive good for the established order of the American slave republic.

IF THE CONSEQUENCES of infidelity within the abolitionist movement were damaging, the consequences for the movement's relations with the outside world must count as catastrophic. In allowing themselves to be identified as infidels, the abolitionists handed their opponents the weapon of their own destruction. The proslavery forces worked overtime to ensure that "abolitionist" and "infidel" were even more tightly conjoined in the public mind than "godless" and "communist" would be a century later.

"I understand modern abolitionists' sentiments to be sentiments of marked hatred against [biblical] laws; to be sentiments which would hold God himself in abhorrence," declares Thornton Stringfellow, a Baptist in Richmond.[35] Abolitionists are one and all "Atheists, Communists, Socialists, Red Republicans, Jacobins," adds the relentless Thornwell.[36] In correspondence with like-minded nabobs, Samuel Morse (1791–1872), the inventor of the telegraph and the scion of a devoutly Federalist family, describes "this monster" of abolitionism as "the logical fruit of Unitarianism and Infidelity." He places the blame for it squarely on "the Theodore Parkers of the day, the leaders, the fierce supporters of a spurious humanitarianism."[37] Reverend Henry J. Van Dyke of the First Presbyterian Church of Brooklyn points to abolitionists to illustrate "the power of fanaticism to embitter the heart." He thought it self-evident that "abolitionism leads, in multitudes of cases, and by a logical process, to utter infidelity."[38] The convergence between the antislavery movement and the nascent women's rights movement confirmed in the eyes of the faithful that abolitionism was simply Satanic. When Frances Wright, a Scottish-born follower of the Epicurean philosophy, stepped out in speeches and essays to announce her abolitionist and feminist program, the papers of New York exploded with vituperation. She was called a "female monster," a "bold blasphemer," and, most memorably, "the red harlot of infidelity."[39]

The defenders of orthodoxy were wielding a blade honed to a very sharp edge in the grinding theological conflicts of the early, New England–based phase of the counterrevolution. Timothy Dwight himself had published his epic poem on "The Triumph of Infidelity" in 1788, and the fundamental goal of the invective had not changed in the decades since: to police conformity in support of a regime whose main reason for being was to defend the propertied against the propertyless.

The ceaseless policing of religious belief was more than a practical matter of silencing dissent. There was also in it a certain kind of joy for the enslavers and their champions, maybe even something erotic. It transmuted the fears to which a conspicuously brutal labor regime necessarily gives rise into a righteous crusade against the individuals who drew attention to the injustice. Religious paranoia was at bottom a way of displacing the doubts and anxieties that the practice of enslavement created. Every reminder of the evil, according to this logic of transference, was an instance of the evil itself; every sign of infidelity an occasion to confirm the faith; just as every hint of resistance on the part of the enslaved was proof of the need to suppress the malign sponsors of bad thoughts still more. Striking back at the sources of this unwelcome consciousness thus becomes a form of catharsis, even a sacramental act, sometimes an unexpected font of ecstasy. With every scream elicited from the objects of their fear—Douglass saw this very well—the enslavers only grew more enthusiastic in their religious exultations.

This was the reality in which Henny and Frederick moved. This was why Douglass called the complicity of American Christianity in slavery "the darkest feature of slavery" and at the same time "the most difficult to attack."[40] Their awareness of the reality, however, only served to deepen the abolitionists' predicament. They could not unsee the outrage. They couldn't help but draw attention to the most twisted features of the system. Such was the nature of their adversary, however, that the louder they shouted, the stronger it became.

The Politico-
Theological Crisis

THERE WAS NOTHING NEW in an alliance between men of property and men of the cloth at the power nexus of the American slave republic. Priests and kings, after all, have colluded throughout history. But there was something new in the form of the first American counterrevolution. Its novel feature was its reliance on seemingly democratic means of popular religion to achieve its antidemocratic ends. The American counterrevolution was thus a postdemocratic event in essential ways. It could only have taken the specific form it did after, not before, the democratic revolutions of the early modern world.

Among the first to glimpse the way in which democracy can turn on itself in this way was Alexis de Tocqueville. On his tour of America in 1831, Tocqueville registered on the one hand the new and striking power unleashed in the new American democracy. "The people reign in the American political world as the Deity does in the universe. . . . Everything comes from them, and everything is absorbed in them," he writes.[41] Other observers have tended to note the same surge of popular power, and they have often identified it with the popular religious awakenings.[42] "The apotheosis of the will of the majority was never greater in the South than in the years 1828 to 1861," says the historian Clement Eaton.[43] But Tocqueville could also sense that the extraordinary power of popular opinion might also yield a new form of tyranny. In the Old World, he explains, the tyrant, "to reach the soul, crudely struck the body"; in the New World, "tyranny leaves the body alone, and goes right to the soul."[44]

Like many modern political theorists, however, Tocqueville lost the thread of the argument in an excessively loose understanding of democracy. The unexamined premise, even today, is that democracy happens wherever the people get what surveys say they want at any point in time. But this is to conflate political action that is based on the shifting opinions of the majority with democratic self-government. In the actual world, nothing can govern itself through unreflective impulse. There is no freedom without reason. A democracy without the capacity for rational deliberation is a contradiction in terms. As counterrevolutionary elites in America came to understand, intuitively at first and then explicitly, the key to perpetuating privilege in an emerging democracy is to deprive the people not of their notional political power but of their faculty of reason. The aim was not to force compliance from without but, as Tocqueville observes, to secure obedience from within.

The assault on abolitionist infidelity was central to this project of securing obedience from within. It was the internal core of the same effort that expressed itself outwardly with the heavier tools of gag rules, censorship of the mails, vigilantism, death threats, and outright murder. "No person can safely reside in the South who is suspected of liberal views on the subject of slavery," Professor Charles Shaw of the University of Virginia explained—in an essay that he preferred to publish anonymously.[45] Even in the relatively free northern press, pressure from vested interests meant that free and fair discussion was often hard to find. Abolitionists were routinely shoved aside to make room for writers with views more congenial to the wealthy and powerful. All these assaults on freedom of thought drew their internal support from the appeal to true religion against the depredations of the infidels. The closing of the American mind was astonishingly swift and thorough.

FREDERICK DOUGLASS understood well the self-deconstructing character of American democracy in the early republic. On the eve of the war, as he was delivering a speech at Boston's Tremont Temple, a vigilante mob attacked the gathering. A battle of hot words and flying chairs ensued. Douglass himself led the abolitionists "like a trained pugilist," and the belligerents dragged him by his hair (his "wool," it was said), until his fellow abolitionists could rescue him.[46] The police sat out the mayhem for three hours and finally moved in—not to arrest the rioters but to clear everyone out of the temple. Unbowed, Douglass appeared a few days later at the Music Hall. "No right was deemed by the fathers of the Government more sacred than the right of speech," he declared from the same stage that Parker had made famous. "Theodore Parker had maintained it with steadiness and fidelity to the last." The defense of this right, he understood, was at dead center in the struggle over slavery. "Slavery cannot tolerate free speech," he told the crowd at the music hall. "Five years of its exercise would banish the auction block and break every chain in the South."[47]

Two years later, in the middle of the shooting war, Douglass spoke again of the riot at the Tremont Temple. In earlier times, he tells the people of New York, Americans "could devise no better way . . . to cure a woman of Quakerism than by the cartwhip." But now we have the principle of free speech. "Such is my confidence in the potency of truth, and the power of reason," he goes on to say, "I hold that had the right of free discussion been preserved during the last thirty years . . . from the first ruthlessly struck down all over the South, . . . we should now have no slavery to breed rebellion."[48] It is a remarkable proposition, especially coming from one who devoted his life's work to the struggle against slavery. As his allusion to the religious persecutions of yore makes clear, Douglass was particularly sensitive to the role of religion, and not merely the formal censorship of speech through law, in suppressing the freedom of thought.

Theodore Parker, of course, had long since grasped and articulated the infidels' predicament. Upon returning from his year-long journey to Europe, where he deepened his connections with the continent's radical thinkers, Parker surveyed the devastation of the intellectual landscape in the aftermath of the battle of the Bible. "In no nation on earth is there such social tyranny of opinion," he observes. "The Democratic hands of America have sewed up her own mouth with an iron thread."[49] And then: "There are no chains like those wrought in the name of God and welded upon their victims by the teachers of religion."[50]

IN AN 1857 SPEECH excoriating the US Supreme Court's *Dred Scott* decision, Abraham Lincoln decries the growing national fervor to extend slavery in perpetuity and notes with dismay that "the theology of the day is fast joining the cry."[51] In 1858, he reads Frederick Ross's work, *Slavery Ordained of God*, and pens a scathing note. On the theology of slavery, Lincoln adds, "The Almighty gives no audable [sic] answer to the question, and his revelation—the Bible—gives none—or, at most, none but such as admits of a squabble."[52] "Here are twenty-three ministers of different denominations, and all of them are against me but three," Lincoln tells a political ally in October 1860: "These men know well that I am for freedom in the territories, freedom everywhere as far as the Constitution and laws will permit, and that my opponents are for slavery. They know this, and yet, with this book in their hands, in the light of which human bondage cannot live a moment, they are going to vote against me." In 1864, he remarks, in that same, ironic tone: "It seems that God had borne of this thing [slavery] until the very preachers of religion came to teach it from the Bible."[53]

It is in this context that one should read the memorable line that appears in his Second Inaugural Address: "Both read the same Bible, and pray to the same God; and each invokes His aid against the other."

The tendency among the ideologues today is to read only the first half of this sentence. At the inauguration of the forty-fifth president in 2017, for example, a US senator from Missouri cited the first clause to suggest that the nation would continue to find unity after the divisive election of 2016 by reading the same Bible and praying to the same God. But the second half of Lincoln's sentence makes quiet mockery of any such interpretation.

In *Ruins*—the book that Lincoln absorbed as young man of the lyceum—Volney offers a "both sides" analysis of his own. He describes a conflict between the Russians and the Turks in which both sides pray to their God and invoke his aid against the other. Volney doesn't bother to hide the obvious conclusion. When the Russians and the Turks talk about God, they aren't talking about anything that deserves the name of God.

In his Second Inaugural Address, Lincoln tells us that he has seen the same reality that Douglass saw in the household of Captain Auld and which Theodore Parker witnessed on the nation's theological battlefields. America's Bible-based version of the Christian religion had fashioned itself into the cornerstone of the counterrevolutionary American slave republic. It became the chief accomplice in one of the greatest crimes against humanity in modern history. The consequence of this politico-theological catastrophe would soon become apparent. The only remaining answer to the terrifying violence of slavery would be the terrifying violence of a civil war.

5

WITH
ALL
NATIONS

The Springtime
of the Peoples

OTTILIE ASSING WAS thirty-three years old when she stepped off the *India Queen* in the summer of 1852. The suicide attempt, the adulterous liaison with a dying actor, and the spiteful glances from the burghers of Hamburg—all that was behind her now. She was going to hurl herself at America. Most of her hopes rested on verbal assurances from her friendly editor at the *Morning Paper for Educated Readers* to publish her reporting back in Germany. She knew it wasn't going to be easy. "The stench of religion permeates all of life" in America, she writes a year after arriving. "I would feel more comfortable if there were more paintings, better drama, and less religion!"[1] No matter; she was determined to tell the world about the good and the bad in the land of the future. She was not altogether deluded in supposing that she was carrying the torch back to its point of origin in the spirit of a liberator.

There was no one quite like Assing, and yet she was not alone. In her educational pedigree, her bourgeois sensibility, and her political radicalism, she was representative of a cadre that landed on American shores around the time she did. They numbered only about 10,000, but they fanned out across the American continent with surprising impact. They brought with them a philosophy that in their own understanding had first burst onto the world stage in the Western Hemisphere. Their impact on events in America has for too long been underappreciated. And they weren't there entirely by accident. The forces that put Assing and her cohort aboard ships such as the *India Queen* had global reach, and the ideals to which they appealed were forged well beyond their point of origin.

Had the United States existed in the kind of splendid isolation that still colors the mythical history, the American slave republic of the middle of the nineteenth century would likely have persisted undisturbed by the noises from the fanatical fringes of abolitionism for many decades to come. Then again, an isolated United States might never have become a slave republic in the first place. The precondition of American slavery in the middle of the nineteenth century, after all, was a global trading system that depended increasingly on cheap American cotton. Lincoln indirectly acknowledged the global context of the conflict in the final sentence of his Second Inaugural Address, which closes with the wish for "a just and a lasting peace among ourselves and with all nations."

It is therefore less surprising than it might at first seem that the same global system that enabled the rise of the American slave republic nurtured the resistance to it, and that the injustices it engendered elsewhere should have rebounded in the direction of America. In any event, the shock did come, it came from the outside, and it arrived partly in the form of ideas, but mostly in the form of people such as Ottilie Assing. After 1848, the reinforcements washed ashore in numbers that no one had anticipated. A nation built by immigrants would have to be rescued from itself by immigrants.

IN 1848, THE SCATTERED embers of the American and Haitian Revolutions burst into open flames in the series of extraordinary, continental-scale disturbances that shook the European order. It started in the restive cantons of Switzerland, then quickly spread to Rome, forcing the pope to flee for safety to the homes of friendly oligarchs, and then leaped over to Venice before exploding on the streets of Paris in February 1848. The monarchy was overthrown, a second republic was declared, and slavery in the French colonies was abolished. In a matter of months, the red tide swept through northern and western Europe. The regimes in Netherlands, Belgium, Prussia, and the seat of the Habsburg Empire in Vienna trembled in what enthusiasts described as "the springtime of the peoples."

Though the disturbances of 1848 were too complicated and multifarious to reduce to any single meaning, the center of gravity around which all revolved was the rising power of working and middle classes. The masses—and especially the more refined elements of them—were fed up with a system that squeezed them at every corner for the benefit of a privileged elite. The old order was on the defensive, and so were the old ideas about the duties of the working people to their long-established overlords.

The new ideas, on the other hand, were not in all cases well formed or universally embraced. The revolutionaries were soon split between those who emphasized liberalizing political reforms and those who also favored more radical visions of economic restructuring. In the eyes of the defenders of the status quo, the presence of economic radicals was all the evidence needed to condemn the entire revolution as nothing more than a plot to steal their riches and destroy civilization at its foundations. Karl Marx—a creature of 1848 to the end—articulated the sum of all fears: "A specter is haunting Europe—the specter of communism."

IN AMERICA, THE FIRST effect of the news of the European revolutions was to tickle national pride. The establishment-friendly historian George Bancroft exulted that "the echo of American democracy" could once again be heard from the other side of the sea.[2] Upon hearing that the marching citizens of Venice were shouting "Long live the United States! Long live our sister republic!"[3] Americans congratulated themselves for having blazed the trail to freedom. American hearts swelled with satisfaction in the knowledge that the United States was the first—and only—major power to recognize the new French republic established in 1848.

The news from Europe, however, reached an America divided against itself and sliding into the grasp of its own counterrevolution. When progressive thinkers looked at events in Europe, they ached for what might have been. "Liberty and equality have long been American ideas; they were never American facts," explains Theodore Parker, with his eye on the "Proclamation of the Abolition of Slavery in the French Colonies" of April 27, 1848. "America sought liberty only for the whites. But France has . . . attempted to make our ideas into facts."[4] In his freshly printed newspaper the *North Star*, Frederick Douglass describes the news of the revolutions as "a bolt of living thunder" targeting with equal force the despots of Europe, the Tories of England, and the slaveholders of America."[5] Like Parker, he saw tremendous hypocrisy in the self-congratulatory celebrations of 1848 in America. "Why should we shout when a tyrant is driven from his throne by Garibaldi's bayonets, and shudder and cry peace at the thought that the American slave may one day learn the use of bayonets also?" he asks.[6]

America's progressives identified profoundly with Europe's revolutionaries. The intrepid journalist Margaret Fuller, on assignment in Europe, went so far as to have a secret love affair with one of them in Italy. (Possibly married him; at any rate, they had a baby.)[7] "I listen to the same arguments against the emancipation of Italy, that are used against our blacks; the same arguments in favor of the spoilation of Poland as for the conquest of Mexico," Fuller writes back from the front lines of the Italian struggle.[8]

The leaders of the American counterrevolution demonstrated just as swiftly that they had little more than a rhetorical interest in the European revolutions. They were all for democracy—but only so long as it was the kind of democracy that protects the rights of property, above all of property in slaves. "The great object of government is the protection of property at home and respect and renown abroad," Daniel Webster reminded Americans, and his fellow men of property in the North and South nodded in agreement.[9]

They soon identified the turmoil of 1848 with the terror that followed from 1789. Here was proof that a proper democracy was a rare thing, possible only on American soil, where a distinctive understanding of the racial order among whites, Blacks, and natives, together with an exceptional faith in the right God and the rights of property, kept the people from getting out of hand with their democratic pretensions. Such a system would never work in the flawed, unbelieving culture of Europe, the wise old men said. The new European revolutionaries, conservatives in the mold of James Henley Thornwell concluded, were socialists, communists, infidels, and—it all meant the same thing—abolitionists. The rot could be traced, they were sure, to 1789. As the South Carolina governor and serial rapist James Henry Hammond pointed out, the union of abolitionism and religious infidelity was "first concentrated to a focus at Paris" with the first (ultimately ineffective) attempt to abolish slavery during the original French Revolution.[10]

THE YEAR 1848 WAS one of those years that stands for a philosophical event, too. One representative of the new spirit was Ottilie Assing's uncle's friend, Alexander von Humboldt. Already famous as an intrepid naturalist, Humboldt achieved superstar levels of celebrity with *Cosmos*, a multivolume 1840s blockbuster that provided a natural history of, well, the entire universe. But he was also a champion of the liberal values of the Enlightenment.[11] He traveled in Cuba and came back loudly excoriating slavery as "the greatest evil that has befallen mankind." Having lived among the indigenous peoples of South America, he was certain that there are "no races which are more noble than others. All are equally entitled to freedom." His science was bold enough that the religious authorities often found it necessary to censor those parts of it that contradicted the Holy Scriptures. Although an old man by the time the revolution came and a good friend of the Prussian king, Humboldt joined in the demonstrations in support of political reform, and the revolutionaries later returned the compliment by holding his works up high as an example of how science and reason would light up the path to a republican tomorrow.

But few doubted that the philosopher of the hour was Ludwig Feuerbach (1804–1872). The spirit of '48 said that the human world would have to be rebuilt on human foundations, not on the rights of property or the claims of some otherworldly religion, and no one appeared to speak more directly on behalf of humans against the tyrannical fictions of their own creation than Feuerbach. The essence of his message was that in all their long history of worshipping God, humans had only ever been investing their hopes in an alienated version of themselves. God is just a confused image of man, he said, and the age of theology must yield to the new, liberal, republican age of anthropology. At a heady moment in the revolutionary process, Feuerbach ascended to the Frankfurt Parliament, which later came to be called—not in a nice way—"the philosophers' parliament."

In America, consequently, the opposition to 1848 soon took on the character of a philosophical and religious police action. In the leading conservative journals of the time, Feuerbach's philosophy is denounced as "godless humanism," "atheistic nihilism," and "vulgar atheism." In the crowd of intellectual malefactors from Europe polluting American thought—the French positivist Auguste Comte and the English philosopher John Stuart Mill were unrepentant humanists, too—Feuerbach unquestionably comes off as the worst of the lot. He is so bad that he even makes Auguste Comte look good. A positivist, a soft atheist, and a utopian political thinker with a cult following, Comte, like Feuerbach, heralds the end of the "age of theology" and the rise of the "age of anthropology." But Comte at least writes favorably of the role of religion in inculcating moral values, some conservatives note, in contrast with the ham-fisted Feuerbach, who "assails Christianity with the ribaldry of old-school infidelity."[12]

THE FATE OF 1848 was decided not in the philosophical journals, however, but on the streets and in the jailhouses. The revolutionaries may have been on the right side of history, but they soon discovered to their dismay that history can take a very long time to make up its mind. By the fall of 1849, the monarchs, the military men, and the holy ministers of the old order had roared back to power. The reaction cracked down hard on those who had cherished hopes for change. In Germany itself, the tragic consequences arguably extended for a full century. Only after two world wars and its own program of genocidal expansion did Germany embrace the liberal, progressive spirit of 1848.

In its second act, consequently, 1848 produced a diaspora of the desperate and the disillusioned. Much of the migration took place within Europe, as refugees shuffled from one benighted country to another. A substantial number, however, departed for new continents, with North and South America at the top of the list. In the years preceding the shooting war over slavery, hundreds of thousands of Europeans emigrated to the United States. Tens of thousands of Germans settled in Missouri, Kentucky, Ohio, New York, Wisconsin, and Texas. To speak of the numbers that count: Germans alone eventually represented one out of every ten soldiers in the Union army, or roughly the same proportion as Blacks.

Most of the immigrants came in search of economic opportunity. Their moves were thus an indirect consequence of the failure of the revolutionary process in Europe to yield meaningful economic reform, combined with the thirst for labor in the New World. Sprinkled among the masses of economic refugees, however, was a special cadre of individuals who were the more direct representatives of the revolution. Numbering perhaps 10,000 or so, these hard-liners came to be known as "the 48ers." Like Ottilie Assing, they came mostly from the educated classes and mostly from German-speaking lands. They were wantonly progressive in their political, social, and religious convictions. In America, they had an immediate and profound impact on the labor movement, public education, publishing, the arts, and abolitionism, and they set the tone for much of the rest of the German community.

The Revolution Will
Be Translated

OTTILIE ASSING'S FIRST STOP upon arriving in America was Friedrich Kapp's living room in Hoboken, New Jersey. That's where the revolutionary vanguard liked to stay. Born in 1824 to a family of educators in the province of Westphalia, Kapp was made to order for the revolutions of 1848. At his uncle's house he formed a tight friendship with Ludwig Feuerbach himself, and he promptly joined the left side of the Hegelian movement as a lawyer and a part-time journalist for a utopian socialist magazine. Inevitably, he ended up on the losing side of the rebellions. After a daring escape from a Prussian prison, he fled to Brussels and then Paris. Hounded out of Paris and then Geneva by police, he settled in the New York City area in 1850.

In America, as far as Kapp was concerned, the revolution continued. He immediately hatched a plot to bring Ludwig Feuerbach over from Germany. (The philosopher was tempted, but ultimately declined.) He threw himself into journalistic crusades and Republican Party politics. After a harrowing trip to Florida, he became an outspoken abolitionist, too, and published a book vehemently denouncing slavery.[13] A critical player in delivering the German vote to Lincoln in the election of 1860, he dreamed of combining "German idealism with American realism."[14] He was blunt—and thoroughly Feuerbachian—about the first step in the program: "The Americans will rise to a much more eminent position as soon as they get rid of Christianity."[15]

He had to like Ottilie Assing. He found her a room in a neighboring apartment in Hoboken, and they remained political and social allies for years to come. In later days, when Assing would sometimes return home with famous friends and secret plots to provoke a civil war, Kapp would prove ready to offer his aid to the cause. Together, they served as a kind of aboveground railroad station in Hoboken for still more refugees from the European crisis. From Kapp's and Assing's living rooms, the 48ers fanned out across the continent, with the largest number landing in the Upper Midwest.

Among the most memorable of the newcomers was August Willich (1810–1878). Rumored to be the love child of a Hohenzollern prince and a Polish actress, Willich was raised as a member of the landed aristocracy of Prussia in the home of Friedrich Schleiermacher—the theologian later blamed for starting the liberalizing tendency that disgracefully climaxed in the works of Strauss and Feuerbach. He grew into an unapologetic traitor to his class. At the age of thirty-six, he resigned his position in the Royal Prussian Army and declared his loyalty to republican and communist principles. In 1848, he became a military leader on the people's side of the revolution, and his aide-de-camp was Friedrich Engels (the other author of *The Communist Manifesto*). Forced to flee when it all fell apart, he moved to London and joined the League of Communists, where he got into a fight with (Engels's coauthor) Karl Marx because he felt that Karl was just too conservative. August challenged Karl to a duel, Karl refused to show but sent a stand-in, and the unfortunate alter-Marx got a hole in the head on a cold beach in Belgium.

In America, Willich bumped along from Brooklyn to Ohio, rising to prominence as a leader of the German community and a tireless advocate for abolition, public education, the Republican Party, and the refounding in America of "a REPUBLIC OF LABOR AND INTELLIGENCE."[16] He figured out soon enough which American leaders were prepared to join him on the journey. At a grand celebration in Ohio, he publicly defended Theodore Parker against attacks from religious conservatives, inveighing that "it is the duty of every German freeman" to stand up for this "American warrior of the mind" as he attempted to educate the benighted American public and liberate it from the grip of slavery.[17]

Never one to be outflanked on the left, Willich soon came to be known as "the reddest of the Red."[18] During the war over slavery, he commanded the 32nd Indiana Infantry Regiment, also known as the "First German," which won national recognition for its discipline and bravery. Even while drilling his soldiers on innovative military techniques, Willich would lecture them on the truths of Marxism (having patched up with Karl). As physically courageous as he was intellectually daring, he had his horse shot out from under him, was captured, released in a prisoner exchange, returned to battle, and played critical roles in the siege of Chattanooga and the Georgia campaign, before getting seriously wounded and sent back to guard the home front in Ohio as a major general.

In Wisconsin and then Missouri, the 48ers had their representative in Carl Schurz (1829–1906), who got his start fighting the Royal Prussian Army in 1848, alongside Willich, Fritz Anneke, and others who would regroup in the Union army. In America he became a powerful advocate for the antislavery cause and the man he took to be its rightful leader, Abraham Lincoln. During Lincoln's 1858 campaign for the US Senate, he translated his hero's debate performances against Stephen Douglas in real time for the benefit of enthusiastic Germans in the audience. In the Union army, he rose to the rank of major general, and in the aftermath of the war, after drifting to the right, he attained still greater political influence as a US senator and a secretary of the Interior. His wife, Margarethe Schurz, established the first kindergarten in America.

In 1854, a group of radicals including Bernhard Domschke (1827–1869) and Karl Heinzen (1809–1880) gathered in Kentucky and produced a succinct statement of the proper German position on the American crisis. The "Louisville Platform" was against slavery, against religion in any of its recognized forms, and for women's rights. Rather boldly, it was also against the presidency itself and the US Senate, proposing to replace these antidemocratic features of the US Constitution with a unitary legislature representing all the people.

Among the 48ers who remained in the Old World, the American scene in all its hopes and contradictions remained the subject of keen interest, and few were more interested or more influential than Karl Marx. From his exile in London, he threw his pen across the ocean, contributing a remarkable 487 articles (with Engels's help) to the *New York Daily Tribune* from 1852 to 1862. The traffic in ideas also flowed in the reverse direction. The 48ers in America kept an eager eye on the homeland, and some eventually returned to carry on with their revolutionary projects in Europe.

THE 48ERS BROUGHT to America not just their radical political sensibilities but their specific philosophical and literary tastes. One of their most successful imports was Alexander von Humboldt. Emerson lionized Humboldt as one of the "wonders of the world." Henry David Thoreau appears to have experienced nature through the great naturalist's writings before discovering it in his own backyard in Concord. Every academy of learning worth its salt in America wanted Humboldt on its list of members, and most of them got their wish.[19]

Americans quickly discovered the political nuggets in the science. "Humboldt's open liberalism and his opinions on slavery are reason enough to make conservatives and Democrats furious," Ottilie Assing pointed out.[20] Frederick Douglass's *North Star* ran a series of glowing articles on the great scientist. Garrison admired him so much that he asked Theodore Parker to produce a piece on the man and his work, which the humanist minister happily supplied. Humboldt, says Parker in the pages of *The Liberator,* "is the Friend of Mankind, always on the side of Progress and Humanity. He takes the side of the Indian in North and South America against his conqueror. He recognizes the natural right of the African."[21]

As influential as Humboldt's progressive naturalism, paradoxically, was Hegel's idealism. For a time, it looked as if Hegel himself would rise like the owl of Minerva to preside over the philosophy of the new republic. In Ohio, Willich joined with fellow dialecticians to form the nucleus of the "Ohio Hegelians." In Missouri, Henry Clay Brockmeyer (1826–1906), a poet and future Union army soldier with a history of run-ins with religious authorities, helped launch the "St. Louis Hegelians." America's Hegelians could rejoice in the words of the master himself, who announced in one of his Berlin lectures that "America is therefore the land of the future, where, in the ages that lie before us, the burden of the World's History shall reveal itself."[22] Walt Whitman eventually got the message: "Only Hegel is fit for America—large enough and free enough."[23]

Arguably a more urgent cause for the Germans than introducing Hegel to Americans was reacquainting them with Thomas Paine. Scandalized by the way Americans in the throes of their counterrevolution had treated the erstwhile hero of the first American Revolution, Willich and 200 of his

closest friends in the German community of Cincinnati organized a celebration in 1859 in memory of the author of *The
Rights of Man*. A growing number of similar celebrations of
Paine spread across the country. The 48ers took to America
so well, in part, because they did not think it was a foreign
country. On the contrary, they sometimes felt that they understood it better—or at any rate remembered its original promise better—than the residents they encountered upon arrival.

MANY 48ERS—Kapp, Schurz, Willich, and Assing among many
others—became abolitionists. Karl Heinzen, to name one, set
up a radical newspaper in New York, then moved with his
paper to Boston to insert his brand of atheism and outspoken
feminism into the antislavery and labor movements. The holy
people were predictably incensed, but the abolitionists welcomed the new addition. Wendell Phillips became a staunch
supporter of Heinzen's efforts, and Garrison praised Heinzen's
Pionier for its "manly and fearless utterance on all subjects."[24]
Like many of his fellow 48ers, Heinzen was as contemptuous
of the racism that pervaded all sections of American society as
he was militant in his abolitionism. Having developed a taste
for direct and sometimes violent action in 1848, he dismissed
many of the white, moral-suasion abolitionists as "peace toot-
lers." Free Blacks, on the other hand, had an "unvarnished
sense of right," he said, and understood much better than
whites the needs and purposes of abolitionism.

Other Germans also married into the abolitionist movement or otherwise contributed to it in personal ways. German émigré Charles (Karl) Follen (who preceded the 48ers)
so inspired William Lloyd Garrison that Garrison named one
of his sons Charles Follen Garrison. (Sadly, Theodore Parker,
having delivered the eulogy for Charles Follen, was called
upon to speak at the funeral of Garrison's eponymous son,

who died at the age of seven.) Then Garrison's daughter Fanny paired up with Henry Villard, born Ferdinand Heinrich Hilgard, the revolutionary-minded teenage son of a reactionary father. Villard had fled Germany after the revolutions of 1848 and changed his name in America to avoid recapture.

But the 48ers did not simply join the abolitionist movement; they changed it in decisive ways. Mostly, they radicalized it. As much by their loud example as by direct interventions in the conversation, they cleared the space into which the revolutionary character of the antislavery project could unfold in all its dimensions—philosophical, religious, economic, and political. To be sure, many American leaders—Theodore Parker among them—took pains to insist that they were not as far out on the limb as the Germans. And yet, by virtue of having the German extreme against which to distinguish themselves, they permitted themselves to step much farther out on that limb than they might otherwise have dared.

The case of the inimitable Moncure Conway illustrates the consequences on the American mind of direct contact with German revolutionaries. Not long after setting up his renegade ministry in Cincinnati, Conway befriended August Willich and promptly developed a fascination with the German community and its culture. He read Strauss intensively and was never the same again. The fruit of this brush with German thought was a schism in his own congregation, which proved to be less liberal than he might have hoped.[25] But Conway pushed on. The Germans of Cincinnati reintroduced him to the work of his own countryman, Thomas Paine, and with that Conway believed he had the guidance he needed to rethink the meaning of the American Revolution. He joined the Germans at Willich's grand and beery 1859 party in honor of Paine, where the crowd passed a resolution in praise of "the heretic clergy" of the day, among whom they named Theodore Parker the leader.

Frederick Douglass, too, developed a fascination with German culture. He snapped up German grammar books and started to teach himself German. He put his daughter Annie, too, in German lessons. "To no class of our population are we more indebted for valuable qualities of head, heart, and hand, than the German," he pronounced.[26] His fondness for these immigrants of the mind had everything to do with where they stood on the only issue that mattered. "A German has only to be a German to be utterly opposed to slavery," he said.

OTTILIE ASSING SET OFF from her Hoboken headquarters and swiftly zeroed in on the noisy contradictions of her newly adopted society. The rights of woman were inevitably among the first subjects of her reporting. The women's movement in America had recently passed through its moment of self-discovery at Seneca Falls in 1848, and Assing was eager to meet the protagonists. She couldn't help remarking in a letter to her sister that many of the women involved were "tactless and vulgar."[27] Soon enough, she concluded that German activists were there not merely to observe American women in action but to guide them toward more sophisticated and effective methods in the quest for justice.[28]

Fascinated by the intersection of race and religion, she next began to travel widely in the African American world. She spent nights in revival tents with people of all colors and attended services in Black churches (for sociological purposes, not worship). She soon focused her reporting onto the extraordinary Reverend James Pennington—the same reverend who presided over the wedding of Frederick and Anna Douglass shortly after they arrived as free people in the North. Awarded an honorary doctorate from the University of Heidelberg, Pennington was already a celebrated figure in Germany.

She next devoted attention to Wendell Phillips, the spellbinding abolitionist orator. He was an inspired choice, but not quite inspiring enough. Phillips was one of those men who could hold a crowd better than he could hold a room, and Assing moved on.

Three years after stepping ashore, Assing came across one of the small number of books that would change the course of her life. The famous ex-fugitive orator Frederick Douglass had just released his second, much more comprehensive autobiography, titled *My Bondage and My Freedom*.[29] Whether Ottilie fell in love first with the man she encountered in its pages can't be known. What is certain is that she had at last found a clear goal around which to organize her energetic presence in America. She was going to translate this masterpiece. And she was going to introduce her readers in Germany to its incomparable author. But first she had to meet him for herself.

At First Sight

A SUMMER'S DAY, 1856. His translator arrives in Rochester, New York, on the train and looks for him first at his printing office in town. She is directed to his home in the outskirts, and so she walks the two miles across a "charming, bucolic landscape." High upon a hill that commands a view of the scene, surrounded by a beautiful garden, she finds a "stately, villa-like home." A man greets her at the door, and his physical presence swiftly overwhelms the printed page. He is a "rather light-skinned mulatto," "of unusually tall, slender, and powerful stature."[30] He has "a prominently domed forehead" to suggest intelligence; an "aquiline nose" that indicates refinement; and "narrow, beautifully carved lips" that speak "more of his white than his black origin." His voice is "mellifluous, sonorous, flexible," and it reaches the listener as if "for the first time to reveal a truth lay unspoken in everyone's heart." His "entire appearance . . . tells a tale of past storms and struggles." At first sight, the translator knows that this man possesses an awesome willpower "that brooks no obstacle . . . in the face of all odds." There cannot be much doubt about it: Ottilie was in love. It was there for all to see in the preface for the German translation of Douglass's autobiography.[31]

At the least, they became intimate friends. The relationship that began with the ascent to the estate of the great "mulatto" lasted through eighteen summers, and it was kept alive with a regular correspondence through the winters. In letters to her sister, Ludmilla, Ottilie represents her union with Frederick as the moral equivalent of marriage. (Douglass's wife, Anna, presumably enjoyed only the legal equivalent.) What Frederick confided in letters to Ottilie cannot be known because, upon her death, he rushed over to her lodgings and made sure to burn them all. It seems safe to say that whatever Frederick wanted in a personal way from Ottilie was not quite the same as what she wanted of him. Assing's unabashed glorification of Douglass as an unimpeachable savior of humanity lent a tragic air to her longing that the hero of her reporting would one day throw it all away to be with her.

The nature of their relationship in the flesh, however, is merely a historical curiosity in comparison with the political partnership that blossomed from that first meeting. This was a match made in an ideological heaven. They each brought distinctive skills and perspectives, yet they saw "eye to eye" on every major issue of the day.[32] Within a year of their meeting, Ottilie was doing her part to promote her new political hero. "The lion of this year's season was above all Frederick Douglass, that extraordinary mulatto," she tells her German readers. "Fire and passion combine with a complete mastery of the issues and admirably correct proportionality; through perfect handling of language, the wealth of ideas is pressed to full effect."[33] Very swiftly, too, Ottilie settled into her self-assigned role of educating Frederick. She chanced a copy of Goethe's works, she tells Ludmilla, "And you can imagine what a joy it is to initiate Douglass into it."[34]

They surely bonded over the rights of women. Douglass had joined the seminal Seneca Falls gathering, and he was well on his way to being recognized as one of America's great advocates of women's rights. In her reporting on the women's movement, Assing observes that the great difference between the European branch of the movement and its American counterpart is that in the new world "many important, experienced, and universally esteemed men have put themselves forward as warm champions of women's emancipation."[35]

In her reporting, Assing also thrills over Douglass's work on what she translates as the *"unterirdische Eisenbahn."* By Assing's reckoning, the "subterranean railroad" was guiding thousands of fugitives every year to freedom—and one of its central stations happened to be located underneath Douglass's own home in Rochester.

They must have discovered early, too, that they also had Toussaint L'Ouverture in common. Indeed, the throbbing heart of their political partnership was the vision that both perhaps first glimpsed in the leader of the Haitian Revolution. If Assing admired the rebel heroes of *Aphra Behn* and *Engagement in Santo Domingo*, Douglass positively exalted Toussaint L'Ouverture. The "Black Spartacus" of the West Indies was everything he wanted to be. Douglass took to enticing subscribers to his journals by offering them complimentary prints of L'Ouverture's image. He saw in his idol not just a champion of the enslaved but an icon of the Enlightenment. Often depicted reading Raynal's *History of the Two Indies*, L'Ouverture stood for the promise, in his own words, that "reason and education will spread across our regenerated soil . . . man will elevate himself on the wings of liberty."[36] From their shared admiration of L'Ouverture it was just a short step to joint support for John Brown—the man whose legacy would outshine even the hero of Haiti in Douglass's mind in later years—for here was one American who staked his life on the idea that Black people had the power and the right to resist the American slave republic.

Assing apparently had no trouble believing in the power of nonwhite arms and minds—on the battlefield and on the political stage. Was it the experience of being half-Jewish? Of being trapped in the body of a woman? Or had she simply come to believe all the pretty words in those philosophical tomes of her youth? All we can know is that she was willing to lay it all on the line. Soon enough, together with Douglass and their mutual friend John Brown, she was in the thick of a plot that would count on Black power to smash the American slave republic.

Maybe the most curious thing about the affair is that Assing did not get to that militant place simply because Douglass was leading her on. To the contrary, it would be more accurate to say that he was just catching up with her. Had they met at an earlier point in his career, it seems unlikely that Frederick would have proved so receptive to the kind of political and philosophical radicalism that Ottilie was offering. His journey as an abolitionist through the rapidly shifting currents of the time had changed his thinking in a way that, though it made sense in retrospect, could hardly have been anticipated in advance. He only realized where he was going around the time that he opened the door and saw her standing there.

6

EVERY DROP OF BLOOD

The Parable of Covey

EVEN AS HIS CAREER elevated him to national prominence, Frederick Douglass returned with renewed intensity to the stories drawn from his youth. None of those stories seemed to matter more than the one about his violent struggle with the enslaver Edward Covey—the struggle that, in Douglass's own reckoning, made him a man. The parable of Covey is without question the climactic episode in the *Narrative of the Life of Frederick Douglass* that stunned American readers in 1845. It expands from about a dozen pages there to more than thirty in the 1855 autobiography that Ottilie Assing set about translating. Douglass told and retold the story to hundreds of audiences around the country and then once again in his final autobiography. Although the event happened when he was seventeen, its meaning seemed to unfold over time. It was never more of the moment than in the years immediately following his encounter with his new German friend.

AROUND THE TIME THAT the summer of religious revival gave way to a winter of pinching frost, Captain Auld had decided that the time had come for Frederick to be broken.[1] He had

had enough of him scrounging for food from the neighbors. Or maybe he just needed to do something about the insolence in those sixteen-year-old eyes. "Breaking" was a common practice in the slave system, and it was the work of dedicated practitioners. On the Eastern Shore, as it happened, a specialist lived not far from the revival campground. His was a small farmer with big dreams, and his name was Edward Covey.

Like Captain Auld himself, Covey enjoyed a local reputation as a "pious soul" and a "professor of religion." He was "my brother in the Methodist church," Douglass wryly observes. But Covey's hopes for wealth and station depended on his ability to rent human beings from his neighbors at a discount. He earned the discount by offering his services as an educator. Specifically, he educated his charges in the meaning of obedience. That is what slave breakers do.

The beatings started on the third day and extended with diligent ferocity over a period of six months. Every week or so, on some pretext or none, Covey laid into Frederick with a lash, raising welts as thick as a finger and causing the blood to drip off his back. Then he worked his slave on the Maryland cornfields until there was no more work left in him. By the summer of 1834, the training seemed complete. "I was broken in body, soul, and spirit," Douglass recalls. "My natural elasticity was crushed, my intellect languished, . . . the cheerful spark that lingered about my eye died." This, he said, is how "a man is made a slave."

On a hot August afternoon, Frederick snapped. He turned around and seized Covey by the throat. He clamped his fingers down hard enough to draw blood. Under a sweltering sun, the two men struggled violently, clawing each other around stacks of hay and piles of manure. Though careful not to inflict serious injury, Frederick refused to stand down. At one point, he knocked his adversary into the mire. At last exhaustion set in, and Covey retreated under the feeble pretense that he had finished the whipping.

Covey later said nothing about the episode. But henceforth he avoided Frederick's eyes and kept his distance. He wanted to pretend that nothing had happened. Frederick guessed that Covey was keeping silent to protect his reputation as a tamer of humans. The slave-master's power, he sensed, was more fragile than he had understood. Frederick himself had never felt better. The spring returned to his step, and he once again felt the determination to escape. This, he writes, is "how a slave is made a man." The fight with Covey was "the turning point in my career as a slave."

THE MOST OBVIOUS lesson that Douglass wished to convey to his abolitionist audiences is that slavery depends on violence. Apologists for slavery (even today)[2] routinely insist that the cruelties associated with enslavement are merely abuses of the system, not indictments of it. Where masters are good Christians, explains the proslavery reverend Thornton Stringfellow, cruelty is unknown on the plantations, except as an occasional act of loving-kindness.[3] "The crime is not slaveholding, but cruelty," adds his fellow Baptist, Richard Fuller of South Carolina.[4] But Douglass rejects this self-serving nonsense. "If it is right to hold a slave, it must be right to do the necessary thing, to withhold education and brutalize the slave," he says.[5] "Nature never intended that men and women should be either slaves or slaveholders, and nothing but rigid training long persisted in, can perfect the character of the one or the other."[6] Theodore Parker agrees: "The relation of master and slave begins in violence; it must be sustained by violence. . . . There is no other mode of conquering and subjugating a man."[7] In still fewer words: slavery is not wrong because it is cruel; it is cruel because it is wrong.

A second, perhaps more pressing lesson of the parable of Covey is that what begins in the threat of violence can only end with the threat of violence. The only way to fight power is with power. Those "who would be free must themselves strike the blow," Douglass repeats in one speech after another.[8] The words are borrowed from Lord Byron, who issued them in the context of his work on behalf of the revolution in Greece, but the insight comes straight from that fight on the Maryland shore. In Douglass's universe, no force from on high and no savior from another country will come to rescue the slave from the Coveys of the earth. Salvation will come in one way or another from the power of the enslaved people themselves.

The most surprising lesson from the parable of Covey, however, concerns the unexpected fragility of the master. The power of the enslaver, Frederick comes to understand, depends less on any real strength than on the perception of strength among his peers and among the enslaved. This dependence on mere perceptions is so great that the enslaver may choose to avoid confrontations so as to hide his weakness from others, and even from himself. The illusions and delusions of the master, Frederick further intuits, explain something of the excess of cruelty in the slave system. Enslaving fellow humans is hard, dangerous, and guilty work. It causes stress, fear, and hatred, rooted in the suppressed awareness that the enslaved individual is a potential equal in power. It is bound to produce resentment, and this resentment is bound to focus on the root source of the fear and loathing; namely, the humanity of the slave. It is on this account, Douglass explains to his audiences, that slavery invites an excess of cruelty, and that this excess could be a source of consolation and joy—and even of religious ecstasy. Vanity, delusion, and the apotheosis of reckless self-destruction are endemic to the condition of the master, just as submission and self-denial are to the slave.

These lessons from the parable of Covey seemed increasingly urgent in the world of the mid-1850s. In the arc that Douglass traced across those fraught years, the growing salience of that parable tracked the profound transformation in his relationship with the one individual who more than any other would come to define the trajectory of his own abolitionist career: John Brown.

Brown's Eyes

JOHN BROWN WAS the kind of man who left his mark at first sight. There was something in his gaze—"so transparent that all men see him through," said Emerson—that made people stop and ask themselves difficult questions about their own lives. Douglass was no exception to the rule. His first encounter with Brown came at a pivotal moment in Douglass's career, but its impact would become clear only many years later. In the home on Cedar Hill in Washington, D.C., where Douglass spent his final years amid busts of German philosophers, no man's image looks back from more of the paintings and photographs lining the walls than that of John Brown.

Douglass first experienced the gaze in 1847, when he stopped at Brown's home in Springfield, Massachusetts, on his move from Lynn, Massachusetts, to Rochester, New York.[9] Brown's eyes were "full of light and fire." He was "lean, strong, and sinewy," as "straight and symmetrical as a mountain pine," and "his bearing was singularly impressive." The house had "an air of destitution," says Douglass; its frugal lines seemed to conform more to the austere character of its owner than to his financial condition. Though a prosperous merchant at the time, Brown lived by choice in a poor neighborhood. The host offered his guest a Spartan meal of boiled beef and cabbage across a table "innocent of paint, veneering, varnish, or table-cloth." Brown's wife and sons waited on him in an almost cult-like atmosphere, obeying him in everything and observing him "with reverence." He was clearly "the master" of his house, Douglass says somewhat warily, "and was likely to become mine too if I stayed long enough."

In the eyes of many of his contemporaries, Brown was a figure walking out of the glory days of Puritan New England: Parker's coconspirator Franklin Sanborn joked that the old man was born more than a century late. He was righteous, he was angry, and he had the harshest verses of the Old Testament always at the ready. But Douglass saw something else in him, too.

No one was more convinced than Brown that his moral conscience revealed absolute truths that were subject to challenge by no authority, whether literal or clerical. Few were less restrained in their disgust with the established churches and theologians over their compromises with slavery. Brown's "awakening" to the slavery issue, by his own account, came from his encounters with the infidel abolitionists around William Lloyd Garrison, who first opened his eyes to a truth hidden from him by his earlier commitment to a complacent orthodoxy. It is at least curious that his closest allies—among them Douglass, Parker, Sanborn, Thomas Wentworth Higginson, and Henry David Thoreau—ranged along the heretical extremes of religious opinion. If their freethinking ways did not ultimately change Brown's Old Testament orientation, they nonetheless appear to have transformed his political theology into something that his Puritan forebears would hardly have recognized as their own.

After consuming their grim repast, Brown and Douglass got down to work. Brown laid out his extraordinary plan for the liberation of America's enslaved people. He began by agreeing with Douglass that the Garrisonian program of "moral sua-sion" would never work. Only the force of arms would do, and that force would necessarily come from the ebony arms of the enslaved people themselves. What was needed was to gather a force of escaped slaves in the mountains and wage a guerrilla war of attrition. Such an unconventional war, Brown prophe-sied, would undermine the institution of slavery by destroying "the money value of slave property."

Brown traced his finger across a map of the Appalachian Mountains. "God has given the strength of the hills to free-dom," he intoned. Blood would spill, he acknowledged, but he excused it all in the language of natural justice. "Slaveholders had forfeited their right to live," he told Douglass, and slaves have "the right to gain their liberty in any way they could."

The astounding vision of a mountain republic was national in scope and international in inspiration. Brown drew explic-itly on the example of guerrilla warfare in the Haitian Rev-olution.[10] His model was Toussaint L'Ouverture. A year after meeting with Douglass, Brown would travel to Europe and gather still more insights from the veterans of the revolu-tions of 1848 in Italy, Poland, and Bavaria. His plan had ele-ments of fantasy, but it did not lack for vigorous research and sophisticated theory.

Brown's vision was also America's nightmare, at least for the stolid majority who remained content to perpetuate the slave system. The expansionary imperative of slavery neces-sarily entailed growth in the number and economic impor-tance of the enslaved people, but the swelling population of slaves was in turn widely (and correctly) perceived as a threat to the system. "We of the South are emphatically surrounded by a dangerous class of beings—degraded stupid savages—who if they could . . . would re-act the St. Domingo tragedy," writes the editor of a Tennessee newspaper in 1837, invok-ing the dreaded specter of the Haitian Revolution.[11] And now here was Brown, acknowledging the threat that everyone recognized—and promising to bring it to life.

Brown left "a very deep impression on my mind and heart," Douglass writes. "My utterances became more and more tinged by the color of this man's strong impression."[12] The subsequent record abundantly confirms the point. Days after that first meeting, Douglass suddenly writes, "slaveholders, as such, can have no rights. They have no rightful existence on earth."[13] One year after the visitation, he shocks a crowd at Faneuil Hall with a startling pronouncement: "I would welcome the intelligence tomorrow, that the slaves had risen in the South, and that the sable arms which had been engaged in beautifying and adorning the South, were engaged in spreading death and devastation."[14]

By 1854, Douglass is saying that violent resistance against slave catchers is "wise and just."[15] In the 1855 version of the parable of Covey, he brings its first teaching into the open: "Human nature is so constituted, that it cannot *honor* a helpless man, although it can *pity* him, and even this it cannot do long, if the signs of power do not arise."[16] Soon enough, he announces that the "peaceful annihilation" of slavery "is almost hopeless." After the *Dred Scott* decision of 1857, he makes clear that only tactical considerations, not moral scruples, now stand in the way of violence: "We . . . contend that the slave's right to revolt is perfect, and only wants the occurrence of favorable circumstances to become a duty."[17] By the time he wrote these words, he could look over to Boston and see that at least one other person had landed on the same page.

Fugitive Justice

ON AN UNSEASONABLY WARM EVENING at the end of October 1850, the members of the Vigilance Committee of Boston gathered in a tense and sweaty room in Faneuil Hall.[18] Word had gotten out that fugitive-slave hunters were prowling around town with a warrant for the arrest of William and Ellen Craft. Theodore Parker was there, and so were Ralph Waldo Emerson and Frederick Douglass. For a thrilling hour, "the swarthy Ajax" of the abolitionist movement, as Douglass was coming to be known, stoked the flames of outrage with an incandescent defense of the natural rights of man against the recently enacted Fugitive Slave Act. The committee, roasting in the heat of its own indignation, resolved to protect the Crafts at all costs. "Every moment is liable to bring with it blood shed and carnage," Douglass scribbled in a hasty note to a friend.[19]

The Crafts were famous around the world for the daring artistry of their escape from Georgia two years previously. Ellen, who was of mixed race and light skinned, disguised herself as a young, infirm, white male planter. William played the part of the personal slave. Scrambling the boundaries of race, sex, and class, they brazenly rode first-class trains and steamboats north to freedom, talking their way through several scrapes with unsuspecting passengers, innkeepers, and old acquaintances who fortunately failed to recognize them.[20]

Upon arriving in Philadelphia, the Crafts appeared on stages alongside Frederick Douglass, William Wells Brown, and other leading abolitionists. William Craft recounted how his father, his mother, and his brother had been sold away when he was young, never to be seen again. Ellen shocked audiences with the whiteness of her skin. How was it, some abolitionists wondered, that so many had so much trouble acknowledging the horror of slavery until they saw it in their own skin? Moving on to Boston, where it was felt they would be safer, they were a natural fit for Theodore Parker's 28th Congregational Society. A skilled carpenter with a ferociously independent spirit, William was a "tall, brave," and "noble" man, observed Parker. When well-wishers suggested that he purchase his own freedom to keep the kidnappers away, Craft retorted, "I will buy myself, not with gold, but with iron!"[21]

For a time, the Crafts survived undisturbed in their new life. But fast on the passage of the Fugitive Slave Act as part of the Compromise of 1850, the Crafts' enslavers commissioned a pair of slave hunters from Georgia to capture the fugitives and return them to slavery. The slave catchers journeyed to Boston and took up residence at the United States Hotel. They were said to be as ugly as they were evil. A handbill distributed by outraged abolitionists alleged that the face of one of these miscreants was "uncommon bad." Parker himself confirmed the description: "I saw the face. It looked like total depravity incarnate."

The Vigilance Committee resolved to meet ugly with ugly. A man was needed to deliver the threat of violence in person to the despicable duo. The name of Theodore Parker was put forward. An objection rang out. This show of force was no task for a clergyman! Parker stood up and announced, "This committee can appoint me to no duty that I will not perform." At that moment, Douglass records, "I got a peep into Parker's soul."[22]

Parker was elected chairman of the Executive Committee of Boston's self-appointed vigilantes, and he quickly got down to business. The first step was to hustle Ellen Craft through the dark hours of the morning to a hideaway house in Brookline. Next, he made sure that William Craft was armed and ready for every eventuality. "I inspected his weapons," Parker writes. "His powder had a good kernel, and he kept it dry; his pistols were of excellent proof . . . I tested his poniard; the blade had a good temper . . . the point was sharp." Parker justifies the fearsome gear with the logic of natural right: "There was no law for him but the Law of Nature; he was armed and equipped 'as that law directs.'" He evinces no qualms about what the Law of Nature commands in this kind of case. "The fugitive has the same natural right to defend himself . . . that he has against a murderer or a wolf."[23]

With William fully prepped, Parker marched him over to the home of Lewis Hayden, a prosperous clothier and the de facto stationmaster of Boston's underground railroad. As an enslaved child, Hayden had seen his father sold away. His mother, who was half Native American and half white, lost her mind after being handed over to a man who bought her for sex. Flogged and imprisoned when she refused her master's demands, she threatened to kill herself and possibly her own son. Later, when he became a father, Hayden sat helpless as his own wife and son were sold away from him, never to be seen again. The purchaser was none other than Senator Henry Clay, a.k.a. the Great Compromiser, a principal architect of the Fugitive Slave Act. Then Hayden himself was traded away for a pair of unremarkable horses. Upon inspecting the horses, he later said, he was insulted to learn just how low his market value was. Hayden, in short, was a man with nothing left to fear in life that had not already happened to him. When the Georgian slave hunters came around for William Craft, he waved a torch over a barrel of gunpowder and promised to blow himself and everyone on the block to pieces if they tried to come in.[24]

A few days later there was a scare about Ellen. Were the kidnappers onto her hideout? Parker fished her out of Brookline. He brought along a hatchet just in case. Then he barricaded her together with William in his own home near Lexington. "I have written my sermons with a pistol in my desk—loaded, a cap on the nipple, and ready for action," he writes.[25] He was quick to draw a direct connection between his personal call to arms and the revolutionary heroism of his forefathers. "When I write in my library at home," he reminded his congregation, "there hangs the firelock my grandfather . . . zealously used at the Battle of Lexington."

Meanwhile, under Parker's direction, members of the Vigilance Committee organized a campaign of harassment against the slave hunters. Five formal complaints were filed in court against the pair in rapid succession for trivial offenses such as smoking in the streets, swearing in public, driving too fast, and slander. The charges were spurious; the point was to force the miscreants to turn up at the courthouse and post bail. At the courthouse, mobs drawn heavily from Boston's free Black population crowded menacingly around the Georgians and shouted, "There go the slave hunters!" The slave hunters, however, let it be known that they would not leave "'til they got hold of the [fugitives]."[26]

Parker decided to make it personal. He marched over to the United States Hotel with a few dozen of his friends and demanded to see the "ambassadors" from Georgia. The would-be kidnappers sent down word that they were otherwise engaged. Parker left the crowd in the lobby, pushed upstairs, and banged on their door. It cracked open and he barged in. "I told them that I had stood between them and violence once—I would not promise to do it again," Parker records.[27] Rather transparently, he was offering to "protect" them from the mob that he had helped to organize. They eyed the plainclothes minister and finally got the message. That same afternoon, the slave hunters were spotted slinking out of town on the train to New York.

The danger had passed, but only for the moment. According to Parker's report, Boston's reactionary industrial elites, led by the likes of Daniel Webster, were determined to show their love for their fellow oligarchs in the South and "thirsted for the blood" of Ellen and William.[28] It was decided that the Crafts would find no safe home in the land of the free. Money was needed to fund their flight to Europe, and so a rescue fund was established. Parker himself contributed $1,000 to the cause. There was one last detail to resolve before sending them off to Canada and then to England. William and Ellen had never been properly married.

On November 7, 1850, Parker performed the wedding ceremony. He brought along a Bible and bowie knife that he had scooped up at the holding house of another fugitive, and he offered the items as gifts for the newlyweds. Never one to fetishize the scriptures, he focused his attention on the blade. He called it a "sword," and he seemed eager for it to be used at any provocation. " 'With this sword I thee wed,' suited the circumstances of that bridal," he later comments.[29]

In England, the Crafts swiftly established themselves as dashing spokespersons for the enslaved. At the Crystal Palace, alongside exhibitions from around the world, they staged a mock slave auction to drive home the horror of buying and selling humans. William was "witty and erudite" and an "accomplished writer," the society reporters said, despite having learned to read only after securing his freedom. Ellen dazzled. She was "very intelligent" and the "chief attraction of the ball-room," they said. "Her conversation stamps her as being possessed of high intellectual attainment."[30]

THE FUGITIVE CRISIS was a clarifying moment for the nation. Many Americans finally jumped off the fence on one side or the other. Among the large part of the population that tacitly supported slavery, the extralegal activism in defense of fugitives such as the Crafts counted as proof that abolitionism was indeed the great disturber of the peace and the incarnate evil of the age. Among the abolitionists' hitherto silent fellow travelers, on the other hand, the brutality of the fugitive law forced a public reckoning with the horror of slavery. Ralph Waldo Emerson, for example, had long been opposed to slavery in principle, but he had also maintained a polite distance from the abolitionists, whom a decade previously he had rather condescendingly dismissed as "sour and narrow," "thin and blind," with "virtue so vice-like."[31] With the passage of the new law, however, he came off his high horse. "The fairest American fame ends in this filthy law," he declared. "I will not obey it, by God."[32] Later, in an essay on "courage," he offers "the leader and the soul of the vigilance committee" as a paradigm of that virtue.[33]

The effect of the crisis on that leader and soul of the Vigilance Committee was no less clarifying. Theodore Parker would never be the same. A roster of fugitives showed up in Boston in the footsteps of the Crafts—Thomas Sims, a man called Shadrack, Anthony Burns—and they produced a string of incidents that sometimes crossed the line into bloodshed. With each new wave of would-be kidnappers, Parker held forth at angry meetings and printed up furious posters to alert the public. He came to be known as "minister at large in behalf of all fugitive slaves in Boston."[34] His activism reached a kind of climax in the case of Anthony Burns, a fugitive from Virginia who had made his way to Boston as a stowaway crammed into a shipboard crawlspace without food for three weeks.

On the evening of May 26, 1854, while Burns languished

under arrest in the Boston courthouse jail, Parker and the Vigilance Committee whipped up a crowd at Faneuil Hall.[35] At the same time, Lewis Hayden marshalled a phalanx of Black abolitionists, and Parker's acolyte Thomas Wentworth Higginson—the most militant of the white abolitionists by some measure—recruited a squadron of white abolitionists. The biracial assault forces headed over to the courthouse with axes and a battering ram and hurled themselves against the courthouse door. The plan was to bring in Parker's crowd from Faneuil Hall and storm through the opening. But the communications failed, or possibly Parker got cold feet. The militants, presumably carried away in the heat of the moment, knocked the courthouse door down anyway, and Higginson surged inside, likely with Hayden at his side. But in the absence of backup from the Faneuil crowd, the marshals defending the courthouse were able to repulse the attackers. In the scuffle, a shot rang out. One of the marshals fell dead. Hayden later confided to friends that it was he who fired what might be called the first shot of the second American Revolution.

Burns was marched down to the dock with an armed guard and shipped back to slavery, but not before his case stirred the passions of Boston and the entire nation. In the aftermath of the assault on the courthouse, criminal charges rained down on the abolitionists. Parker himself was indicted, and in the year following the disturbance, the self-appointed minister of fugitives faced a trial and the real prospect of imprisonment.

EVEN AS HIS antislavery activism turned militant, paradoxically Parker's racialism continued to inflect his work. "The African is the most docile and pliant of all the races of men," runs a typical Parker commentary. "The stroke of an axe would have settled the matter long ago. But the black man would not strike."[36] And: "The African has the largest organs of generation in the world, the most erotic heat."[37] (He promoted arguably more negative stereotypes of the Irish, among whom he thought "lying, begging, stealing" counted as natural instincts.)[38] Notwithstanding his commitment to universal rights, Parker believed in racial differences, and the pinnacle of the racial heap in his mind belonged to "the Anglo-Saxon race"—or more exactly, the New England branch of that race, which was manly, bloodthirsty, and endowed with an "ethnological instinct for Freedom."[39]

By 1856, the Black abolitionist Charles Lenox Remond had heard enough.[40] If their taste for carnage and oppression made Anglo-Saxons "the superior race," then this could only be because they manifestly lacked "common humanity and decency."[41] At an 1858 celebration, the Black abolitionist John Rock confronted Parker and demanded that he stop with the talk about "docile Africans" and "bloodthirsty Anglo-Saxon" freedom lovers. Parker reportedly explained to Rock that he was speaking of the behavior of Blacks in the past, not the future.

Days after the encounter, Parker wrote to the historian George Bancroft urging him to include more stories about Black heroes in his chronicles of the American Revolution.[42] Though Parker never gave up on his racialized stereotyping, he remained unusually keen to celebrate Black violence in the service of justice for the enslaved. When fugitives from Maryland murdered their enslaver as he pursued them into Pennsylvania, Parker scandalized white America by rising to defend these Black fugitives for standing their ground. His ally Frederick Douglass, who helped the fugitives escape to Canada and wound up in possession of the very gun that was used to kill the enslaver, in turn defended Parker's position as "consistent and right."[43]

Even as he peddled racist tropes, Parker's closest collaborators included most of the leading Black abolitionists of the time—William C. Nell, Lewis Hayden, William Wells Brown, and, not least, Frederick Douglass. Douglass, at any rate, was prepared to exonerate Parker. "He would shed his blood as quickly for a black fugitive slave pursued by human hounds as for a white President of the United States," Douglass writes in 1885. "It has lately been attempted to class him with the contemners of the negro. Could that be established, it would convict him of duplicity and hypocrisy of the most revolting kind. But his whole life and character are in direct contradiction to that assumption."[44]

Drawn by the Sword

JOHN BROWN AND HIS BAND of abolitionist warriors descended on the prairie homes of proslavery settlers in the hot Kansas summer of 1856 and hacked five men to death with broadswords in their own backyards. Exactly what moral principle the murderous assault in Pottawatomie was intended to serve can still be debated, but no one at the time doubted that vengeance was part of the story. The attack came three days after proslavery militants had burned and sacked the town of Lawrence, Kansas, and two days after Preston Brooks brutally caned Charles Sumner on the floor of the US Senate. A total of twenty-nine people died that year in the cycle of retaliation and counterretaliations across Kansas. One of them was Brown's son Frederick. By the end of summer, Brown himself was a wanted man and rather dangerous to know.

Douglass wasn't sure about the Pottawatomie event—he called it "a terrible remedy for a terrible malady"—but that did not stop him from receiving his old friend when John Brown rolled into Rochester in late 1856.[45] He was also quite happy to introduce Brown to Ottilie Assing. The reporting coming from Assing's pen at the time reads like John Brown with a German accent: the "slaveocracy" has captured the American political

171

system; the nation cannot long survive half-slave and half-free; violence is unavoidable, she warns her German readership.[46] At some point, through Brown, Douglass and Assing met with a man by the name of "Colonel" Hugh Forbes. An English "soldier of fortune" and supposed veteran of the revolutions of 1848, Forbes proposed to regularize Brown's highly irregular troops with expert military advice. But first he needed money to save his destitute relatives in Europe, or so he claimed.

Douglass passed the fund-raising task to Ottilie Assing, whom he describes in his last autobiography as "a German lady deeply interested in the John Brown scheme." Assing in turn shopped Forbes among her German friends in New York. They were sure to have the money needed to keep Brown's new lieutenant aboard. Douglass had his doubts about the "Colonel," and Assing soon did, too, but neither doubted Brown. Both knew he intended to make a spectacular move very soon, and both were evidently eager to help him.

UPON LEAVING NEW YORK, John Brown swooped into Boston like a prophet out of Deuteronomy.[47] He wanted money, and he wanted guns. On the evening of January 4, 1857, he showed up in Theodore Parker's living room. William Lloyd Garrison was there, too, along with a small crowd of reformers.

It was the first time that Parker and Brown met in person, though the two were far from unknown to each other. As a leader of a group of Massachusetts antislavery activists who called themselves "the Kansas Committee," Parker had sent Thomas Wentworth Higginson down to Kansas with money, guns, and a clutch of antislavery companions. Fresh from his violent interventions in the case of fugitive Anthony Burns, Higginson sent back a fistful of reports on the conflict there. He had no reservations about crossing whatever lines might have divided the occupations of journalist, advocate, and guerrilla fighter. Much of his reporting in Kansas took its inspiration from Brown's deeds. His evident purpose was to toss fuel on the fire that Brown had started. Higginson later confessed that he "loved" Brown.

The gathering of Parker, Brown, and Garrison in Parker's living room may serve as a marker of the transformation in the antislavery movement that had started with the fugitive crisis and the Craft affair. The views of these three abolitionist leaders had grown like intertwined yet distinct trees, planted in very different philosophical soil, reaching for the same sky but bearing very different fruit.

In the 1830s or 1840s, Garrison might have been expected to dominate the conversation. But as the 1850s careened from one triumphant "compromise" on behalf of the slaveholders to another, he came to seem more like an onlooker with respect to the movement he had helped set in motion. He remained committed to his moralizing program. Slavery remained a "sin"—a temptation placed before white souls like a bottle of demon rum. The onus consequently fell upon slaveholders to repent, and the duty of the abolitionists was to harangue them until they did so and to shun them if they did not.

We must not "resist evil with evil," Garrison insisted, his words aimed squarely at Parker and Brown. "Do not get impatient, do not get exasperated, do not make yourselves familiar with the idea that blood must flow."[48] He was immune to all evidence that this program of moral suasion had yielded the opposite of its intended effect. America's slaveholders were more convinced than ever of the righteousness of their cause, and the moderate mass in the middle mainly regarded the abolitionists themselves as the fanatics in the dispute.

In their fireside debate at Parker's home, Brown answered Garrison's version of New Testament wisdom with the wrathful pages of the Old Testament. He was far more interested in the vengeance of the Lord than in turning the other cheek.

Only blood will answer for blood, he surely would have said—and settlers in Kansas could testify that he meant what he said. Given the wrought-iron personalities involved, it is hardly likely that ground was gained on either side of the debate in Parker's living room.

Parker had little use for either side of the Bible, of course, and he was as wary as Douglass of Brown's prophetic voice. By January 1857, however, he had moved decisively to Brown's side in the debate over tactics. Already in 1854, Parker is writing, "I expect a Civil War." In November of 1855, he predicts that "in 1860 comes the real struggle between North and South." After the election of the proslavery James Buchanan to the presidency in 1856, he tells Herndon: "Now we are to make our choice . . . between the *Ruin of our Democratic Institutions* and *Civil War*. Do you doubt which we shall choose?"[49] When blood begins to flow in Missouri and Kansas, he says simply: "We are in a Civil War." At the gathering in his living room, he told Garrison that the time had come to inject "a bit of Lexington into the controversy."[50]

A new and bracing form of abolitionism was emerging, and in the minister of the 28th Congregational Society it found one of its loudest and most effective voices. In the person of Parker and his allies, abolitionism had come to an end in a certain sense; it no longer stood for a coherent political program. It merely marked the end point of a broader, more determined movement that would pursue any available strategy that might lead to the extinction of slavery. In the new antislavery movement, moralizing stances would no longer do; only action that produced results. Political action was to be preferred, naturally; but physical violence could not be ruled out as a matter of moral principle. Civil disobedience—already championed in theory by Henry David Thoreau among others—began to cross the line into incivility.

A distinctive feature of the new antislavery was its comprehensive character. Opposition to slavery could no longer be represented as one among many reform projects, to be listed on a menu including prison reform, education reform, and women's rights. Parker himself had always kept his hand in a variety of reform agendas, but in the aftermath of the fugitive crisis he made clear that the struggle against slavery was the battlefield on which all the others would be decided. At his home in Lexington one day, he convened activists of all stripes in the Boston area, and for six hours (with a short interval for tea), "a most spirited conversation was held on all the great Reform subjects of the day." But the message that Samuel May, a Garrisonian, took home was definitive: "I am more convinced than ever that Anti-Slavery Reform carries all others with it, and that its triumph will be theirs."[51] As Higginson put it in the days after the Craft affair, "I tell you the conflict with Slavery is not reform, it is Revolution."[52]

The other distinctive feature of the new abolitionists was their determination to claim for themselves the legacy of the first American Revolution. In this respect, they differed self-consciously from Garrison, whose abolitionism despised the Constitution as a pact with the devil, urged the free states to secede from a union with slaveholders, and wished for a speedy end to the American experiment. Garrisonianism was not unlike those modern views holding that slavery (or at least white supremacy) was stamped into the American project from the beginning, and that the logical thing to do is therefore to demolish the whole system. Parker and his fellow antislavery activists, on the other hand, saw in slavery a betrayal, not a realization, of the nation's founding ideals and documents. "Slavery tramples on the Constitution; it treads down states' rights," Parker inveighs.[53] The Constitution "was formed . . . 'to secure the blessings of liberty'; Now, the Constitution is *not* to secure liberty; it is to *extend slavery*." Gerrit Smith, Lysander Spooner, and Frederick Douglass, among many others, came to the same view. No symbol came easier to Parker in this respect than his grandfather's rifle, which metonymically united his newfound taste for violent activism with his unshakable conviction that he was championing "the idea of America."

As the debate with Garrison wound down, no doubt Parker waved in the direction of the trusty flintlock hanging over his desk. John Brown, who also took pride in his forebears' revolutionary heroism, could only have responded with an amen. Their commitment to violent methods—at least in principle—was an extraordinary and perhaps shocking development in American history. Even more remarkable, however, is the fact an American president would recast this development as necessary, and perhaps even divinely sanctioned. In his Second Inaugural Address, Lincoln allows that God might very well require that the war continue "until every drop of blood drawn with the lash shall be paid by another drawn with the sword."

7

ALL THE WEALTH . . .

. . . Piled by 250 Years of Unrequited Toil . . .

THE STORIES THAT AMERICANS still tell themselves often have this in common with the stories the slaveholders told the nation: that slavery is the font of great wealth. Yet Frederick Douglass resisted this narrative from the beginnings of his abolitionist career. He took as his starting point an insight gleaned in his first days in New Bedford, as a free man with a new last name.

The first thing that struck him about the town was its seemingly effortless prosperity.[1] As he walked along the town's famous wharves, he marveled at the "industry without bustle, labor without noise, heavy toil without the whip." Passing through the tidy neighborhoods in search of employment, he realized that laborers in the North often lived better than slaveholders in the South. The discovery came as both a joy and a shock, for it contradicted an assumption that he had absorbed in his youth. Like many fugitives—and indeed like most southerners and northerners, enslaved and free—Frederick had grown up in the certainty that "slavery [is] the basis of wealth."

In the Old South, the conviction that slavery alone is the path to wealth and station was written into the hopes and dreams of daily life. "The only heaven that attracted them," W. E. B. Du Bois observes of the people of the South, "was the life of the great Southern planter."[2] They took for granted "that labor is evil, that work is degrading," Douglass adds, while "idleness is the badge of respectability."[3] The same dogma was also written—and theorized and even celebrated—in the extensive literature of apologies for slavery. "In all social systems there must be a class to . . . perform the drudgery of life," argues John Henry Hammond of South Carolina on the floor of the US Senate in 1858.[4] You may as well build a house on air, he says, as build a society without this "mudsill of society." The northern economy operates on the same principle, he opined, and the wage-laborers of the factory system are a kind of mudsill, too.[5]

At the foundation of "the slave theory of wealth," to give it a name, lies a set of premises as old as civilization and as irrefutable as the Bible, or so many believed. "Servitude is the condition of civilization," the proslavery ideologue William Harper announces; so much "was decreed, when the command was given, 'be fruitful and multiply . . . ,' and when it was added 'in the sweat of thy face shalt thou eat bread.'"[6] Scarcity is the fundamental condition of human existence, or so the logic goes; labor is an evil imposed upon humans in consequence of their innate depravity; and the wealth of nations is the fixed sum of things extracted from this penitentiary labor. All wealth originates in domination, according to this line of thought, and the only question of interest is who by divine decree is entitled to occupy which end of the timeless relationship between master and slave.

But in New Bedford, Frederick saw the slave theory of wealth refuted in the streets. Here the mudsill was absent, but the houses were sturdy. Labor was free from domination, yet work was productive. Although he perhaps overlooked the fact that the wealth of New Bedford mostly came in on its fleet of whaling ships, he soon observed the same contrast with southern life in other northern towns. He glimpsed for the first time the intuition that the slave system is not a means of producing wealth but of diminishing it—that the absence of domination is not a path to poverty but a means of escaping it. He also grasped that the common religious consciousness obscures the economic reality, and that the solution to the economic problem of slavery therefore necessarily involves a kind of spiritual and intellectual reform. The philosophical labor required, Douglass understood, would be substantial. Fortunately, his German was improving by the day. "The work before us," he explains, "is nothing less than a radical revolution in the modes of thought which have flourished under the blighting slave system."[7]

IN THE AFTERMATH of his vigilantism in Boston. Theodore Parker's career as a speaker of national stature took flight. He embarked on long tours through the Northeast and Upper Midwest, sleeping on trains, powering through traveling colds, and dining on soggy crusts at faraway inns. He made it as far south as Delaware, though he was greeted there with death threats. By the middle years of the 1850s, he was reaching audiences of "sixty or a hundred thousand persons" per year, according to his own estimate.[8] His list price—$25 a talk—put him in the exalted company of Ralph Waldo Emerson and Henry Ward Beecher as one of the hottest tickets on the circuit. Parker was increasingly active behind the scenes, too, and became a significant player in the conversations that produced the Republican Party. His correspondence reached across the country, to Connecticut, New York, Pennsylvania, and even to ambitious lawyers in Illinois.

The critics were all love or all hate. When they weren't denouncing his "fanaticism" and "brazen infidelity," they were hailing his performances as "luminescent in thought" and a "mental and moral feast."[9] Parker's lectures ranged widely over topics both ephemeral and eternal, but at bottom they were harangues, sometimes repetitive, often purple, always circling back to slavery, drawing on every rhetorical implement he could grab, and wielded like a sledgehammer on the national mind. The personal transformation that began with his sermon on the transient and the permanent in 1841 was complete. Parker then was a moralist; Parker now is a revolutionary.

The conventional expectation today would be that any sermon by an abolitionist minister would involve much talk of sin and repentance. Slavery was an immensely profitable activity for the nation, or so the usual story goes, and only an appeal to conscience could persuade white America to set aside this material interest. But the sermons on slavery that Theodore Parker delivered in the early 1850s don't read like sermons in this conventional sense at all. They are more like the works of an unusually vexed professor of economics. They marshal battalions of statistics and bristle with spreadsheet-hungry analysis. They aim to pound into their listeners a fistful of lessons about the true origins of the wealth and poverty of nations. His central thesis is that slavery is a means of impoverishing nations, not enriching them, and it is driving America to ruin.

Parker starts by making the case that in the decades after the American Revolution, the slave states dramatically underperformed their free-state peers in every reasonable measure of economic prosperity. He carefully analyzes the rates of population growth in the two sections of the country; the rates of increase in the value of land and housing stock; average wages and productivity; the aggregate value of farm tools; the production of manufactured goods; total miles of railroad track laid; tons of shipping; military capabilities; enrollment in schools; levels of illiteracy (among the free population only, as it was a criminal offense to teach slaves to read); number of newspaper titles; circulation of newspapers; number of patents; number of professors and schoolteachers; number of books in libraries; number of books exported; and number of works of recognized literary and scholarly quality. In every one of these indicators of wealth, Parker finds, the free populations of the slave states (never mind the enslaved populations) perform worse than those of the free states—often by shocking margins.

He repeatedly returns to the contest between Virginia and New York. In 1776, he points out, Virginia was the largest state in population and wealth. By general acclaim, it was the leading state in national politics and the birthplace of presidents. It enjoyed every natural advantage over New York: a warner climate, more fertile soil, more abundant resources in timber and mineral deposits, and more easily navigable rivers and ports. Yet by 1846, New York had grown tenfold in population, while Virginia had not even managed to double in size, and it lagged its northern rival on every meaningful axis of achievement.[10]

Other observers confirmed Parker's assessments of the state of the South. Frederick Law Olmsted, famous now mainly as a landscape architect, toured the southern states and sent back damning reports to the *New York Daily Tribune*: "The citizens of the cotton States, as a whole, are poor. They work little, and that little, badly. They buy little, they sell little; and they have little—very little—of the common comforts and consolations of civilized life."[11] William Goodell, in his reports from an earlier tour, comes to substantially the same conclusion: "Though many individuals are enriching themselves by the system, the southern country, on the whole, is becoming impoverished by it."[12] The Virginia-born Moncure Conway confirms that in the South, "wretchedness and brutal igno-rance" prevailed among the free population. Perhaps the best evidence that this economic critique was on the mark is the fact the former slave states continued to underperform their free-state peers down to the present, a century and a half after slavery was abolished.[13]

In 1857, Hinton Rowan Helper of North Carolina attracted great fame (and death threats) when he published a book reproducing the same economic indictment of the slave sys-tem in the South.[14] "The liberation of five millions of 'poor white trash' from the second degree of slavery, and of three millions of miserable kidnapped negroes from the first degree of slavery cannot be accomplished too soon," he writes. The lower-income whites' "unparalleled illiteracy and degradation is purposely and fiendishly perpetuated" at the hands "of a vil-lainous oligarchy" that seeks its own power at the cost of uni-versal misery. Helper's book went through multiple editions and became a bestseller. Over in Springfield, Illinois, Lincoln and Herndon read it avidly. In truth, however, it was mostly a summary of what Parker had already blasted across the land-scape in his lecture tours.

BUT PARKER'S CRITIQUE extends well beyond empirical obser-vations about the southern economy. He offers a thorough analysis of why slavery impoverishes—and then he extends the argument to the entire national economy. The so-called free states do not escape the dead hand of chattel principle, he insists; slavery impoverishes the entire nation. "America is poorer for slavery," he insists.[15]

The argument begins with an insight that Frederick Doug-lass absorbed in his youth. The slave's true master is not the man with the whip. It is the surrounding society that exercises its power through his arm. It is the policemen, the militias, the judges, the slave hunters, the watchful neighbors, and the lynch mobs; it is the battalions of preachers that sustain the conviction of the system's righteousness; and it is the squadrons of family members, such as the white half of Ellen Craft's family, who diligently humiliate their enslaved siblings and cousins in order to keep them in a state of subordination. All these people serve the slave system, and yet the cost of their service is never reflected in the enslavers' accounts. The Fugitive Slave Act, for Parker and his allies, was proof that the uncompensated services of the free states, too, were central to the perpetuation of slavery. The way for the slaveholders to keep their institution profitable was to have the rest of the country pay the bill for enforcing their practice.

The unaccounted-for costs of the slave system, in Parker's view, include not just the cost of enforcement but the conditioning and deprivation required to reduce naturally equal human beings to an unnatural state of obedience. Douglass emphatically agrees. The education foregone diminishes the potential contribution of enslaved people to society; the cruelty required to dominate them converts them into agents of opposition. In some of the modern commentary on slavery, paradoxically, the suggestion is made that slavery was profitable because it coerced more labor out of the enslaved population than it might otherwise have been willing to supply.[16] Douglass and Parker would have found such claims laughable. Torture doesn't make for better workers; it is a heavy cost incurred for the sake of avoiding the still heavier cost of shirking, sabotaging, and running away.

The costs of slavery are also paid in the coin of national security. Slavery must expand or die, and so it drives the Union toward needless and costly wars of aggression. In a "Sermon of War," Parker again rallies armies of statistics to demonstrate that the militarism resulting from slavery diverts resources from productive economic activity to fleets and arsenals: "They weave no clothe, they break no bread." Slavery also renders the Union more vulnerable to outside attack. Enemies can always threaten to mobilize slaves against their oppressors—as in fact happened to some degree in the War of 1812 and in the American Revolution. "How weak slavery makes a nation!" Parker exclaims.[17]

All these uncounted costs of slavery distort the markets for what does enrich the nation. Free labor finds it impossible to compete with subsidized slave labor, and so the enormous white underclass of the South and even the northern working class to some extent are condemned to unproductive and undercompensated working lives. The value of the land counts for little against the artificially subsidized value of the slave labor that tills it, and so it, too, is despoiled and then left behind in an expanding circle of ecological devastation. The technological innovations that might reduce labor are of little interest in a society that depends on uncompensated, coerced labor.

The use of the term "capital" to describe claims over the product of enslaved labor—claims whose aggregate trading value was as high as $4 billion nationally on the eve of the war—stands in the way of a clear perception of the source of the riches that accumulated in the plantation houses of the South. "Capital" in this instance was, as it so often is, a selective legal fiction. It attached great value to claims that did not add to the actual wealth of the nation (titles to steal the labor of enslaved people, for example) and no value to activities that did (the labor of child-rearing, for instance). Had it been possible to "capitalize" and trade the value of the work performed by the free laborers and farmers of the North, that $4 billion of capital on the slaveholders' balance sheets would have seemed small as a share of the nation's actual wealth. Instead, as Parker points out, "capital" accumulated in the hands of southern planters in direct proportion to their ability to diminish the long-term wealth of the nation.

The accumulation of this species of pseudo-capital was the fundamental source of the financial instability that afflicted the republic from its inception. Parker argues—on solid empirical evidence—that the Panic of 1837 and other such devastating disruptions of the economy had their origins in the speculative excesses made possible by the slave system.

At the root of the ills of the slave system lies the extreme economic inequality that it inevitably produces—not just between the races but among the white population. The slaveholding oligarchy does not merely profit from preexisting racism, reactionary religion, political corruption, sexual aggression, and genocidal expansion. It actively invests its publicly subsidized gains in promoting all those hateful processes. The richer it becomes, the better it gets at dividing the nation and pillaging the future. Extreme inequality and extreme poverty go hand in hand in the American slave republic as they have in human history since the Bronze Age, and for all the same reasons. The ultimate target of extreme wealth, Parker comes to understand, is reason itself. The gag rules, the censorship, the disdain for higher education, and above all the relentless attacks on religious infidelity follow from the elemental fact that reason can never support the participation of a whole society in its own impoverishment. So long as reason is against the oligarchs, the oligarchs will be against reason.

The toxic reach of the southern oligarchy, in Parker's view, was glaringly visible in its hold on the emerging industrial elite of the North. The would-be oligopolists of the North, he argues, follow the example of their southern peers in demanding public support for supplies of artificially cheap raw materials for their factories, all of which comes at the expense of the people. "The cottonocracy," says Parker, "hate THE PEOPLE."[18] "The slave power has its vassals all over the North. They abound in the great cities—Cincinnati, Philadelphia,

New York, and Boston," he inveighs.[19] "The Money Power and the Slave Power go hand in hand."[20]

The representatives of the Money Power certainly appeared to agree with Parker's analysis. They, too, believed that the perpetuation of great concentrations of wealth in the North depended on continued collusion with the even greater concentrations in the South. The so-called Cotton Whigs roundly condemned the abolitionists and vowed to enforce the Fugitive Slave Act with the full power of the state. The *New York Journal of Commerce* warned of the "mischief which mad abolitionists . . . wantonly perpetrate."[21] The wealthy Boston industrialist Amos Lawrence crystallized the anxiety of the Brahmins when he said that the choice between slavery and antislavery was a choice between law and disorder. The southern papers were rather more direct; they called for Theodore Parker to be hanged.

The crucial upshot of Parker's analysis is that the wealth accumulated by the enslavers has an illusory quality. The great mansions of the South were created by turning the surrounding foundations of prosperity to mud; soon the earth would take them back. In his 1862 speech to the Massachusetts Anti-Slavery Society, John Rock—the same John Rock who had quarreled with Parker over his use of racist stereotypes—marvels at the accuracy of this prognostication. "Through 240 years of indescribable torture, slavery has wrung out of the blood, bones and muscles of the negro hundreds of millions of dollars," says Rock. "At the same time, it has developed a volcano which has burst forth, and in less number of days than years has dissipated this wealth and rendered the Government bankrupt!"[22]

IF SLAVERY IS the paradigmatic source of the poverty of nations, then what is the source of their wealth? In his lectures on the economic crisis of the American slave republic, Parker's first and most impassioned claim is for the value of education. The true foundation of wealth is not to be found in the appropriation of other people's labor, he argues, but in the development of the laborer's mind. "The wealth of New England runs out of the School-houses of New England," he says.[23]

Out of this insight into the importance of the laborer's mind, Parker champions the idea of "free labor" that would come to play a central role in the formation of the Republican Party. "There are some who count labour a curse and a punishment," Parker declares in his "Thoughts on Labour," pointing a finger directly at the proslavery ideologues.[24] "They regard the necessity of work as the greatest evil brought on us by the 'Fall.'" They believe "that work degrades." This depreciation of labor, Parker suggests, in turn leads to an illusory conception of wealth and advantage. Idle mastery, or domination without toil, is the ideal in a society that fails to appreciate the value of labor. The central idea of free labor, on the other hand, is that labor is a "noble" aspect of human self-realization. The essential precondition for this kind of noble labor, it further says, is the equality of mutual regard among members of society. "When one claims it right to have others do for him what degrades them in his eyes, their eyes or those of society, there is the spirit of slavery," says Parker.[25]

The strongest and wealthiest society, Parker concludes, is one that can organize itself into a genuine democracy. By this he means not merely a form of government with opportunities for majority voting, but a form of society that governs itself through rational self-determination. In a characteristically optimistic finale to one of his sermons, he lays out his ideal: "As soon as the North awakes to its ideas, and uses its vast strength of money, its vast strength of numbers, and its still more gigantic strength of educated intellect, we shall tread this monster [of slavery] underneath our feet." Americans will then arise as "the noblest people the world ever saw—who have triumphed over Theocracy, Monarchy, Aristocracy, Despotocracy, and have got a Democracy—a government of all, by all, and for all."[26]

. . . Shall Be Sunk

WILLIAM HERNDON WAS AWARE of the risk he was taking in reaching out to a lightning rod such as Theodore Parker.[27] In his first letter to Parker, dated 1854, he declares that his only purpose is to invite the minister to include Springfield, Illinois, on one of his national speaking tours. In subsequent missives, however, Herndon lets on that he is hoping to establish a correspondence with Parker "on Mr. Lincoln's account." He also requests, and promptly receives, assurances that Lincoln's interest in their exchanges will remain secret. "Base politicians would charge him with sending you matter," Herndon intimates to Parker.[28]

Parker's duties as minister to fugitives in Boston prevented him from accepting Herndon's initial invitation to Springfield. "My 'trial' takes place in March," he explains in a hasty note from January 1855; after that, "who knows where I may be?"[29] Under indictment for his involvement in the Anthony Burns affair, he was busy composing a ferocious 230-page defense of his actions. He intended to read it before a jury of his peers and thereby to put slavery itself on trial. He evidently sought to cast himself as a latter-day Socrates and turn his case into an indictment of his country's crimes.

Parker's plans for a showdown in the courthouse came to an unceremonious end when the trial was canceled. The various other proceedings issuing from the Burns affair likewise unwound in a string of acquittals and mistrials. The juries and the judges of Boston proved that they were, after all, Bostonians first and foremost. But this piece of good news was not about to stop Parker from taking on the mantle of the American Socrates. He converted his defense brief into a book in the model of Plato's *Apology* and published it as *The Trial of Theodore Parker*. Herndon read every word and ranked it among the great works of world literature. In his first note to Herndon, Parker summarizes the message of the draft in a sentence that would be repeated in many variations through their several years of correspondence: "Unless we exterminate Slavery, there is no Freedom possible."

"Blast slavery if you can—aid freedom to stand erect, and with the forces of nature floating every where, man will yet enter goodness, and develop greatness, along the lines of time, and on the realms of space," Herndon exhorts. Parker's responses indicate that he is indeed blasting slavery in every way he can. Herndon urges Parker to think big, to fight for equality, to go utopian: "*May you see what another has said—a day when the state shall be without a King—Society without an aristocracy*—a church without a priest and a family *without a slave*," he writes. The great man whom Herndon here pretends to paraphrase, as both would have known, is Parker himself, who uses the same words in one of the lectures passed along to Lincoln.

As their correspondence flourished, Parker only grew in moral stature in Herndon's estimation. Soon the renegade minister occupied a position second only to Lincoln in Herndon's pantheon. Herndon palpably longed for approval from his new spiritual mentor. Above all, he wished to engage Parker in the exalted realms of philosophy. Together, he and his new idol would serve as Lincoln's philosophical council and guardians, or so Herndon seems to have imagined. Indeed, Herndon's most sacred task, by his own account, is to serve as the midwife for Lincoln's philosophical rebirth. Together with Parker, he hopes to coax the future leader into embracing a fully enlightened position on the question of slavery. "I adhered to Lincoln, relying on the final outcome of his sense of justice and right," Herndon writes. "Every time a good speech on the great issue was made I sent for it. Hence you could find on my table the latest utterances of Giddings, Phillips, Sumner, Seward, and one whom I considered grander than all the others—Theodore Parker."[30]

A FEW LINES DOWN in Lincoln's Second Inaugural Address, in the sentence that impressed Frederick Douglass more than anything any other president had ever said, a first trace of Herndon's pedagogical efforts may possibly be glimpsed, where Lincoln conjectures that "all the wealth piled by the bond-man's two hundred and fifty years of unrequited toil shall be sunk." Lincoln offers this suggestion as a hypothetical; but coming very near the end of the war, after the burning of Atlanta, it cannot have been intended as such nor would it have been heard as such.

William Herndon certainly thought he knew where Lincoln got this idea:[31]

I remember once, after having read one of Theodore Parker's sermons on slavery, saying to Mr. Lincoln substantially this: 'I have always noticed that ill-gotten wealth does no man any good. This is as true of nations as individuals. I believe that all the ill-gotten gain wrenched by us from the negro through his enslavement will eventually be taken from us, and we will be set back where we began.

Some historians suggest that Lincoln only set about ending slavery after war had exhausted all the other options. In his Second Inaugural Address, however, Lincoln presents as a conclusion drawn from the war a premise about the futile riches of slavery that he had embraced well before the shooting started.

8

THE JUDGMENTS OF THE LORD

A Brief History of God

"FREDERICK, IS GOD DEAD?" Sojourner Truth asked with dismay from the back of the hall in a voice that brought the audience to a standstill. It was as if "some one had thrown a brick through the window," Douglass later recalled.[1] They were attending an antislavery convention in Ohio, and Douglass, fresh from his first meeting with John Brown, was in the middle of a speech expounding his "sanguinary doctrine" that "slavery could only be destroyed by blood-shed."[2]

It was a reasonable question. The first lesson from the parable of Covey is that no force from on high will reach down to rescue the slave. He who would be free cannot count on God to strike the blow. This was not a thought that fit well with the kind of faith-based abolitionism that Sojourner Truth championed. A devout believer, she remained loyal to Garrison and his moral-suasion school (though she did relinquish the pacifism after the war broke out).

"No," Frederick replied, "and because God is not dead slavery can only end in blood."

What Douglass did not explain to his "good old friend" Sojourner was that "God," if yet alive, now stood for something that she and her fellow believers would not have recognized as divine. It referred instead to a certain idea of nature—the same idea of "God or nature" that presided over the intellectual world of the first American Revolution.

How THE GODS were invented, blended, unified, divided, exported, and recruited for various purposes over many millennia—all this belongs to earlier chapters in the history of God and can be safely set aside.[3] The part of the history that matters for the American struggle over slavery begins with the death of an author in Germany in 1781.[4]

Gotthold Ephraim Lessing (1729–1781) left the world at the age of fifty-two as a respected playwright, critic, and philosopher. Soon after his death, the word got out that his Jewish friend Moses Mendelssohn (1729–1786) planned to write a friendly biography. A young intellectual socialite named Friedrich Heinrich Jacobi (1743–1819), however, thought he knew the real story. A sworn foe of the Enlightenment rationalism that had once seduced him as a young man and that he now saw as a threat to genuine religion and the established hierarchies, Jacobi penned what he knew would be a poisonous letter to Elise Reimarus (1735–1805), the sparkling hostess of Berlin's leading salon.

Lessing, said Jacobi to Reimarus, had confessed to him in late life that he was a Spinozist. To be a Spinozist, as Lessing himself observed, is to hold firm to the principle that the ancient Greek philosophers first announced: that nature always explains itself. Everything we see and feel, even our own thoughts and minds, according to this radical line of thought, comes into being and passes away through necessary and intelligible laws of nature. All things in the universe are thus part of a single interconnected whole that operates according to the necessary laws of its own nature. Because nature always explains itself, according to this line of thought,

"God" can be neither the name of an agent that stands outside of nature and acts against its laws nor the name of an agent within nature that acts according to its laws. It can only be another word for the whole of nature. In more technical language: God is the sole "substance" of the world, and all things, ideas, and individuals are just "modes" of this substance.

According to Jacobi, all "consistent philosophy is Spinozist, hence pantheist, fatalist, and atheist." Together with some like-minded reactionaries, he therefore set out to make war on philosophy. He was representative of a cycle of enlightenment and counter-enlightenment that characterized European intellectual life at least since the emergence of Spinozism, and perhaps even since the dawn of philosophy in ancient times. The English deist Alexander Pope (1688–1744), in his *Essay on Man* of 1734, supplies the vocabulary for the Spinozistic vision that dominated radical philosophy through the nineteenth century:[5]

All are but parts of one stupendous whole
Whose body Nature is, and God the Soul

Pope identifies this stupendous world-soul-whole as "Nature's God." The same God later makes its most celebrated appearance in Thomas Jefferson's Declaration of Independence. Spinoza's sympathizers at the time called this system "pantheism," but his detractors, who were far, far greater in number, called it "atheism." Pope, who picked up his Spinozism from the philosopher-statesman Lord Bolingbroke, rapidly became the target of attacks by Swiss, French, and English defenders of orthodoxy.

In Mendelssohn's day, just as in Pope's day, to be branded a Spinozist was the moral equivalent of being accused of feasting on live babies. In hundreds of sermons and dissertations that poured from the pulpits and the lecterns, Spinoza was represented as "the Euclid of atheism" or, more to the point, "Satan." When Mendelssohn got wind of Jacobi's foul insinuations about Lessing's beliefs, he was distraught. To disparage Lessing was to impugn his friendly biographer. The libel was all the worse because Mendelssohn was Jewish—which, according to the prejudices of the time, implied both that he was somehow responsible for Spinoza and that he might be guilty of something even worse than Spinozism.

Mendelssohn fought back with private letters to Jacobi, in which he argues, among other things, that certain varieties of pantheism are compatible with theism and therefore are perfectly safe for public consumption. This was a mistake. It amounted to an admission that Mendelssohn was the kind of dissimulating pantheist that Jacobi said Lessing was. In 1785, in a gleefully malicious breach of protocol, Jacobi went public with their exchanges.

Now Mendelssohn was truly mortified. But at least he had an answer all written down. His biography of Lessing was ready, and it could explain everything. Lessing was a cuddly pantheist with excellent family values, Mendelssohn could prove, not a pantheist of the infanticidal kind. He was so concerned to get his response to the publishers that on a frozen New Year's Eve in Berlin he rushed out of his home without his winter coat. He fell ill and died four days later. With his demise the "pantheism controversy," also known as the "Spinoza controversy," exploded into the German republic of letters. Jacobi, some said, had killed Mendelssohn in a dialectical way.

There were more victims to come. Not one to be put off by accusations of philosophical homicide, Jacobi trained his polemical guns on the famous philosopher Immanuel Kant (1724–1804). But the sage of Konigsberg was so high in the worldwide hierarchy of philosophical prestige as to be untouchable. Kant enjoyed the added benefit that the baroque complexity of his philosophical system, which now serves as a kind of employment system for academic philosophers, shielded from view its profound engagement with Spinozism. Jacobi moved on to Kant's not-so-famous self-proclaimed disciple, Johann Gottlieb Fichte (1762–1814) and scored a direct hit on this softer target. Amid heated talk of critical religion theories in the academy and accusations of downright heresy, Fichte was forced to resign from his professorship at Jena. (Ten years later, he made a comeback by wrapping his heresies in nationalist rhetoric about the superiority of German culture; he intended for Germany to lead an "empire of spirit and reason" in which "crude physical force" would play no part, but that was not how later nationalists read him.)[6]

With Fichte down for the count and Kant cocooned in his unintelligible critiques, Jacobi shifted his attention to the philosophical prodigy Friedrich Wilhelm Joseph Schelling (1775–1854). At the age of twenty, Schelling had already declared to his friend G. W. F. Hegel, "I have become a Spinozist!"[7] But Schelling fought back with a more aggressive version of Mendelssohn's argument and managed finally to put Jacobi in his place. Pantheism, he insisted, pairs perfectly with a plain vanilla belief in almighty God.

The disintegration of the French Revolution was widely interpreted as an argument in favor of the Counter-Enlightenment—or at the very least in favor of keeping one's mouth shut—and in its aftermath the pantheism controversy appeared to retreat from the front pages of the literary magazines. A more accurate assessment, however, is that the revolution, having failed on the ground, ascended into the air. The paradoxical effect of the pantheism controversy was not to kill off the ghost of Spinoza but to make his secret philosophy at once more secretive and more seductive. A whole generation of German philosophers experienced clandestine conversions. Following Kant's lead, they learned to speak in a way that shoved their most important ideas safely over the edge of intelligibility.

In the half-century century following Mendelssohn's death, German philosophers filled the halls of the world's greatest universities with strenuous claims that their philosophy was not what it in fact was. On the one hand, they promised a reconciliation with the Christian tradition (in one or the other of its squabbling varieties) and an endorsement of all the good things in the established order. On the other hand, they kept hankering for a revolution, and their revolutionary hopes rested unavoidably on a naturalism that, within the vocabulary of the time, was inextricably associated with atheism in general and Spinozism in particular. German philosophy thus became a relentless effort to make circles look like squares, and the resulting exercises in geometry were as extraordinary as the intellectual talent devoted to the effort.

Hegel was the undisputed master of this phase in the history of God. His dialectical philosophy is characteristically generous to both sides of the argument. On the one hand, it tells us that Spinozism is "the only philosophy" and the "essential beginning of all philosophizing." On the other hand, it appears to imbue the Christian religion as it manifested itself in the churches of Berlin around 1820 with the character of absolute truth. The issue comes down to how one understands the "Spirit" that occupies the apex of Hegel's philosophical imagination. Is "Spirit" just another reincarnation of the old "God" or is it the thing that emerges after the death of God? Is his philosophy Christian or anti-Christian or does it, in its dialectical wisdom, simply identify Christianity with the negation of Christianity? The rebarbative prose of the Hegelian dialectic, notoriously, allows plenty of room for all interpretations. Even so, in his lectures on the philosophy of history—surely his home turf—Hegel lets slip some damning hints. "The province of the spirit is created by man himself," he says.[8] And if that were not enough: "The universal spirit is essentially present as human consciousness. Knowledge attains existence and being for itself in man."⁹ Which, translated back into the old religious language, is a lot like saying that man creates God, rather than the other way around.

THE PAX HEGELIANA could not last. In 1835, four years after Hegel's death and nearly fifty years after Jacobi gloated over the corpse of Mendelssohn, the liberal poet Heinrich Heine ripped off the Band-Aid. "Pantheism," said Heine, is "the secret religion of Germany."¹⁰ All too predictably, the post-Hegelian dialecticians divided into two dialectically opposed camps. The "Right Hegelians" took up the side of God and country; the "Left Hegelians" put their chips on freedom and progress.

The suggestion that there was some sort of equivalency or symmetry between the two sides of the post-Hegelian debate, however, is misplaced. The right-wingers did end up with the tenured professorships and higher salaries in the emerging German university system. But they constituted a group only in reaction to their far more ambitious, coherent, and impecunious opponents. The Left Hegelians were the ones who went on to shape the revolutions in Europe and America. They included David Friedrich Strauss and the train of Bible critics that followed in his wake; Ludwig Feuerbach and a coterie of like-minded humanists; and communists such as Karl Marx—perhaps the most underrated champion of the original liberalism of America's first revolution.

In partial alignment with the group, in effect if not in intention, was Alexander von Humboldt, the world-famous scientist, naturalist, and explorer. In his bestseller *Cosmos*, Humboldt offers in part a throwback to the empiricist origins of the Enlightenment, and it was welcomed by many as an antidote to the headache of Hegelian idealism. Yet in the cosmos Humboldt celebrates, every particle of the universe from the bottom of the ocean to the farthest star, and every phenomenon, from the reproduction of plants to the operations of the human mind, forms part of a stupendous whole whose secrets can be known only to those with the patience to pursue genuine science. Humboldt's commitment to the old monistic habit of radical German thought was quiet but flagrant. As a contributor to *Frederick Douglass' Paper* observes, "His great distinction is the comprehensive view he takes of the laws and facts of the physical world."[11]

The same combination of scientific spirit and holistic naturalism overwhelmed the philosophers and theologians who inherited the leftward side of the Hegelian tradition. The liberal theologian Friedrich Schleiermacher (1768–1834) indirectly pursued the same agenda and left behind a string of theological heirs whose works shaped the young Theodore Parker. The Protestant religion may extend its life, Schleiermacher argues, on the understanding that religion is properly grounded in a "subjective feeling," not in objective truth. God, he was content to suggest, is basically a mood. The poison fruit of Schleiermacher's efforts, or so many conservatives believed, was David Friedrich Strauss, the first of the Left Hegelians to achieve infamy. As critics and sympathizers understood, Strauss's rationalist biblical scholarship essentially served to add academic weight to Spinoza's claim in the *Tractatus Theologico-Politicus* that the Bible offers only moral truths in the form of myths adapted to the popular mind.

The decisive break from the Hegelian slumber, however, came with the publication of Ludwig Feuerbach's 1841 bestseller, *The Essence of Christianity*. "The spell was broken; the 'system' was exploded and cast aside," Karl Marx recalls. "One must himself have experienced the liberating effect of this book to get an idea of it. Enthusiasm was general, we all became at once Feuerbachians."[12] And, most memorably: "There is no other road for you to truth and freedom except that leading through the brook of fire [Feuerbach]." [13] Feuerbach's accomplishment, says Marx, is to "abstract from Hegel's abstraction . . . and talk . . . instead . . . of man." [14]

In Feuerbach's words, God is the "species-essence of Man." What humans in the past have called "God"—and what the Hegelians obtusely called "Spirit"—is just a word that stands for our common humanity. It is an artifact of human consciousness, not the creator of it. Feuerbach thus reduces theology to anthropology and declares that the aim of the philosophy of the future must be to liberate humanity from its enslavement to the fictional deities of its own making. "God himself is a materialist," he adds for good measure; and "Spinoza is the Moses of modern free-thinkers and materialists." [15]

A significant part of Feuerbach's appeal is the intellectual ruthlessness with which he advances his claims. Turning on Schleiermacher, for example, he sticks the knife in: "If feeling is subjectively what religion is chiefly about, then God is objectively nothing but the essence of feeling." [16] Feuerbach agrees that "God is pure, unlimited, free feeling," but then he leaves no doubt that "feeling is atheistic in the sense of the orthodox belief, which attaches religion to an external object." [17] Which amounts to saying: Schleiermacher is just a mealymouthed Feuerbachian. (Schleiermacher may not have cared that much; he himself concedes, to the scandal of his contemporaries, that it is perfectly possible to imagine a feeling of the divine without supposing the existence of its object; that is, to have "a religion without God.")

This is the final stopping point of Hegel's dialectics of Spirit and the destination of German thought at least since the Enlightenment, or so it seemed to many observers. No wonder the intellectual policemen of the established order who took up Jacobi's mission anew were alarmed. Forget about Spinoza, they said: Satan has a new name, and it sounds like a river on fire.

ALL UNDERSTOOD THE timeless truth that debates about the nature of the lord in heaven are, at bottom, debates about who is entitled to rule on Earth. The ultimate sin of Feuerbachian atheism, in the eyes of the defenders of the faith, is a political crime. In keeping with its Spinozistic origins, it centers the political order not on an unimpeachable command from above but on an evolving standard of political legitimacy originating from below. The old idea was that the powers that be are ordained of God; the new idea is that they are ordained of the people.

In the philosophical language passed down through the Radical Enlightenment of the early modern period, the standard against which the legitimacy of the political order is to be tested goes under the name of "the laws of nature." These laws are not commands, properly speaking; they are simply rational inferences about what humans must do to survive and prosper under the natural conditions of human life. They are, to use Thomas Hobbes's term, "dictates of reason." It is a law of nature, for example, that one should not drink to excess if one is to live a long life. Or, that one should prefer peaceful collaboration with others over war. Laws of nature in this sense belong to a category entirely different from that of civil laws. The laws of nature refer to reasons; civil laws are commands. Civil laws are made to be broken, and they have little meaning without a penal code. The laws of nature, on the other hand, cannot be violated; they can only be ignored. They involve no "punishment" other than what follows logically and naturally from the "crime" itself. The laws of nature are also quite distinct from the "natural law" of medieval theologians, which amounts to an effort to discover supposed civil laws in nature.

According to the logic of the Radical Enlightenment, the "unalienable rights" of man follow from the laws of nature. The right to breathe the air and the right to seek the truth, for example, follow from the natural powers of human beings to breathe and think for themselves. Such rights may or may not be recognized within any given code of civil laws, but they are unalienable in the sense that they cannot be taken away without also doing away with the bearer of those rights. They are distinct from civil rights, which amount to a duty imposed on pain of civil punishment to recognize other people's rights in specified ways.

In the deistic rhetoric that often accompanies the Radical Enlightenment, the laws of nature and their associated unalienable rights are attributed to "Nature's God," and in this way they acquire a sheen of theological piety. But the laws of nature come from the deity in the same way as the laws of physics do. They are valid insofar as they follow from the nature of things, not insofar as they express the supposed will of a superior being. They are accessible through reason and experience, not through any kind of revelation or dispensation. The role of Nature's God in the political theology of the Radical Enlightenment is not to tell humans how to live but to guarantee only that the world is a place in which it is possible to live and prosper in accordance with reason. Alexander Pope sums it up in *Essay on Man* by the very couplet that introduced "Nature's God" to the English-speaking world: "Slave to no sect, who takes no private road / But looks up through Nature to Nature's God."[18]

The Feuerbachian philosophy belongs to this line of political theology grounded in laws of nature, but, owing to the post-Hegelian philosophical context within which it emerges, it brings with it a certain shift in emphasis. It centers the laws of nature above all on the laws of *human* nature. Realizing the "species-essence" of man, says Feuerbach, is key to human freedom and self-realization. The most important aspects of this species essence have to do with the development of human consciousness through equal mutual regard. Feuerbach therefore calls for a liberal, republican political order with the explicit object of human self-realization through equal mutual regard. He lays out his political philosophy in the book that Ottilie Assing picked up in a New York bookshop in 1859 and brought over to her special friend, Frederick Douglass.

Nature's God Redivivus

AT AN 1850 MEETING of the American Anti-Slavery Society, several Garrisonians put forward a brazen resolution:

> If the Bible sanctions slavery . . . the Bible . . . ought to be . . . regarded as the enemy of Nature and Nature's God, and the progress of the human race in liberty, justice, and goodness.[19]

In 1851, Parker's own Vigilance Committee of Boston passed a series of loud resolutions denouncing the Fugitive Slave Act as "a daring outrage on the laws of Nature and Nature's God." The revival of Nature's God in the American antislavery movement naturally came with a certain amount of theologizing, and much of the relevant speculations are ready to hand in the works of Theodore Parker.

In his theological discourses, Parker draws a distinction between "the God of the philosophers" and the God of ordinary religion. Though one might at first suppose that he will grant equal legitimacy to both varieties of God, it soon becomes clear that his sympathies lie mostly on the side of the philosophers. "Spinoza and his followers," he concedes, "do not call it God but Nature." Yet these Spinozists "have a higher idea of the quality of God than the Christians."[20] Though careful to dissociate himself from the memory of Thomas Paine, his words at times read almost as if recited from Paine's *Age of Reason*: "In nature . . . God speaks for ever. . . . The Universe is his Scripture. Nature is the prose, and man the poetry of God."[21]

Having identified Nature's God with the laws of nature in the manner of Paine and his German admirers, Parker goes on to acknowledge that he himself is a partisan of the laws of nature: "Everywhere I find law," he writes.[22] "The law of nature . . . represents the modes of action of God himself, his thought made visible."[23] The "consciousness" of a God that acts only through laws of nature, he adds with a metaphorical twist, must differ from our own consciousness as much as the constellation of a bear differs from a bear.[24] He is too well-read not to be aware that the metaphor of the constellation and those "modes of action" of God are so close to Spinoza that they could count as plagiarisms.

At a telling moment in a sermon defending the philosophical conception of God, Parker puts his bursts into poetry. The God of the philosophers, he avows:

Warms in the sun, refreshes in the breeze,
Glows in the stars, and blossoms in the trees;
Lives through all life, extends through all extent,
Spreads undivided, operates unspent.

The lines come unacknowledged from Alexander Pope's *Essay on Man*, where they follow directly on the couplet cited earlier that begins with "All are but parts of one stupendous whole / Whose body Nature is, and God the soul."

The somewhat clotted erudition through which Parker burrows his way back to the presiding deity of America's founding generation was quite possibly the consequence of his evident need to maintain some sort of ministerial pose. Often, he allowed his hard-won scholarship to get in the way of wisdom and leave him short of the kind of fluid statement that might have ensured the sort of impact that Paine had on his contemporaries. He was in some ways trailing his congregation rather than leading it. Less constrained individuals such as Margaret Fuller had long been avowing sentiments along the lines of: "I had only to live in the idea of the ALL."[25]

The appeal of the new pantheism had a lot to do with its corresponding political theology, of course, and specifically with its take on slavery. Volney articulates the critique of slavery well in his *Ruins*—the work that Jefferson (partially) translated and that Lincoln assimilated into his thinking as a young man. "All men, having equally eyes, hands, mouths, and ears, and the necessity of making use of them, in order to live, have, by this reason alone, an equal right to life, and to the use of the aliments which maintain it," Volney reasons.[26] Slavery, which pretends to give one human absolute control over the body of another, fails to acknowledge this law of nature and therefore fails the test of reason. Parker repeats the claim almost word for word.[27]

Consistent with the logic of the Radical Enlightenment, Parker distinguishes ordinary civil laws from "the Higher Law" by which they must be judged. "I respect the statutes which men have made only so far as they embody Justice and conserve the Unalienable Rights of men," he writes to Samuel May, an earnest abolitionist of much more conventional religion.[28] For "man owes allegiance to . . . the Laws of his own Nature and to the Constitution of the Universe." In much of the historiography, the "Higher Law" trope is presumed to represent some sort of religious commitment to a legal code emanating from doctrines taken upon faith. But the genealogy of Parker's philosophy rules out such a conventionally pious interpretation of the Higher Law doctrine in his case.

Parker's engagement with Feuerbach illustrates well the gravitational pull of German radicalism on his thought. On the one hand, Parker makes clear that he intends to defend some form of religion against "the *Feuerbachianer*," as he refers to the crowd of 48ers making so much noise in the streets of American political and religious discourse. Feuerbach reduces God to a "whimsy of man" and thus involves the "the denial of . . . all forms of God," Parker complains. Feuerbach clearly goes too far. Parker affirms contra Feuerbach that religion is "natural to man." It is "an instinct" and a "sentiment" grounded in the "spiritual faculties in the soul."[29]

On second reading—what is the difference between Feuerbach's alleged assertion that God is "a whimsy of man" and Parker's declaration that religion is a "sentiment" emerging from human "spiritual faculties"?[30] As far as "Germanicus" Hedge and the reactionary critic and Catholic convert Orestes Brownson were concerned, no more proof was needed that Parker was a particularly devious Feuerbachian atheist—the kind that holds onto the name of God even as he destroys the thing.

It gets worse. We learn from Parker that Feuerbach is a "speculative atheist," and this is something very different from and much better than a "practical atheist." Feuerbach is a good man who means only to save religion from its abusers. The "atheistic Feuerbach," Parker explains, believes himself answerable to "eternal laws of matter and mind." He and the 48er crowd therefore respect the "objective restraint" required for a moral life. "The 'atheism' of . . . Feuerbach," Parker argues, "is higher and better than the theological idea of God, as represented by Jonathan Edwards, the great champion of New England divinity."[31] As a matter of fact, Feuerbach and people like him aren't really atheists at all: "When a philosopher says there is no God, I do not believe he thinks so, only that he thinks that he thinks so."[32] We should be grateful to "live in an age when mankind has outgrown the popular theology," Parker exults—apparently unconcerned that the narrative of progress from theology to anthropology he offers is the same one that Feuerbach promotes.[33]

AMONG THE ANTISLAVERY LEADERS who embraced the renewed political theology of Nature's God, Frederick Douglass stands out for the clarity and forcefulness of his expression on the subject. "Every man is the original, rightful, and absolute owner of his own body," he writes in a letter to his former master, Thomas Auld.[34] "I must breathe for myself, and you for yourself." Human rights, he argues, do not descend from the command of a deity on high but arise from the natural condition of humans themselves. "Our natural powers are the foundation of our natural rights," he writes in the context of his defense of women's rights. "Man can only exercise the powers he possesses, and he can only conceive of rights in the presence of powers."[35] He comes close to declaring outright that, in a certain sense, might is indeed right: "Power is the highest object of human respect. Wisdom, virtue, and all great moral qualities command respect only as powers."[36] He makes no apology for his insistence on the legitimacy of all means of resistance to the slave oligarchy: "Power concedes nothing without a demand. It never did and it never will."[37]

The case against slavery, according to the logic Douglass pursues here, comes down to the "self-executing laws of eternal justice."[38] In its futile attempt to violate the laws of nature, he predicts, slavery will ultimately be the architect of its own destruction. The guarantee that the laws of nature are in force comes from Nature's God—because Nature's God presides over a universe that is explicable through reason. What Sojourner Truth perceived as a call to violence, in this light, looks more like a prediction. Slavery will bring about its own, violent end, Douglass was telling his fellow abolitionists—and we had better prepare.

By 1854, Douglass was able to see the laws of nature at work, not just on the institution of slavery, but in the rise of the anti-slavery movement. Abolitionism, he says, did not emerge out of some mere sentiment or arbitrary doctrine. Rather, the factors that produced it, "like the great forces of the physical world, fire, steam, and lightning, have slumbered in the bosom of nature since the world began." Where did these elements come from? He asks. "I trace them to nature and to nature's God."[39]

In the final pages of his last autobiography, Douglass makes clear that the philosophy of Nature's God not only illuminated his experience as an abolitionist but also emerged naturally from it. "Schooled as I have been among the abolitionists of New England," he says, "I recognize that the universe is governed by laws which are unchangeable and eternal, that what men sow they will reap, and that there is no way to dodge or circumvent the consequences of any act or deed." He has devoted his life, he adds, to spreading this emancipatory message. "In my communication with the colored people, I have endeavored to deliver them from the power of superstition, bigotry, and priest-craft," he writes.[40] "In theology, I have found them strutting about in the old clothes of the masters, just as the masters strut about in the old clothes of the past." In this valedictory writing, his commitment to the laws of nature could hardly be more emphatic: "All the prayers of Christendom cannot stop the force of a single bullet, divest arsenic of poison, or suspend any law of nature." It was precisely this commitment to reasoned inquiry, of course, that put Douglass in a position to understand immediately the message Lincoln conveys in his Second Inaugural Address.[41]

Three Pantheists
Meet in the Woods

IN A LONG LETTER of January 24, 1857, Herndon draws a curious picture of what he takes to be the metaphysical vision that he and Parker share. After congratulating the minister on his unparalleled contributions to humanity, he sets off on a several-page "ramble in the forest with my dog and gun" to "see what I could *see*."

The first thing he sees, on this bitterly cold day, is his own breath. It "glitters like millions of small globes blazing in the air." Then he pushes on through the underbrush "now moving this brush, now that limb." Rabbits scamper into their holes, fish fight for a patch of open water in the ice, and beautiful black oak trees stand out "boldly against the infinite blue." Along this journey through nature, the transcendental epiphanies burst unbidden like flocks of birds startled to life. "Man is the Lord of all he surveys! *He* is the King!" Herndon exclaims. "And yet he bows humbly to the outstretched arm of bird and bush. Great lord is he!" Herndon struggles mightily to convey his intuition that all things in nature strive to persist in their own, utterly unique essence. "Man acts like man not because it is in the nature of man to do so; but *because he is a man . . .* ," he chants. "Everything is a law unto itself—matter and man—fish and bird."

One such letter obviously would not suffice. Herndon continues the exposition in a follow-up that takes us deeper into his metaphysical wilderness. "I have an idea that there are no laws in nature as usually understood," he announces. "I infer this from your most excellent sermons." Straining to articulate the distinction between civil laws and natural laws, he adds, "Law is a generalization of and in the mind, is a subjective concept in the Reason [*sic*]. Place it there and I am content. Law is not in nature as a property, attribute, quality, or essence." [42] All things, he further explains, are "governed by modes of constant operation," of which God is "the immediate cause."

It's not a bad rough-cut sketch of Parker's thought. It's also not a bad paraphrase of Spinoza's doctrine of the "conatus," according to which the power through which all things strive to persist in their own being is just the power of God, or Nature, which is the immanent cause of all things. "This is my philosophy," Herndon intones. "Drive the ultimate upwards and downwards around the circle till they meet in God." At certain points in these misty wanderings through the philosophical woods, Herndon hopes to signal the elevated nature of the discussion by reaching for a German name or two. He praises Parker for his pure "reflections in the Kantian sense."

In his reply to Herndon, Parker offers no comment on the hillbilly pantheism. Possibly Herndon understood Parker's reticence to stem from the wise conviction that there are certain truths that philosophers must pass over in silence. Parker does however offer praise for Herndon's political judgment. Both were political junkies, eagerly trading insights on the odds and the handicaps of the political stars of the day. Much of the chatter centered on Lincoln's great rival, the "little giant" Stephen Douglas. Even so, Herndon's backwoods philosophizing left its mark, for a version of the secret pantheism that he shared with Parker can be found in the writings of his law partner and "pupil," Lincoln.

LATE ONE EVENING near the end of Lincoln's first term, an English professor of law named George Borrett and a pair of fellow tourists got it into their heads to call upon the president at the cottage in the Old Soldiers' Home where he and his family often escaped the Washington, D.C., weather.[43] To their astonishment, they were allowed in and seated in the living room. The lanky president soon descended in a pair of carpet slippers, with hair ruffled and very sleepy eyes. After an amiable discussion of the US Constitution and the differences between American and English law, the conversation turned to English poetry.

Just before their arrival, Lincoln told his visitors, he had been "deep in [Alexander] Pope." The Englishmen were astonished to learn that the president was "a great admirer of Pope, especially of his *Essay on Man*, going so far as to say that it contained all the religious instruction which it was necessary for a man to know." Then, reciting from memory without hesitation, Lincoln challenged his visitors to show him any finer lines of poetry than those ending with:

All nature is but art, unknown to thee;
All chance, direction, which thou canst not see;
All discord, harmony not understood;
All partial evil, universal good:
And, spite of pride, in erring reason's spite,
One truth is clear, Whatever is, is right.

This climactic passage from the *Essay on Man* follows almost immediately upon the lines from the *Essay* recited by Parker in his sermon on "the God of the philosophers." It represents

Alexander Pope's extended description of Nature's God—the "stupendous whole / Whose body nature is, and God the soul."

In the same, reflective weeks that he was reciting metaphysical poetry to English visitors, Lincoln was composing his Second Inaugural Address. In that final speech, he invokes an "Almighty" that has its "own purposes" only partially understood by both parties to the conflict. Lincoln's deity gets that slavery is the source of division in the United States, but this deity may very well have permitted the division for reasons Americans themselves can't see. All discord, as Pope would have said, is harmony not understood. Then follows the sentence that Douglass esteemed above all other sentences, in which Lincoln allows that God may be content to allow every drop of blood drawn with the lash to be repaid by another drawn with the sword, and all the wealth piled up through slavery sunk. The implication, as Frederick Douglass was quick to see, is that Lincoln's God is one that allows crimes to punish themselves through the self-executing laws of nature. It presides over a universe ruled by force that answers only to reason. In Lincoln's Second Inaugural Address, Douglass could hardly fail to hear a restatement of the philosophy found in the parable of Covey, passed along to Sojourner Truth, and openly expounded by Theodore Parker.

Lincoln's other writings make clear that the critique of slavery embedded in his Second Inaugural Address does indeed draw on the same political theology that inspired Douglass, Parker, and other leaders of the antislavery movement. "God gave man a mouth to receive bread, hands to feed it, and his hand has a right to carry bread to his mouth without controversy," Lincoln writes in an earlier reflection—paraphrasing Parker paraphrasing Volney.[44] "If anything can be proved by natural theology, it is that slavery is morally wrong." The unjust character of slavery, he repeats elsewhere, "is clearly proved by natural theology . . . apart from revelation."

Lincoln concludes the most interesting sentence of his Second Inaugural Address with the affirmation of the world that such a pantheistic intuition requires. Where Pope says, "whatever is, is right," Lincoln says, "the judgments of the Lord are true and righteous altogether."[45] Perhaps judiciously, and not uncharacteristically, Lincoln here disguises the source of his thought with an allusion to a passage drawn from the Psalms in one of its pantheistic moments. As in his long-ago handbill from the campaign of 1846, the orthodox reference masked a heretical doctrine.

To those among his listeners privy to his theological journey from the beginning, the God of Lincoln's Second Inaugural Address would hardly have come as a surprise. The deity of the address is recognizably descended from the God of Lincoln's freethinking youth, when, as Herndon puts it, he was "an elevated pantheist." In later years, as Herndon explains, Lincoln "rose to the belief of a God, and this is all the change he ever underwent," and the God of the Second Inaugural Address, who has purposes even if they are unknowable, appears to track this shift.[46] In the abstract classifications favored by philosophers, one could say that Lincoln started off an atheist and then moved toward deism. His later writings, and certainly his public speeches, evince belief in some sort of supreme being, typically along the familiar lines of the moderate deism of America's founders.

The underlying heresy, however, remains unchanged. As Jesse Fell explains, the mature Lincoln believed in "a Creator of all things," but this Creator "had neither beginning nor end," and "possessing all power and wisdom, established a principle, in Obedience, to which, Worlds move and are upheld, and animal and vegetable life came into existence." Fell points out that Lincoln's "Creator" has little to do with the Gods of any variety of Christianity. The doctrine remains that of Volney and Ethan Allen—and Theodore Parker, as Fell himself suggests.[47]

9

THE SWEAT
OF OTHER
MEN'S FACES

The Dialectic of the Master
and the Shipyard Worker

WHEN FREDERICK WAS twenty or so, his enslaver Hugh Auld
(Thomas's brother) permitted him to hire himself out as a
caulker in the shipyards of Baltimore. He had learned the
skill of crafting watertight seals on wooden hulls, and he was
now the recognized master of a kit of mallets, chisels, and
hooks. He collected as much as $1.50 a day, working as many
as six days a week. His skillset placed him within a privileged minority of the enslaved population, and his income
would have compared favorably with the median income of
the immense white underclass of the South.[1]

But every Saturday evening, Frederick would return to
his enslaver Hugh Auld and hand over all his earnings for
the week. Master Hugh would finger the cash meticulously
under the lamplight, stacking up the nickels and dimes. Then
he would look Frederick in the face—"as if he would search
my heart as well as my pocket"—and ask reproachfully, *"Is
that all?"*[2]

That money, Frederick just knew, was rightfully his own.
Hugh Auld had nothing to do with it. "I contracted for it; I

earned it; it was paid to me."³ Auld's claim on the money was no better than "the right of the grim-visaged pirate upon the high seas."

On a good week, Auld would push a small coin or two back across the table, as if to commend Frederick for a job well done. But the gratuities only stoked the young man's anger: "The fact, that he gave me any part of my wages, was proof that he suspected that I had a right *to the whole of them*." Auld's consciousness of the situation, as much as his own, was the object of Frederick's intense concern. He worried that by taking the extra pennies he might permit Auld to conceive of himself as "a pretty honorable robber, after all!"

Measured in terms of physical comfort and liberty of movement, Frederick's last year of servitude was surely the most comfortable. He ate well, slept in his own bed, and was largely exempt from the kind of torture he had endured out on Covey's farm, and to which enslaved field hands were routinely subjected. Indeed, his enslaver was now the chief source of protection against the remaining threat of physical violence in his life, which came from his white fellow laborers. Free white workers often attacked Black and enslaved workers, out of a combination of racial animus and the (largely correct) perception that enslaved laborers were being used to compete away their wages.

And yet Frederick discovered that, even as his living conditions improved, his longing for freedom only grew more intense. He became aware that, although the kind of violence he had experienced on Covey's field was now out of sight, it would never be out of mind. The whippings had always been performative; their purpose was to keep him in a state of fear about what would happen should he fail to turn over his wages, so that he might discipline himself. And everyone in society was in some way involved in keeping him in the trap. The ministers who urged him to obey in the name of Jesus, the slave catchers who would hunt him down if he ran away, even the children on the street who might whisper to others about his whereabouts. "I am the slave not only of Master Thomas," he had earlier observed, "but I am the slave of society at large. Society at large . . . had bound itself to assist Master Thomas in robbing me."[4]

The more he thought about his situation, the less content he became. The rub of the problem, he came to think, was consciousness itself. To keep a slave happy, you must never let him see his own reflection in thought. "If there be one crevice through which a single drop" of awareness can fall, "it will certainly rust off the slave's chain."[5]

In Frederick's case, that crevice was the gap between his independent workweeks and the Saturday night robberies. Out in the shipyards, laboring in his own right on wooden planks with his mallet and his chisels, Frederick became conscious of himself in a certain sense as a free agent. He was "a someone" who could shape raw materials into useful objects and get paid for it. This consciousness of himself as a free being only grew with the recognition that others provided in acknowledging his work—a recognition that Auld himself could not withhold as he shuffled gratuities back across the table. But on Saturday nights, Frederick was compelled to witness his own lack of freedom—even as he was asked to supply his enslaver with the kind of recognition that only a free person can offer. Why would Auld care if Frederick thought he was "a pretty honorable robber" if he did not already suppose that Frederick was a free man able to pass judgment on him as an implicit equal?

In later years, Douglass's experience at Hugh Auld's table served as an important source of illumination in his reflections on the question of slavery. He grasped in a visceral way that consciousness and slavery are natural enemies; that his enslaver, too, persisted in his own kind of false consciousness; that their mutual liberation turned on a recognition of their mutual equality. It took Douglass some years—and some amount of philosophical reflection—to articulate the implications of this insight and then fold them into the radical strategy that ultimately served to guide the antislavery movement. But the heart of the matter was undoubtedly clear enough when he sat across from Hugh Auld on those Saturday nights.

Twenty-year-old Frederick Bailey had no trouble identifying the chief vulnerability of the property regime in which he found himself trapped. In the eyes of the system, he may have been merely a wage-earner not entitled to the wages he earned. But in his own eyes he was a man with a will, desires, and powers of his own. He possessed a faculty of consciousness—and he also had a pair of legs. His value as a species of "capital" in somebody else's pocket was only as good as the system's ability to prevent him from picking himself up and running away. By the end of the year, he had secured his ticket on the underground railroad and escaped to the North.

Freedom Renewed

A CERTAIN THEORY OF FREEDOM—call it the atomic theory—is perennially popular among those with property and privilege to defend. It says that freedom is a predicate of individuals alone, in the way that momentum pertains to individual atoms. A distinctive feature of freedom in this atomic sense is that it is entirely independent of equality and even inclined to oppose it. Any attempt to make the atoms more equal—to speed some up and slow others down—can only come at the expense of freedom, or so the thinking goes. Even advocates of (limited) equality, such as the political theorist John Rawls, pursue their arguments from a defensive crouch mandated by this atomism. Their case for a welfare state boils down to reasons why we should sacrifice some degree of liberty and prosperity for some degree of equality. It isn't hard to explain why the men of property tend to favor the atomic view, of course; it confirms them in their belief that the freedom and prosperity they enjoy belong to them and them alone, just as momentum pertains to every atom—and that the cries for equality are therefore merely a cover for theft.

Frederick Douglass and his antislavery allies, however, embraced a very different theory of freedom. It wasn't so much a new theory as a revived version of an old one, though it acquired a new suite of conceptual tools and a renewed hold on the mind in its passage through the furnaces of nineteenth-century Germany philosophy. Its point of departure is that human beings are not, after all, atoms but rather creatures of consciousness. We are reflective beings, or beings that come into existence by looking into a mirror as it were, and so our degree of freedom is in some yet-to-be-explained sense coextensive with our degree of self-understanding. Call it then the reflective theory of freedom. This new-old theory of freedom, along with its attendant theory of consciousness, matters—because it was this theory that guided Douglass and the antislavery leaders as they engineered America's second revolution.

THE LOCUS CLASSICUS of the reflective theory of freedom appears in G. W. F. Hegel's first and most original major work of philosophy, *The Phenomenology of Spirit*, in a chapter that has come to be known as "the master-slave dialectic." (A more accurate translation of the chapter title would be "The Independence and Dependence of Self-Consciousness: Lordship and Bondage," but it is best here to focus on how Hegel was read rather than on what he intended to write.) In what can seem like a strangely abstract retelling of the kind of experience that must have been common on the ground in the shipyards of antebellum Maryland, the chapter begins with two forms of consciousness seeking freedom and engaged in a "struggle of life and death"[6] with one another for domination. One seeks freedom by becoming the lord or master, the other hopes to survive by acquiescing in becoming the bondman or slave. (A cautionary note: Hegel's refractive philosophical prose resists any reduction to a psychological plotline or historical narrative; the story he tells isn't a generalization over the actual experience of masters and slaves so much as an analysis of the contradictions that shape some aspects of the consciousness of masters, slaves, and all people to some degree.) As the dialectic proceeds, a kind of reversal takes place, wherein the master's form of consciousness is shown to be deficient while the slave achieves a more complete form of consciousness grounded in a deeper understanding of freedom.

To make sense of Hegel's unusual philosophical allegory, it is necessary to know something more about the idea of "consciousness" that his predecessors had prepared for him and of which he makes use. His most important predecessor in this regard was Johann Gottlieb Fichte (who took himself to be summarizing and clarifying the message from Immanuel Kant, who was himself borrowing much from a still earlier generation of philosophers). Fichte's philosophical system begins and ends in the quest for freedom. His starting point is therefore the self or "I" that seeks to realize itself, or become what is, as a genuinely free or self-determining being. The complication, according to Fichte, is that this "I" is "only active . . . never passive." That is, it "has no being proper, no subsistence, for this is the result of an interaction."[7] Fichte's "I" can see itself only in the mirror, as it were, and what it sees in the mirror can only consist of its engagement with some object that is independent of consciousness. In a formula: the "I" can only construct itself out of a reflection on the "bump" or shock of its encounter with a "not-I."

Following Kant, Fichte initially analyzes this "not-I" as something sensuous or material and answering to basic concepts of substance and causality. For the "I" to come into being, it must inhabit a world that operates in a lawful way according to causes, for otherwise it will find no place within which to situate itself. The same principles that keep the caulk on the planks and the hulls floating in the water, for example, are the ones that allow the shipyard worker to emerge as an actor in the world. So far, so Kantian, one might say. But then, drawing on some underdeveloped suggestions in the Kantian philosophy, Fichte opens up a bold new dimension to the analysis of the relation between the "I" and "not-I."

To be an "I," Fichte argues, is to pursue goals, and not merely to respond to an existing world populated with physical objects. It means acting for reasons, not just from causes. All consciousness, he argues, is in some way normative or purposive. But these reasons around which the "I" comes into being must necessarily come to it from the "not-I." Otherwise they would be arbitrary and ever changing, the vacillating hallucinations of a hermetic "I," and thus no reasons at all. Fichte further supposes that such "I-creating" reasons can be provided only by what has the character of consciousness. It follows that the "not-I" must have the character of consciousness, too, if it is to give the "I" the character of consciousness. Thus, the "I" can construct itself only in the reflection of its encounter with another "I," an "I" that is "not-I." When we suppose that we are giving ourselves reasons for action, according to Fichte, we are dividing ourselves from ourselves and listening to the reasons that can only emerge from a consciousness imagined to be on the other side of the table, as it were. Fichte's conclusion is characteristically pithy and startling: "A human being becomes a human being only among human beings."[8] Still more compactly: "No thou, no I; no I, no thou."[9]

Fichte uses the term "summons" (the German is *Aufforderung*) to describe the voice of reason to which the "I" answers in constructing itself in its quest for freedom. The term is closely linked to the idea of a "vocation" or "calling" (the Germans would say *Beruf*, from *rufen*, "to call")—for, according to the traditional theological vocabulary, a "summons" may also be understood as a "calling" from God. In this reappropriation of terms, it is possible to glimpse the profoundly secular implications of the philosophical tradition that Fichte inhabits. In Fichte's analysis, the "summons" that makes us what we are emerges out of consciousness itself, or, more precisely, out of the intrinsically social or interactive nature of consciousness. The religious sense of the term, as a summons from on high, can only be derivative, not original—a metaphorical representation, or maybe a "self-alienation" (to use Fichte's own term), of the self-consciousness that arises from human acts of mutual recognition. As his successors such as Feuerbach would grasp, what Fichte offers is not a secularization or "disenchantment" narrative involving a supposed loss of religious meaning or that strange nostalgia that intellectuals sometimes have for premodern life under feudal theocracies. Rather, it is a "recovery" narrative, inasmuch as it proposes shedding the artifice of religion in order to return to the naturally godless roots of meaning and purpose in human experience.

HEGEL'S MASTER-SLAVE DIALECTIC picks up where Fichte leaves off. Self-consciousness, says Hegel, is freedom, and yet this self-consciousness exists in and for itself "in that, and through the fact that, it exists in and for another self-consciousness, that is, it *is* only in being 'recognized.'"[10] "Recognition" here, from the German *anerkennen*, involves something more than merely identifying the other in a cognitive sense; it requires changing one's own disposition or practical attitude with respect to this other being; that is, it means transforming oneself into the kind of being that will treat this other being as what it is. The process whereby self-consciousness comes into being by recognizing itself in and through its other—this "unity in its duplication"—has many sides to it, according to Hegel, and his almost-unreadable *Phenomenology of Spirit* is intended to lay them all out. The "Spirit" that arises at the end of this strange new work of philosophy is the unified collection of all the forms of self-consciousness that come into being through their reflection in one another, and it stands for a kind of absolute freedom. In Hegel's words, Spirit is "the unity of the different independent self-consciousnesses which, in their opposition, enjoy perfect freedom and independence: the I that is We and We that is I."[11]

The master-slave dialectic captures a particularly important phase in this struggle for the self-realization of consciousness. The consciousness of the master (more precisely, the side of consciousness that conceives of itself as master) seeks to secure the recognition it requires to realize its freedom by reducing the consciousness of the slave to an instrument of its will. For example, the consciousness of the master demands that the enslaved consciousness turn over its wages from its work in the shipyards. The consciousness of the slave, upon experiencing the fear of death at the hands of the master, acquiesces and labors in the world on behalf of the master, grudgingly shuffling the nickels and dimes across the greasy table. At first blush, it appears that the master, having commanded its own recognition, thereby achieves full self-realization, whereas the slave, unrecognized, loses its existence as consciousness.

It soon becomes clear that the consciousness of the master involves a twofold misconception about consciousness itself. The first misconception has to do with the way in which consciousness relates to the material world. It is through its work in the world, through the trace of its mallets and chisels on the wood and caulk of experience, that consciousness can leave a mark. And it is only through reflection on this mark, in its recognition of a caulking job well done, that consciousness may discover itself. In labor, to put it in Hegel's turgid prose, "the negative relation to the object passes into the form of the object, into something that is permanent and remains." Labor is "desire restrained," or "evanescence delayed," yet it is only by stretching itself out in time, or postponing its gratification, that consciousness can construct itself out of experience. The awareness that Hegel describes here is no doubt akin to what a young craftsman might experience in the shipyards as he applies his skills to building sturdy boats and becomes conscious of himself as a "someone."

While the slave, not the master, realizes himself through labor in this way, the master intends to keep for himself the pure enjoyment of things, leaving the slave to deal with the independence or otherness of those things. The master seeks wealth without labor, yet to pursue desires without labor is to be trapped in an unending state of "evanescence": a cycle of impulses that, encountering no resistance from the material world, lacks permanence and objectivity. The slave, on the other hand, has at least the opportunity to find himself in the world through the material trace of his labor.

Feuerbach, who follows Hegel following Fichte, draws out the important implication that consciousness in this Hegelian sense is not some disembodied state of being but rather always characterized and limited by that of which it is conscious. "We know the man by the object, by his conception of what is external to himself; in it his nature becomes evident," he argues. Consciousness in this sense is always partial and always comes in degrees. "A being's understanding is its sphere of vision," Feuerbach explains. "The consciousness of the caterpillar, whose life is confined to a particular species of plant, does not extend itself beyond this narrow domain."[12]

The slave, to continue with Hegel's analysis, is well positioned to grasp this inherently conditioned or dependent nature of consciousness. Death is "the absolute master," says Hegel, and in laboring under the threat of death the slave "has been unmanned, has trembled in every fiber of its being, and everything solid and stable has been shaken to its foundations." In its awareness of the prospect of annihilation, the consciousness of the slave becomes aware of what it truly is—an "I" and not a thing, an existential "I" that creates itself as it externalizes itself in a particular history of engagement with the world. This new consciousness, as Frederick Bailey might have said, is not necessarily pleasant; it may look more like the "horrible pit" of despair one experiences upon realizing that one may be a slave for life. One might even wish that consciousness itself would go away—but of course the very act of wishing it so ensures that it will not.

Now a second and still more important reversal takes place in the master-slave dialectic, and it has to do with the way in which consciousness relates to other consciousnesses. The master demands recognition, yet even as it stacks up the coins on its side of the table, it cannot escape the reality that this recognition must come from another, independent consciousness. Like Hugh Auld looking for Frederick's implicit approval, the master wants its gratuities to be received with gratitude, so that it may know itself as a good master. But in compelling the slave to provide this recognition, the master ensures that the slave is no longer free to give it. In exchange for a few dimes shuffled back across the table, the master hears only the empty echo of its own desire for domination. Its demands for recognition yield only self-deception.

The slave, on the other hand, is in a position to gain a degree of recognition. Having supplied through its labor something that satisfies the desires of another consciousness, it sees that its work is recognized. It has contracted for work, it has caulked the hull of a ship, it has been paid in some form by someone—even if the wages for that work were later stolen as if by a pirate. The sudden awareness of the master's demand for recognition in the form of thanks for a job of mastering well done serves to confirm the slave's understanding that it is not just a "someone" but an "equal." The slave thus has what the master does not—a recognition of mutual equality from a consciousness that is utterly independent of itself. "Through this rediscovery of itself by itself," says Hegel, the slave becomes conscious "of having and being a 'mind of its own.'" It begins to yearn for freedom, and it soon understands that it must run away, to the North.

Karl Marx[13] thought Hegel's dialectic of human self-realization was just "great," but it was Feuerbach who broadcast the results in a way that resonated across the middle decades of the nineteenth century. The fundamental unit of consciousness, Feuerbach explains, is not the individual mind but the idea or act of understanding, and these ideas are intrinsically universal. Thus, consciousness is not an organ of the individual, like the foot or liver, as the atomic theory of freedom supposes, but an activity through which the individual transcends itself and arrives at something universal. "My thought is not mine, but is rather thought *in and for itself* so that it can just as well be mine as that of someone else," Feuerbach writes. Reason is therefore "the unified ground of all individuals."[14] Consequently, the I "attains to consciousness of the world through the consciousness of the Thou," he adds.[15] "Were my self-awareness not also at the same time a comprehension of other men, then I would not be a man." The Feuerbachian summary of Hegel's master-slave dialectic, not surprisingly, is thoroughly humanistic: "In thinking, I am bound together with, or rather, I am one with—indeed, I myself am—all human beings."[16]

THE POINT OF HEGEL'S dialectic of freedom is not to show that it is better to be a slave. Rather, its polemical edge rests on the claim that the conceptions out of which we form relations of mastery, servitude, freedom, and equality are often deeply flawed, and they lead not toward genuine freedom but toward some form of self-deception and instability. In this respect, Hegel's master-slave dialectic is best seen as a way of mapping out a certain terrain of philosophical insights. It tells us that the discipline of service, or the deferral of desire, is essential in the construction of the self. It says that the genuine fear that arises from the encounter with an outside, independent, and uncontrollable reality, too, is a necessary aspect of self-development. It suggests that a complete form of conscious-ness must in some way incorporate both the self-assertion of the master and the responsibility of the slave. But the insight that sparkles brightest in this dialectic has to do with the con-nection between human freedom and equality.

The trouble for the master, as Hegel points out, is that the relationship is "one-sided and unequal." If he is to win rec-ognition, his commands must be reasonable, not arbitrary; they must be "honorable," as Frederick says, and they must be seen as such by the other. Which is to say, that at least for a moment the master must be able to see himself through the slave's eyes. As Hegel explains, "for recognition proper, there is needed the moment that what the master does to the other he should also do to himself, and what the slave does to him-self, he should do to the other also." This equality of mutual regard, according to the logic Hegel unravels here, is at bot-tom a fundamental precondition for freedom. On this conclu-sion, Hegel is refreshingly lucid: "It is necessary that the two selves opposing each other . . . should recognize themselves as what they are in themselves . . . namely, not merely natural but rather free beings. Only in this does true freedom come about, for this consists in the identity of myself with the other. I am only truly free when the other is also free and is recog-nized by me as free." [17]

According to the reflective theory of freedom, then, equality (of a certain variety) and freedom are not to be traded off against each other, but necessarily reinforce one another. The variety of equality that matters is that of mutual regard—or what today sometimes goes by the name of equal dignity. As Feuerbach underscores, equality in this sense is bound up with rationality, for it necessarily involves grounding our own existence as free beings within the kind of universal language that makes reasoned discourse possible. In sharp contrast with the atomistic theory of freedom—which takes for granted that equality can only be purchased at the expense of prosperity—the reflective theory says that equality not only empowers individuals but puts them in a position to engage in rational cooperation. A society that enjoys the equality of mutual regard, according to this logic, will be richer and stronger, not poorer and weaker, than a society ordered into masters and slaves. Which of course is what Theodore Parker saw in the public schoolhouses of New England and what Douglass observed on the streets of New Bedford.

THERE IS ONE interpretation of Hegelianism—strongly associated with the man who ascended to the chair of philosophy at the University of Berlin around 1818 and went on to celebrate the virtues of the reactionary Prussian regime that had been so kind to him—that numbers it among the enemies of the open society.[18] There is another interpretation, more popular among the 48ers who crossed the Atlantic and their American allies, that finds in Hegelianism a profound defense of a certain kind of liberalism. The dialectic, as ever, does not take sides, but history is not quite so ambidextrous. The Hegelianism that matters is the liberal one that shaped America's second revolution; the other one simply took the name and slapped it on nationalist urges that came mostly from other sources. This Hegelian liberalism is at odds with much of what passes for liberalism today (or what typically travels under the very misleading name of neoliberalism), but it is quite close to—indeed it is a rich paraphrase of—the original liberalism of the first American Revolution.

The essence of the connection is laid out in *The Philosophy of Right*, Hegel's major work of political theory, which purports to show how the idea of reflective freedom can be realized in the world. The part of the argument that matters here is that which revolves around what Hegel calls "civil society." Although the term now tends to stand for any social phenomena outside formal government and business,[19] Hegel's civil society is in fact the arena within which liberalism rules. It describes that sphere of social life in which individuals may enter contracts with one another, perform labor and services, organize associations, get married if they wish, and in general act in such a way as to "make a name" for themselves, as a skilled shipyard worker, for example, and become a "someone."

Within Hegelian civil society, the idea of "property" plays an important role, for consciousness must be able to objectify itself in some way in the world by claiming certain things as "mine." The shipyard worker needs to be able to say: this is my work, my wages, my food. The "property" in question, however, is not an absolute claim over material things for all time but a publicly recognized claim to what forms a part of the individual's freedom or self-realization. The foundation of property is thus not "my" will, as the atomic theory of freedom implies, but a "common will."[20]

More important even than "property"—and the start of the thread that would tie German philosophy with the ideology of Parker, Lincoln, and the new Republican Party—is the role of "labor" in Hegelian liberalism. Working in the shipyards isn't just a matter of collecting a few nickels; it is a way of performing a service of value and thereby winning recognition as a productive individual. "Labor is of all and for all, and the enjoyment of its fruits is enjoyment by all," says Hegel. "Each serves the other and provides help. Only here does the individual have existence, as individual."[21] In a well-ordered civil society, he concludes, "the livelihood, happiness, and legal status of one man is interwoven with the livelihood, happiness, and rights of all." In the northern sections of the United States, this vision of a society that comes together around free labor and values human rights above property rights would have quite some appeal.

In its foundations and in its evolution, the liberalism of a Hegelian civil society is quite distinct from the pseudo-liberalisms associated with atomic theories of freedom. The latter tend to identify liberalism with a set of formal laws, mostly having to do with property such as it happens to be encoded in this or that regime, that fix individual rights for all time. Hegelian civil society, on the other hand, is legitimate, and works, only to the extent that individuals within it may embrace its rules as the reasonable extension of their quest for self-realization. The rules in question include not just formal laws but also the customs and practices through which individuals find meaning; in particular, the system of education. These wide-ranging rules are inherently social, and they also always have a provisional character. They may be tested against the requirements of equal mutual regard. Where the rules conflict with the fundamental human right to freedom—a possibility of which the atomic versions can rarely even conceive—it is the rules that must be revised. Civil society is therefore also, according to Hegel, a historical achievement, not a natural state of things. It accumulates over time, as actual human societies discover and develop the rules that make it possible for all to work together in a manner that respects the rights of each. It is in the final analysis a measure of a society's willingness to educate itself.

Although Hegel and his more overtly republican successors packaged their liberalism in an idiosyncratic vocabulary, it is probably best understood as an extension of the liberalism that emerged from the Radical Enlightenment of the seventeenth century and shook the order of the world in the revolutions at the end of the eighteenth century in America, France, and Haiti. The same liberalism survived the Hegelian winter as it were, burst forth in the springtime of the peoples in 1848, and then sailed to America aboard overcrowded vessels such as the *India Queen*. This liberalism relies upon the idea that consciousness is not a thing but an activity; that its elemental constituent is not some soul-like substance but the activity of understanding; that it knows itself and the world only imperfectly, through its reflections on the world and itself; that its freedom is a matter of degree and a function of its understanding; that its freedom or rational self-determination is coextensive with the freedom of those with whom it forms a society; that democracy, understood as the rational self-determination of the sovereign people, is both the most free and the most powerful form of government. All these intuitions lay at the core of the ancient philosophy that was revived in the early modern world in the works of Spinoza and his successors.

To Americans such as Frederick Douglass, hungry for answers in a dark time of counterrevolutionary triumph, the imported Hegelianism offered an invitation to rethink the rights of labor and rights of property—and what to do when the two are in conflict. It called for a new and better understanding of the actual sources of prosperity in human society. What would it take, the revolutionaries wanted to know, to recognize our mutual equality—especially across the color line?

Reflections on the Color of Labor

THE CHILDHOOD OF A SLAVE is a happy one, Frederick Douglass declares in the autobiography that Ottilie Assing wished to translate.[22] The slave child isn't scolded about how to use a knife and fork; he eats with his hands. He has no need to keep his clothes clean; all he wears is a sack. No one corrects his grammar because no one expects him to speak in proper English. His freedom is nearly absolute, and his life is "uproarious." Best of all, he is likely to be surrounded with playmates with whom he can share the fun times.

Among Frederick's childhood pals was a boy his age named Daniel. The two bonded in the usual ways: over games, jokes, and cake purloined from the manor house. Daniel did the treat-stealing because Daniel, as it happens, was the youngest son of Colonel Lloyd, the owner of the plantation on which Frederick happened to be enslaved. "In Mas' Daniel I had a friend at court, from whom I learned many things which my eager curiosity was excited to know," Douglass recalls.[23] From his playmate, Frederick learned to mimic the vocabulary, intonations, and assumptions of the planter class. Daniel, one presumes, absorbed something of the language of the enslaved people.

As for the color of their skin—according to Douglass, it just didn't matter. "*Color* makes no difference with a child. Are you a child with wants, tastes and pursuits common to children, not put on, but natural? Then, were you black as ebony you would be welcome to the child of alabaster whiteness," he writes.[24] "The equality of nature is strongly asserted in childhood." Humans must first be taught to see color and invest it with prejudice, Douglass reasons, before they can learn to despise one another on its account. In the case of Mas' Daniel, the process of racial conditioning was complete within the customary time frame. As they graduated from their childhood games, Frederick and Daniel moved into their alien worlds, divided by color, one to receive the finest schooling available in the manners of the master class and the other to work in the fields and shipyards. Their earlier bond dissolved into mere memory.

In his theoretical works, Douglass elevates the conviction of natural color indifference to a fundamental principle of his political philosophy. In an influential essay of 1881 on "The Color Line," he argues that, even while the color line is undeniably an aspect of American society, "this color prejudice" is far from "the natural and inevitable thing it claims to be."[25] Racism, he maintains, "is American, not European; local, not general; limited, not universal, and must be ascribed to artificial conditions, and not to any fixed and universal law of nature."[26] In his final autobiography, he insists again: "Colors alone can have nothing against each other."[27] The deepest problem with slavery, Douglass elaborates, is not that it treats different colors differently but that it invents color difference in order to treat people differently: "I have held all my life and will hold to the day of my death, that the fundamental everlasting objection to slavery, is not that it sinks a Negro to the condition of a brute, but that it sinks a *man* to that condition."[28] In describing the American ideal, to the last days of his life, he does not cede an inch on the founding principle of universal equality: "My mission now, as all along during nearly fifty years is . . . to hasten the day when the principles of liberty and humanity expressed in the Declaration of Independence and the Constitution of the United States shall be the law and practice of every section, and of all the people of this great country without regard to race, sex, color or religion."[29]

Douglass hardly intended to minimize or deny the reality of racism in American life. In his career as an itinerant abolitionist speaker, he was hounded out of railway carriages, humiliated in churches, insulted in the streets, confined to lower decks on steamships, chased away from speaking events with sticks and bricks, physically assaulted by racist thugs, and treated with condescension even by some of his own colleagues. Having witnessed the full force of race hatred extend through the terrorism of the Jim Crow era, he writes, "There is nothing in the history of savages to surpass the blood-chilling horrors and fiendish excesses perpetrated against the colored people of this country."[30]

Yet he stuck to the principle of natural color indifference that he absorbed as a child to the end. He could see the hate; he still wanted to understand how it operated. He thought it vital to elaborate a certain theory of what racism is: where it comes from, how it functions; above all, how it intersects with economic conflict. His theory of racism rests on the reflective theory of freedom passed along by his German friends, and it decisively shaped not just his understanding of slavery but also the tactics he would embrace in the effort to overcome it.

IN A LECTURE delivered just after the start of the shooting war, Douglass begins by insisting that he wants to leave the fraught matters of race and conflict behind and talk instead about other, happier topics. Then he pauses to ask if what he is proposing to do is even possible. His reflection on the question reveals something essential about his theory of racism.

"When I come upon the platform the Negro is very apt to come with me. I cannot forget him: and you would not if I did," he says. "Men have an inconvenient habit of reminding each other of the very things they would have them forget."[31] He elaborates on this compressed insight with an anecdote from life in the city. One day as he was walking the streets of New York with a white friend, he recalls, the friend turned to him and said, "Frederick, I am not ashamed to walk with you down Broadway." Douglass turns to his listeners and confides: "It never once occurred to him that I might for any reason be ashamed to walk with him down Broadway. He managed to remind me that mine was a despised and hated color—and his the orthodox and constitutional one—at the same time he seemed to be endeavoring to make me forget both." "Pardon me," he adds sardonically, "if I shall be betrayed into a similar blunder tonight." And indeed, the rest of Douglass's lecture on happier topics turns out to be an indirect way of reflecting on race and conflict in America.

The theory of racism upon which Douglass relies here says that racism appears only in the reflections upon color and not in any properties inherent in color. More exactly, according to this "reflective" theory, racism lives in the frame of our perceptions rather than in anything perceived. This frame, moreover, is inherently social. As in the case of the friend who experiences only complacent delight in feeling no shame while walking with Douglass, it figures in the shared assumptions that structure experience and not in experience itself. This structure of experience matters because it is where the normative dimension of consciousness resides—where the differences between an "orthodox" person and a "hated" one live next to ideas about "constitutional" and "despised" colors in the public mind.

A first inference from this analysis, according to Douglass, is that there is no "negro problem"; the Black person "has as little to do with the cause of the Southern trouble as he has with its cure. There is no reason, therefore, in the world why his name should be given to the problem."[32] A related insight is that racism perpetuates itself not merely through acts of overt discrimination but through public performances of the symbolic framework within which it is encoded: Douglass's New York friend did not infringe on his civil rights, and yet his friend's comment served mainly to reinforce the code that divided the races. Douglass's idea here is perhaps closest to that of James Baldwin, who famously said in an interview: "I am not a 'nigger.' I am a man. If you think I am a nigger, it means you need him. . . . if I am not the nigger here, and you the white people invented him, then you've got to find out why."[33]

A further and perhaps even more profound inference is that racism necessarily divides consciousness against itself. It requires treating the equal as unequal—the human as inhuman—and in doing so it constructs a subject that must recognize itself in the other even as it denies the humanity of the other. As in the case of the "master" consciousness of the Hegelian dialectic, racism constrains the capacity of the racist subject to realize its own freedom. It offers not genuine mastery but rather an illusion of mastery. In the case of the poor southern white man, Douglass observes, it introduces an irreconcilable conflict, for he is told that he belongs to a superior caste, and yet he lives in a society that treats him like—and even calls him—trash.

A parallel but very different and more searing division afflicts the consciousness of the object of racist belief. Like the shipyard worker who must surrender his wages to his enslaver, this kind of consciousness comes to be in a world that values his work yet despises him as something less than human. He must see himself through the eyes of those who refuse to see him. W. E. B. Du Bois explains the matter definitively in his version of the same, essentially Hegelian theory. "It is a peculiar sensation, this double-consciousness, this sense of always looking at one's self through the eyes of others, of measuring one's soul by the tape of a world that looks on in amused contempt and pity. One ever feels this two-ness—an American, a Negro; two souls, two thoughts; two unreconciled strivings; two warring ideals in one dark body."[34]

According to Douglass's theory, racism is therefore not a neutral or harmless variation of consciousness, like a pair of tinted spectacles that preserves the shape of the world while changing one of its attributes. On the contrary, it is a deficient mode of consciousness. It necessarily involves systemic misrepresentations of the individual and the individual's reality. Precisely because it is always a deficient mode of consciousness, racism in Douglass's theory is always part of some system of power. Ignorance is always a form of unfreedom, and to be unfree is to be the passive object of external forces. Racist ideas, according to this logic, must therefore arise from sources having little to do with color per se, and they naturally extend their influence into matters that also have little to do with supposed racial difference.

In antebellum America, Douglass could plainly see, the root cause of racism was the slave system.[35] The oligarchs at the commanding heights of the American slave republic did not enslave people because they were of a different color; they invented color the better to enslave people. To secure their claims over the offspring of enslaved mothers and the safety of their "property" as it was marched across the expanding slave territory, they worked to reinforce that racial division. Racism might well outlive the cause that brought it into being, and it most certainly afflicts those who derive no economic benefit from it, according to this view; and yet race conflict and economic conflict are inseparable. So, too, are the solutions to these conflicts. The antislavery struggle, according to Douglass's synthesis, must pursue revolutions in labor and in the perceptions of color at the very same time—for they are part of the same revolution.

THE THEORY WAS in some sense just catching up with the reality on the ground. The antislavery movement and the labor movement were slowly aligning themselves, if not always consciously. Like two sides of the same coin, they looked out in seemingly opposite directions and yet always landed in the same place. This convergence of labor activism and antislavery activism ultimately drew both in the direction of the same reflective theory of racism.

The process was already in evidence in the run-up to 1848, when the same free spirits that were drawn to abolitionism also took great interest in the utopian schemes of European socialists such as Henri Saint-Simon, Charles Fourier, Étienne Cabet, Wilhelm Weitling, and Robert Owen.[36] When ten idealistic families set up a wage-free utopian commune in Northampton, Massachusetts, in 1842, it swiftly became a magnet for abolitionists, including William Lloyd Garrison, Sojourner Truth, and underground railroad stationmaster David Ruggles. Frederick Douglass especially liked what he saw at the Northampton Association and confessed that he felt "a strong leaning towards communism as a remedy for all social ills."[37] Douglass went on to become a vocal supporter of Chartism, the working-class movement that flared in England in the 1840s.[38]

After 1848, the dalliance between labor activism and abolitionism blossomed into a tentative yet powerful alliance. At the Tremont Temple in Boston in 1848, the assembled abolitionists and reformers insisted that the "right to live" trumped "the right of property."[39] A gathering of antislavery leaders passed a resolution identifying "the rights of the laborer at the North with those of the Southern slave" and calling on all "the working-men of the North to espouse the cause of the emancipation of the slave and upon the abolitionists to advocate the cause of the free laborer."[40] Antislavery speeches by Parker and others suddenly bloom with terms such as "the idea of fraternity," "human brotherhood," and "social revolution."[41] In the new, labor-conscious abolitionism, William Craft himself had a particularly constructive role to play. As a skilled artisan whose craftsmanship was widely appreciated, he could be held up as an example of a worthy member of any working-men's association. In his personal career, he made the case for a union of the working classes across the color line.

The labor activism of the antislavery movement was generally not that of the dispossessed proletariat of industrial class warfare, and racism among northern working-class whites prevented it from ever reaching its potential. Abolitionism was mostly a middle-class phenomenon. Apart from eccentrics such as Gerrit Smith and the Tappan brothers, it attracted few adherents from the tiny top of the economic ladder, just as it failed to bring in large numbers from the lowest economic classes of whites. Its ranks were filled with men and women who looked like Parker and the people of his 28th Congregational Society. They were the educated children of white farmers, they were wives and daughters who wanted a seat at the table, and they were the free Black people who fought their way against the odds into the schools, trades, and professions. They were the vanguard of the silent revolution from the middle that powered American prosperity up through the last quarter of the twentieth century.

In his compelling 1862 speech to the Massachusetts Anti-Slavery Society, the Black abolitionist John Rock offers a concise overview of the intersection between racism and class warfare in the slave republic in both North and South. "The educated and the wealthy class despise the negro, because they have robbed him of his hard earnings, and they believe if he gets his freedom, their fountain will be dried up," he says, referring to the oligarchs and their minions of the North as well as the South. "The lowest class hate him because he is poor, as they are, and is a competitor with them for the same labor," he continues, referring to both the white underclass in the South and the white laborers in the North. "The poor ignorant white man . . . does not understand that the interest of the laboring classes is mutual," he observes.[42]

Douglass commits himself to the same analysis. "Fearfully as slavery bears upon the blacks of the South, its effects on the vast majority of whites is no way less dreadful," runs a typical editorial in the *North Star*. "Slavery degrades all labor, and with it all laborers." The Black slave "belongs to one slaveholder," while the white "belongs to all slaveholders collectively. . . . Both are plundered, and by the same plunderers."[43] The white underclass of the South lives in abject squalor, says another editorial published in Douglass's newspaper, because "ignorance, prejudice, and crime are a triumvirate of tyranny."[44]

Douglass anticipates the analysis offered by Du Bois, who argues that southern whites were bought off with "the wages of whiteness." They were paid off, not in real money, but with the psychic benefits that flow from believing themselves to belong to a purportedly superior race. Jefferson Davis, the president of the Confederate States of America, offers essentially the same take but with a happy spin. The beauty of racism, he writes, is "that it dignifies and exalts every white man by the presence of a lower race" and is therefore "essential to the preservation of the higher orders of republican civilization."[45]

The conclusion at which Douglass and his fellow antislavery leaders arrive is the same one that Karl Marx articulates in the tome he published after the war: "In the United States of America, every independent movement of the workers was paralyzed as long as slavery disfigured a part of the republic. Labor cannot emancipate in the white skin where in the black it is branded."[46] In Douglass's mind, recognition is the key to a better future—the kind of recognition that secures freedom for the free by guaranteeing freedom for all. The nation needed to do what Mas' Daniel had unlearned how to do and what Hugh Auld had refused to do: to see the Black child as a child and the Black worker as a worker. But how to accomplish this? In the prewar years, Douglass put his shoulder into various plans to improve the skills and opportunities for Black laborers. When the war came, he threw himself into another, far more violent and ambitious plan to achieve recognition for America's Black citizens.

THAT THE ERSTWHILE Unitarian minister who had once sermonized on the transient and the permanent in Christianity should have led an effort to supply a wanted terrorist with rifles and cash is remarkable enough. Yet Theodore Parker's support for John Brown in the wake of their January 1857 meeting in Boston rested on a still more remarkable theory of what exactly slavery is and how it must be overcome—a theory that Douglass happened to share.[47]

Slavery is not, as conventional wisdom would have it, the rule of the "strong" over the "weak," or so both Douglass and Parker believed. Rather, it persists only because a great many citizens who are not themselves slaveholders and who do not benefit at all from the practice nonetheless sustain the enforcement and the conditioning, the cultural norms, and the religious and political hierarchies required to keep the system running. The essential prerequisite for any slave system (and arguably any form of fascism) is to condition the whole of the population in the profoundly unreasonable and ultimately self-destructive habit of not recognizing one segment of its membership as human.

According to this logic, the end of slavery will come not from above, through ostensibly noble acts on the part of enslavers, as the Garrisonians took for granted; it must come from below, from the unrealized power of the enslaved population itself. This power may conceivably realize itself in a variety of ways: through individual acts of resistance, organized rebellion, or a negotiated settlement. In the context of an oligarchy as entrenched in political and religious life as that of the American slaveholders, both Douglass and Parker eventually conclude that rebellion is the only viable option. Parker underscores the conclusion in blunt letters to friends: "I should like of all things to see an insurrection of the slaves. It must be tried many times before it succeeds, *as at last it must.*"[48] Elsewhere, Parker suggests that it is just a matter of time before "three millions or thirty millions of degraded human beings, degraded by us, must wade through slaughter to their unalienable rights."[49]

The distinctive (and the most Hegelian) aspect of the theory is the role that it assigns to the performative aspect of the exercise of Black power in emancipation. If the unrealized power of the enslaved population is the key to the rebellion, Parker reasons, the key to unlocking this hidden power is to change the way in which Americans (both enslaved and free) perceive the Black population (both enslaved and free Blacks). This transformation in perceptions—that is, the recognition of natural equality—would not only empower the Black population but would also induce the white population to alter the self-destructive behavior through which it sustains the power of the slaveholding oligarchy. The new recognition would thus itself become the source of a renewed national power.

The best or perhaps the only way to precipitate this transformation in perceptions, Parker concludes, would be to arm

Black people so that they can demonstrate their claim to natural equality. When Black arms are at last raised in battle, he argues, white minds will change. The act of recognition, more than the act of war itself, would transform both the beholder and the beheld, and in this way, it would give rise to a new power. The argument, as Parker would have known, is thoroughly Hegelian.

The role of the antislavery movement, according to this vision, is therefore not to prick the conscience of a superior race of enslavers, as the old Garrisonians imagined, but to elicit a public demonstration of power on the part of those whom society has falsely marked for enslavement. A first step in the program, Parker seems to have realized belatedly, was to recognize the role that Black abolitionists were already playing in the struggle. In a speech to the New York Anti-Slavery Society, Thomas Wentworth Higginson makes the point for him. "White Anglo-Saxon abolitionists," he observes, have been "too apt to assume the whole work," and to think that the rescue of the slave was something to be done "not by him but for him." But this was to "ignore the great force of the victims of tyranny." If the slaves were ever to claim their freedom, he concludes, taking the words straight from Douglass's mouth, they "must strike the first blow."[50]

Parker's theory of slavery and antislavery exists in tension, not to say contradiction, with the racialist assumptions that had characterized his thinking from the beginning of his career—and there is some indication that Parker himself was becoming aware of this. No doubt the Black abolitionists with whom he worked had some influence on his thinking. William Wells Brown and William C. Nell, both of whom had swung from Garrisonian beginnings to a conviction that the time had come for violence, insisted in conversation with Parker that the enslaved Black population would demonstrate its valor if given a chance to fight against its enslavers.[51] Frederick Douglass and John Rock, of course, continued to push the same message.

The Man before the Dollar

"I USED TO BE A SLAVE," Lincoln writes in a note to a friend.[52] It's hyperbole, of course, but it captures a tough nut of truth about Abraham's formative years. When he was young, his father rented him out for work as a rail-splitter, flatboat operator, and all-around farmhand. He earned as much as 31 cents a day, but when he came home, he was compelled to turn his wages over to his father. At least until he reached the age of twenty-one, Abe had something in common with young Frederick—and Douglass knew it. "All day long he could split heavy rails in the woods, and half the night long he could study his English Grammar by the uncertain flare and glare of the light made by a pine-knot," says Douglass in one of his eulogies for Lincoln. "He was a man of work. A son of toil himself, he was linked in brotherly sympathy with the sons of toil in every loyal part of the Republic."[53]

Lincoln's origins in the laboring classes, Douglass correctly surmised, was one of the keys to his antislavery politics. So much was evident in the contrast between Lincoln and his predecessor in the White House. James Buchanan had made clear that he would not risk war to preserve the nation, still less to end slavery. He and his fellow northern elites were content to negotiate their way to a Union dedicated to the perpetuation of slavery. "Happily for you and me," writes Douglass, "the judgment of James Buchanan, the patrician, was not the judgment of Abraham Lincoln, the plebeian."[54]

Lincoln, like Theodore Parker, was a champion of "free labor." At the foundation of his ideas on the subject lies the thesis that the development of the mind and the development of the body are two sides of the same project. Lincoln makes the point explicit in his folksy way: "Free Labor argues that, as the Author of man makes every individual with one head and one pair of hands, it was probably intended that heads and hands should cooperate as friends; and that that particular head should control that particular pair of hands."[55] As he explains the role of labor in allowing the self to realize itself in the world, he sounds almost explicitly Hegelian: "The effect of a thorough cultivation upon the farmer's own mind, and in the reaction through his mind, back upon his business, is perhaps equal to any other of its effects. Every man is proud of what he does well." On this metaphysical foundation, Lincoln follows Douglass and Parker in making the case for education: "By the mud-sill theory it is assumed that labor and education are incompatible. . . . According to that theory, a blind horse upon a treadmill, is a perfect illustration of what a laborer should be," he tells the farmers of Wisconsin.[56] "But Free Labor says 'no!' . . . In one word, Free Labor insists on universal education."

The labor with which Parker, Lincoln, and Douglass are concerned is quite distinct from wage labor (even though it may include a subset of that form of labor in some ways). "The hired laborer of yesterday, labors on his own account to-day; and will hire others to labor for him to-morrow," Lincoln explains.[57] He clearly imagines a world in which wage labor functions as a way station on the path to individual proprietorship. You work for wages for an artisan until you acquire your own skills, at which point you can turn around and help another young person get a leg up. The plan was perhaps more plausible in the economy that prevailed in the middle decades of the nineteenth century, and a case could be made that it willfully overlooks the realities of the emerging industrial system in the North, where wage labor was often a ticket to a lifetime of overwork and undercompensation starting in childhood.

Even so, the fundamental idea of labor in Lincoln's thought not only remains distinct from wage labor but may even serve as the basis for a critique of the wage-labor system. And this is precisely what Lincoln provides, at least in an implicit way. The wage-labor system effectively subordinates labor to capital by reducing it to a thing that capital chooses to purchase or not. But Lincoln reverses this essential feature of the wage-labor system. "Labor is prior to, and independent of, capital," he says in his first annual message to Congress. "Capital is only the fruit of labor, and could never have existed if labor had not first existed. Labor is the superior of capital, and deserves much the higher consideration."[58]

If all this makes Lincoln sound vaguely Marxist—well, maybe that's because that is how it sounded to Karl Marx himself. In his letter to Lincoln of November 1864, Marx redescribes the so-called Civil War as essentially "a general holy crusade of property against labor."[59] Should the Confederacy succeed, as he explains elsewhere, "the white working class would be gradually forced down to the level of helotry."[60] The war, in short, is "nothing but a struggle between two social systems, the system of slavery and the system of free labor. It can only be ended by the victory of one system or the other." Marx's admiration for founders such as George Washington and Benjamin Franklin was great, but it paled in comparison with his adulation of Lincoln. Upon reading a draft of the Emancipation Proclamation, he announces that

Lincoln is "a *sui generis* figure in the annals of history," and his proclamation "is the most important document in American history since the establishment of the Union, tantamount to tearing up the old Constitution."[61] In that 1864 letter to Lincoln, Marx gushes, "It fell to the lot of Abraham Lincoln, the single-minded son of the working class, to lead his country through the matchless struggle for the rescue of an enchained race and the reconstruction of the social world."[62] In brief: as far as Karl himself was concerned, Lincoln was America's first Marxist president.

LINCOLN'S PHILOSOPHY of labor receives perhaps its most elegant expression in his response to an invitation from the Republicans of Boston to join them for a celebration in honor of Thomas Jefferson in early 1859. It may seem strange today that the leaders of an antislavery party should have wished to celebrate a founder now identified as the prototypical racist slaveholder. But Lincoln didn't think it was odd. He was unable to make the trip to Boston, but he supplied the group with one of his most powerful letters.[63] The Democratic Party that Jefferson founded, Lincoln begins, has "nearly ceased to breathe [Jefferson's] name." And the reason isn't hard to see. The Democratic Party believes above all in slavery, and so it derides Jefferson's "self-evident truths" as "self-evident fictions."

On the other hand, Lincoln continues, the northern regions that formerly regarded Jefferson as anathema now celebrate his name and his immortal Declaration of Independence. The new Republican Party, says Lincoln, possesses "superior devotion to the personal rights of men, holding the rights of property to be secondary only." Knowingly or not, Lincoln here paraphrases Theodore Parker's thoroughly Hegelian summary of the case for free labor: "The genius of America . . . puts the rights of man first, and the rights of things last."[64] Lincoln then puts the matter in his own memorable words: "[The Democratic Party] of to-day hold the liberty of one man to be absolutely nothing, when in conflict with another man's right of property. Republicans, on the contrary, are for both the man and the dollar; but in case of conflict, the man before the dollar."

IN HIS SECOND INAUGURAL ADDRESS, Lincoln compresses the struggle of the preceding decades between slavery and free labor into a single line. Following upon the observation that "both read the same Bible," he says:

It may seem strange that any men should dare to ask a just God's assistance in wringing their bread from the sweat of other men's faces; but let us judge not that we be not judged.

But Lincoln did judge. Near the end of his final debate with Stephen Douglas, he leaves no doubt that wringing bread from the sweat of other men's faces is not just tyrannical but the essence of all tyranny: "It is the same spirit that says, 'You toil and work and earn bread, and I'll eat it.' No matter in what shape it comes, whether from the mouth of a king who seeks to bestride the people of his own nation and live by the fruit of their labor, or from one race of men as an apology for enslaving another race, it is the same tyrannical principle."[65]

Lincoln's line is particularly remarkable in the way that it handles the allusion to the Bible. In the passage of Genesis to which Lincoln refers, man is condemned to earn his bread "by the sweat of his [own] brow." That passage was a favorite with the proslavery theologians, who used it to suggest that servitude is the natural condition of humanity and labor an intrinsic evil. Lincoln's reversal of the phrase signals that free labor stands in opposition to the proslavery theologians' theory of labor. More important, in directing our attention from the sweat of our own brow to the sweat of *other men's* faces, Lincoln points to his radical, alternative philosophy, which revolves around the fact enslaved people, too, have faces—that they can see and be seen in acts of mutual recognition with all humans; that freedom, not servitude, is the natural condition of humanity.

10

AND
THE WAR
CAME

The Secret Six-Plus

THE FACT OF THE MATTER WAS that John Brown wanted money and guns. Theodore Parker told Brown he knew where to get the funds, "no questions asked." Sometime in 1857, Parker and friends formed the "Secret Six"—the group that, after the plot exploded into the national headlines, was fingered as the conspiracy supporting John Brown. Except that there were surely more than six. The nominal members of the group, according to the breathless reports in the newspapers, were Parker, Thomas Wentworth Higginson, Gerrit Smith, Franklin Sanborn, George Luther Stearns, and Samuel Gridley Howe. But the fiery Lewis Hayden appears to have been a seventh member of the group. Frederick Douglass could also be counted a member, given his role in road-testing ideas for Brown. So, too, could Ottilie Assing. In 1857, as a matter of fact, Assing was the one evidently handling the fund-raising in connection with Brown's unlikely aide, "Colonel" Forbes.

Brown crisscrossed the last years of the 1850s with the conviction of a man of destiny and almost enough cash to make it happen. He was a man in ceaseless motion, traveling in the country in search of still more money, men, and arms. The Secret Six (or Six-plus) ultimately supplied him with $4,000 in money, guns, and supplies. "We must fight with iron tools to root slavery out," Parker explains to one correspondent.[1]

In the winter of 1857–58, Brown materialized at Douglass's home in Rochester, New York. He insisted on casting himself as a rent-paying lodger. He remained several weeks, giving the two men time enough to write up a joint letter to Brown's wife, in which "Fred" invites her and the kids to come visit someday soon. Brown spent his days in Rochester writing up the constitution for his dream republic in the Appalachian Mountains. He seems to have wanted it recorded that Douglass was a meaningful figure in his plans. It is more than likely that he was counting on his host to serve as the new regime's first president and the first Black head of state on American soil. It is not implausible to suppose that Douglass entertained the fantasy—however much his common sense warned him that the plan was dangerously unrealistic. In any event, Douglass was clearly allowing himself to be used as fuel for Brown's incendiary imagination. At some point during Brown's stay in Rochester, Douglass scribbled him an innocuous note. For reasons unclear, Brown decided to preserve the note in his folder of special papers.

In May, the constitution was ready, and Brown convened a "Constitutional Convention" in Ontario together with many of his closest friends and followers. While there he recruited into his army the formidable Osborne Perry Anderson, a printer and a Black graduate of Oberlin College who would later serve as a noncommissioned officer in the Union army. In June, Brown was back in Boston, his hand out as always. He checked into the American House Hotel. He told Parker to look for "Mr. Brown," not "Captain Brown"—for he was going incognito.[2]

The plan was evidently getting bolder and bloodier with every passing month. The specifics may have been fuzzy, but the gist was razor sharp. Later historians, unable to fathom how a nice man like Theodore Parker could have gotten mixed up in a terrorist plot, would suggest that the Secret Six were unaware of the nature of Brown's intentions. In fact, they knew what he intended to do, not necessarily in every detail, but certainly in degree. They knew that the arsenal at Harpers Ferry was the target, and they knew about the vision of an Appalachian republic composed of fugitive slaves. It cannot have been hard to imagine that the ultimate goal was a violent slave insurrection across the southern states. It was all set to go off in the summer of 1858.

Suddenly it was Assing who hit the brakes.[3] She had heard from her German friends that Colonel Forbes had been relentless in his begging for money. He turned out to be a grifter in revolutionary clothing. Having squeezed Brown's German sympathizers dry, she learned, he was attempting to expose the plot to newspaperman Horace Greeley and to government agents. Alarmed at the possible exposure of the plot, she passed the intelligence along to Douglass, who later acknowledged in the passive voice that he "was the first to be informed of [Forbes's] tactics." Douglass flashed the message to Parker, Brown, and the rest of the Secret Six.

Forbes's betrayal threw the Secret Six into disarray. Higginson wanted to forge ahead, as was his wont. He was a man hungry for battle from the siege of the Boston courthouse in 1854 through the end of the Civil War. But Parker got cold feet. He counseled patience and advised putting off the operation for the time being. Brown reluctantly heeded Parker's call for the delay. Neither he nor the Six appear to have lost their determination to do something big when the opportunity presented itself.

Parker and Douglass had to know that Brown's plan was bound to fall short of his extraordinary vision. Yet they were still willing to roll the dice. Why? Because they had come to the view that, for Brown to succeed politically, he did not necessarily need to succeed militarily. According to their Hegelian theory of the crisis, a violent, mostly Black incitement of the sort that Brown hoped to organize would be helpful not necessarily on account of any likely military advantage it might yield but on account of its performative aspect. Not the proposed act itself but the reflection of that act in the public mind was the point of the plot. Indeed, this conclusion explains the curious fact that in the year and a half that followed that initial meeting in January 1857, Parker's confidence in Brown's operational plans diminished even while his material support for Brown's efforts only increased.

A House Divided

IN MARCH 1858, while Parker was busy raising money "no questions asked" for Brown, William Herndon was headed east to meet with Parker and other Republican leaders. Lincoln had just announced his candidacy for US senator for Illinois, and Herndon aimed to make a personal case for his man.

When Herndon arrived, the 28th Congregational Society was in full swing. "There he saw Theodore Parker on his throne, his vast audience before him, his ample discourse a kind of brilliant scene painting—large, rapid, and vivid, with masses of light and shade," enthuses one of Herndon's biographers. "What a galaxy of men gathered about the man of the Music Hall!"[4] Herndon joined the adoring throngs and then went backstage to meet with the rock star in person. Parker was predictably keen on Lincoln. Upon returning to Illinois, Herndon records, "I brought with me additional sermons and lectures by Theodore Parker, who was warm in his commendation of Lincoln."[5]

One of the titles Herndon brought with him was a lecture on "The Effect of Slavery on the American People."[6] According to Herndon, Lincoln read it with interest and returned it. In another lecture that caught Lincoln's attention, Parker describes his vision of a future society without an aristocracy and a church without a priesthood. This one went over well, too. Then Lincoln seems to have had a look at an 1854 sermon on "The Dangers Which Face the Rights of Man in America."[7] In that talk, Parker ransacks world history to examine the causes through which "states may perish." "Shall America thus perish?" he asks. "We needs must learn, or else perish." The thing we must learn if our government "of all, by all, and for all" is not to perish from the earth, Parker argues, is that slavery must end. According to Herndon, with this collection of works, Lincoln "liked especially the following expression, which he marked with a pencil, and which he in substance afterwards used in his Gettysburg Address: 'Democracy is direct self-government, over all the people, for all the people, by the people.'"[8]

America, Parker explains in his 1854 talk on the rights of man, is divided between two utterly contradictory ideas.[9] On the one hand, there is "the idea of Freedom." It is the idea that all humans are natural equals, that they recognize one another and realize themselves through collaboration in the world, and that legitimate government derives from the consent of the governed. "It appears in the Declaration of Independence; it re-appears in the Preamble to the American Constitution," he says. "I used to call it 'the American Idea.'" On the other hand, there is a second idea: the "Idea of Slavery." It says that there is a natural order of subordination in the universe, that the strong are entitled to do with the weak whatever they want, and that our happiness depends on obeying orders from the powers that be as if they were ordained of God. This idea, says Parker, now happens to be "the law of the Presidency" and "of the Supreme Court." The Constitution once supported the idea of freedom; but the Constitution has been betrayed, and it is now used to promote the idea of slavery.

"It is plain America cannot long hold these two contradictions in the national consciousness," Parker concludes.[10] Then he condenses the case to a memorable phrase: "Unless there is national unity of idea in fundamentals, a nation is a 'house divided against itself'; of course it cannot stand."[11] (The quotation marks are there, of course, to signal to Parker's audience that the words come chapter and verse from the ancient text that he regarded as a repository of useful myths: specifically, Matthew 12:25 and Mark 3:25.)

IN THE WEEKS following Herndon's return from Boston with his stash of Parker literature, Lincoln was working on the speech he planned to deliver to the Republican State Convention in Springfield upon accepting the nomination for US senator for Illinois.[12] In that speech, Lincoln declares: "A house divided against itself cannot stand. I believe this government cannot endure, permanently half slave and half free. I do not expect the Union to be dissolved—I do not expect the house to fall—but I do expect it will cease to be divided."

It wasn't the first time that Lincoln had used the "house divided" phrase in his life, and it also wasn't the first time he had questioned the prospects of a nation persisting "half slave and half free."[13] Even so, the parallels with Parker run deep. In his sermons, Parker invites us to consider "national institutions" as a "machine." Where slavery is present, he adds, it may be that "the machinery is defective, made after false ideas."[14] He goes on to trace the history of slavery in the United States up through 1854, the time of his writing, as something like the operation of a machine.

In his House Divided speech, Lincoln, too, tracks the advance of the idea of slavery through the political system. Addressing those who would question his prognosis on the fate of the Union, he says, "Let any one who doubts, carefully contemplate that now almost complete legal combination—piece of *machinery* so to speak—compounded of the Nebraska doctrine, and the Dred Scott decision. Let him consider not only *what* work the machinery is adapted to do, and *how* well adapted; but also let him study the *history* of its construction."

In his 1854 sermon, Parker does not end on a down note, despite the foreboding message. There is something very American in his optimism. "But we shall not fail!" he declares. "I look into the eyes of fifty thousand men and whom, whom, in the last eight months, I have spoken to, face to face, and they say, 'No! America shall not fail!'"

Lincoln says it this way: "We shall not fail—if we stand firm, we shall not fail."

According to Herndon, Lincoln read the draft of his speech out to him before delivering it at the Republican State Convention.[15] Naturally, Herndon found the substance of the speech thrilling. Herndon later claimed he hit the pause button when Lincoln reached the "house divided" line.

"It is true, but is it wise or politic to say so?" he asked.

Lincoln wouldn't budge. He told Herndon he was going to keep the phrase, and then he went on to read the advance copy of the speech before a collection of fellow Republican leaders, with Herndon present. Herndon alone approved of the speech. The rest thought it was political suicide. One pointed to the "house divided" and called it a "damned fool utterance."

Lincoln still wouldn't budge.

"If it is decreed that I should go down because of this speech, then let me go down linked to the truth—let me die in the advocacy of what is just and right," he said. At the Republican State Convention, he delivered the speech as drafted.

At least one person took delight in the speech. In a letter of July 18, Theodore Parker thanks Herndon for sending over a copy of "*the admirable speech of Mr. Lincoln.*" In August, he enthuses once again about "the *noble speeches* of Mr. Lincoln."

Over in Illinois, however, the reception of Lincoln's bold oration was rather different. Stephen Douglas wielded the House Divided speech against his opponent in the Senate race with all the subtlety of a bullwhip. It made Lincoln sound like a madman, said Douglas. Crazy Abe was going to demolish everything white America had built. If he had his way, Black men would soon attempt to marry white virgins, or maybe just rape them without ceremony, or so Douglas managed to insinuate.

Appalled and perhaps feeling remorse over his role in the fiasco, Herndon advised his law partner to distance himself from the speech by blaming the offensive "house divided" phrase on Jesus. Get back out on the hustings, Herndon urged, and say, " 'Douglas why whine and complain to me because I am not the author of it. God is. Go and whine and complain to Him for its revelation and utterance.' "

But Lincoln looked at Herndon for "one short quizzical moment," and replied, "I can't."

Instead, Lincoln dug himself a deeper hole. On a hot July day in Chicago, with his eye on the critical German voting bloc, Lincoln pointed out that, while Americans had every reason to celebrate their founders on the Fourth of July, "among us perhaps half our people . . . are not descendants at all" of America's founding generation. Yet these new Americans can look to the Declaration of Independence and say that they, too, are united and fully equal as Americans. And then Lincoln took the next logical step and extended the American idea from immigrants to the enslaved and the nonwhite population. "Let us discard all this quibbling about this man and that other man—this race and that race and the other race being inferior. . . . Let us discard these things, and unite as one people throughout this land until we shall once more stand up declaring that all men are created equal."[16]

Outside the German precincts, this was pure electoral

poison. "Disgusting," the newspapers said; Lincoln was hoping to build his career on "the most repulsive disunion nigger equality principles."[17]

In Herndon's eyes, Lincoln's defeat in the election of 1858 was a devastating setback for the antislavery cause. Although the loss to Douglas was narrow enough that any number of factors could be cited in explanation, the consensus among political observers then and historians now is that without the House Divided speech, Lincoln would have become the US senator from Illinois.

Lincoln was not the only Republican politician to take the plunge with Parker's thesis, as it happens. At the end of October 1858, US senator William Seward of New York, perhaps feeling upstaged on the left by his rising Illinois rival, attempted his own version of the speech in Douglass's hometown of Rochester.[18] The confrontation between slavery and democracy, Seward declaims, is rooted in "an irrepressible conflict between two opposing and enduring forces." "The United States must and will, sooner or later, become either entirely a slaveholding nation, or entirely a free nation." The consensus at the time and of historians since is that the speech was a career disaster. Once a serious contender for the presidency, Seward was branded both as a hot-headed, uncompromising warmonger and as a vacillator—because, being a leading politician, he often did in fact seek compromise.

The story was not yet over. The conflict of which Parker and Lincoln spoke was already under way by the time Lincoln gave his speech. Missouri was in turmoil, Kansas was bleeding, and Virginia was next. Had Lincoln won the Senate seat in 1858, possibly he would not have been available for higher office in the rapidly changing world of 1860. Had Douglas lost, he might not have had the political power to divide the Democratic vote as the presidential candidate for the North. Had Seward held his tongue, he might have been the shoo-in for the Republican nomination that everyone thought he was. Theodore Parker would not live to see it, but in inspiring his political ally in Illinois to take a losing stand on principle, he may have put Lincoln on an entirely unexpected path to the presidency.

The Lord of the
Bumblebees

IN THE FIRST MONTHS OF 1859, the charges Parker had accumulated against his own body came due. His tuberculosis was in an advanced stage, and he was now coughing up blood regularly. Then he developed a merciless anal fistula. The only procedure for addressing such a condition at the time was a form of surgery that today might be classed as unmedicated mutilation. The prognosis, his doctors said, was bleak.

In the evangelical churches, they prayed for him to die. "If he is beyond the reach of the saving influence of the Gospel, remove him out of the way, and let his influence die with him," they said.[19] Charles Grandison Finney, perhaps still smarting from the hostile reception from Parker during his 1857 revival tour of Boston, was especially vocal in calling on God to rid the nation of the heretic.

Parker responded in what he took to be the model of his grandfather at Lexington. "I laugh at the odds of nine to one," he tells his diary. "I mean to live and not die." To his congregation, he announces: "I have still much to do."[20]

The surgery on the fistula went better than expected. But

Parker's tuberculosis worsened, and the doctors remained grim. The only conceivable therapy, according to the medical practices of the time, was a mixture of hope and denial: sunshine, country air, and rest. Parker accepted that the time had come for him to set off on a final voyage.

In February 1859, Parker embarked from Boston Harbor for the Caribbean. The plan was to remain in the West Indies for a few months and then, health permitting, sail to Europe for the summer. The destination was Italy in time for the following winter. Secret Sixer Samuel Gridley Howe and his wife, Julia Ward Howe, the latter soon to be the author of a famous battle hymn, boarded the boat with him and accompanied him down to Havana. They parted ways in Cuba, where Parker transferred to a boat bound for the island of St. Croix.

"I still carry in my mind the picture of his serious face, crowned with gray locks and a soft gray hat as he looked over the side of the vessel and waved us a last farewell," Samuel writes.[21] Parker wasn't yet fifty years old, but his last photographic portraits show a man who looks twenty years older.

In St. Croix, Parker at first complained of laziness and inefficiency among the recently freed population. The old habit of racial stereotyping died hard. As his health improved under the Caribbean sun, however, his letters took on a more friendly and optimistic variety of racialized thinking. "I shall have nice things to say about the success of emancipation and the refined look of the Negroes," he writes to his Boston friend Joseph Lyman.[22]

In the spring, he sailed for London. There he enjoyed a warm reunion with Ellen and William Craft, who were raising a family and participating in antislavery societies there. He called on various scholars, among whom he enjoyed a degree of fame as an American man of letters. Then it was on to Paris. His weight was dropping to dangerous levels, and the cough was getting meaner. But there was still time for a glorious summer in Neuchatel. For a moment, Parker seemed to be enjoying a revival of spirits amid Alpine blossoms.

On October 12, he arrived in Rome. A few weeks later he made a final move to Florence. In Italy he could count on memorable breakfasts with Robert and Elizabeth Barrett Browning, Harriet Beecher Stowe, and Nathaniel Hawthorne.

During his travels, he composed two autobiographical memoirs that read like long farewells. His pen hardly slowed as his body failed. The need to explain himself to the world only grew more urgent. Only in these final confessions does Parker appear to come clean on the transient and the permanent in Christianity. "I do not believe there ever was a miracle, or ever will be," he declares; "I do not believe in the miraculous inspiration of the Old Testament or the New Testament." The Bible "was the work of man," he flatly announces; the Christian Church "was no more divine than the British State, a Dutchman's shop, or an Austrian farm."[23] Somewhere near the end, he pens an extraordinary satire titled "A Bumblebee's Thoughts on the Plan and Purpose of the Universe."[24]

A million years ago, it seems, a population of Bumblebees gathered to hear a sermon by one of their number, a distinguished individual known as the "MOST MAGNIFICENT DRONE." The august personage describes the great chain of being in the world, with mere matter at the bottom and the world of mind at the top. At the apex of the system, he enthuses, stands the mighty Bumblebee. How impenetrable is our armor! How sweet our honey! How strong our stingers! How exquisite the chemistry of our digestive processes! How far more wonderful is the Bumblebee's mind! By contrast, he sneers, "there is no logic in the crickets' senseless noise." In conclusion, "THE BUMBLEBEE IS THE PURPOSE OF THE UNIVERSE!" The gloating insect, for Parker, is the perfect stand-in for those "practical atheists" who believe that providence exists to cater to their insect-like desires and delusions.

He knew he was dying. His last letters have something of the bitter grandiosity that one expects of a self-appointed truth teller. He turns his focus away from the elites from whom he had always been denied a favorable judgment. He puts his hopes for vindication instead on some recognition from the broad mass of people, the kind who filled up the music hall at the high tide of the 28th Congregational Society. He remains resolutely focused on the promise of America. "How many centuries will it take to bring the actual America up to the ideal of the Declaration of Independence?" he asks his friend Lyman.[25]

Yet he remained an optimist to the end. He was sure that the Lord of the Bumblebees would eventually yield to progress in theology, just as he was sure that the American idea would win out. By the time he reached Florence, he knew that he would not live to see it. After the news that flashed across the ocean on October 16, 1859, however, he did have time for one last act.

The Summer of Feuerbach

IF A LUCKY FIND in a New York bookshop could ever change history, then it must have done so in the winter of 1858–59, when Ottilie Assing chanced upon Marian Evans's fluid translation of Ludwig Feuerbach's *Essence of Christianity*, or so Assing came to believe. Later famous as a novelist under the nom de plume George Eliot, Evans (1819–1880) was part of a circle in England devoted to fanning the flames of Germanic atheism. A committed philosophical radical, her other translations included the principal works of Spinoza and of David Friedrich Strauss. Her lover, George Henry Lewes (1817–1878), meanwhile, was writing long essays on Hegel.

Here now was the textbook that Ottilie needed for educating Frederick. Her relationship with Douglass was deep, she explains in a revealing letter, "but there was *one* obstacle to a loving and lasting friendship—namely the personal Christian God."[26] For all his talk about welcoming infidelity and atheism, it seems, the lion of the second American revolution had yet to come clean in matters of theology. "The stench of religion," Assing complains, can be detected even in the great minds of America.[27] A touch of Feuerbach would be just the thing to round out Frederick's claim to greatness.

The summer of 1859 was so special that Assing just had to telegraph the experience to the German public. "Among those who fled the dusty streets of New York in the summer months was your correspondent, who went in search of a country get-away that no German journalist and absolutely no representative of German letters has hitherto penetrated. This is the house of Frederick Douglass, the famous colored speaker."[28]

And so, while Theodore Parker was searching for a cure among the Alpine blossoms and Abraham Lincoln was recovering from his electoral defeat in Illinois, the two freedom fighters of the human mind curled up in Rochester with Feuerbach's masterwork. According to Assing, the effect was nothing short of revolutionary. Douglass was less explicit on the point, but the impact of German atheism on his thought turns out to be very easy to read in between the lines—provided one looks in places where he appears to be discussing unrelated topics, such as the art of photography.

COMMERCIAL PHOTOGRAPHY arrived with the invention of the daguerreotype in 1839. Within a decade it had become an international fascination. Soon the American landscape was speckled with photographers hauling boxes of fragile plates and toxic chemicals across country lanes and commanding their unsmiling subjects to sit perfectly still as long as three minutes for portraits intended to last a lifetime. Among those who sat most frequently for such portraits was Frederick Douglass—one of the most photographed individuals of the nineteenth century, according to historians.

Douglass sat for so many photographs because he was among the first to grasp the psychological and political power of photography. The fine clothing, the careful positioning of the face and eyes, the intense, often direct, sometimes ferocious, always intelligent gaze that he puts on for the portrait photographers—all were conceived and executed to make a statement about something other than Douglass himself. He understood perfectly that his own image would serve as one of the universal images of Black America, and he was determined to make the contrast with existing prejudices as sharp as possible. He knew that the power of his likeness was not in the fidelity of the images to his actual appearance but in the relation between the stories his pictures told and the narratives in the public mind. His sittings were always a political performance; his aim was not merely to reflect reality but to shape it.

In a series of remarkable lectures on "Pictures and Progress," Douglass takes his ideas about photography in an explicitly philosophical direction. The first lecture was delivered on December 3, 1861, in Boston's Tremont Temple, at a commemoration of the second anniversary of the hanging of John Brown. Appropriately enough, the lecture was part of a series established to celebrate the life and teachings of Theodore Parker, whose transition in the public mind from outspoken infidel activist to tragic, prematurely deceased seer was by now well under way. At the time of the first lecture, the first Battle of Bull Run had already left thousands of dead, and it had destroyed any hope for an easy end to the conflict. Robert E. Lee's Army of Northern Virginia was preparing to take the fight to the North. Douglass went on to deliver revised versions of the lecture on at least four more occasions, the last of which took place in the months between Lincoln's reelection and his second inauguration. It is in this unlikely setting that Douglass leaves the traces of the summer of Feuerbach that he shared with Assing in 1859.

Not surprisingly, Douglass begins his first version of the talk with the question that must have been at the back of many minds. Why take on a subject so seemingly light in spirit as the philosophy of photography while the nation is in the throes of a war between "republican institutions" and "a remorseless oligarchy"?[29] It soon becomes clear that appearing to avoid the storm outside is a way of bringing it up.

Just as with the photographic portraits of himself, Douglass's preoccupation with photography has to do with everything that remains outside the picture but somehow appears within it. A photograph, Douglass tells us, is a great equalizer. It humanizes the enslaved just as swiftly as it exposes the pretensions of rank. It allows the washerwoman to have a likeness of herself more accurate than that of any princess of the past. More abstractly, he says, a photograph is never just about its subject. It always comes with a frame. It registers the consciousness of the viewer; and, in the case of a portrait, it takes as its object the consciousness of its subject. In returning the viewer's gaze, it unites the viewer and the viewed in mutual regard. It is a piece of consciousness detached from the individual, always implicitly addressing the question of what it means to be human. It is a frozen moment of the kind of self-awareness that, as Douglass knew from his days with Auld, slowly dissolves the chains of slavery.

Douglass's thoughts on photography rely on a novel theory of consciousness, and in his lectures, he articulates that theory. "Man is the only picture-making animal in the world," he writes.[30] "Rightly viewed, the whole soul of man is a sort of picture gallery, a grand panorama, in which all the great facts of the universe are . . . painted." Consciousness, according to Douglass, inhabits the frame of things; it finds itself only by stepping outside of itself and seeing itself in and through its encounter with the object. Douglass then states this theory concerning the inherently reflective nature of consciousness in language that is pure Feuerbach: "The process by which man is able to invent his own subjective consciousness into the objective form, considered in all its range, is in truth the highest attribute of man's nature." In the book Douglass read with Assing, one finds: "we know the man by the object."

Douglass extends the point with a paraphrase of the Hegelian master-slave dialectic: "A man is worked upon by what he works on."[31] And: "Men only know themselves by knowing others," he declares.[32] That is, inasmuch as consciousness knows itself only through its reflection on its own reasons and purposes, it knows itself only by standing outside of itself and seeing itself through the eyes of another rational, purposive being. The marvel of photography, according to Douglass, is that it gives us a chance to step outside ourselves and see ourselves in just this way. This capacity for self-transcendence, he goes on to say, is the essence of our humanity and the source of all progress: "self-criticism, out of which comes the highest attainments of human excellence, arises out of the power we possess of making ourselves objective to ourselves." All of which is to adorn with colorful language the central thesis of Feuerbach's philosophy that "my self-awareness" is "at the same time a comprehension of other men."

"Truth is too large to be described by one man," Douglass continues.[33] "It belongs, like the Earth, to all the Earth's inhabitants." Or, as Feuerbach had put it, "only all men taken together live human nature." Douglass adds: "We scan every new face, listen to every new voice, weigh and measure every man who steps forward on the stage of observation, that we may at last gain a rational solution to the mysterious powers and possibilities of the species." The use of the term "species" in this context is impossible to separate from Feuerbach's celebration of the same term.

From Douglass's theory of consciousness, it follows that consciousness expands in degree to the extent that it widens its sphere of experience. A child, Douglass observes, finds a new way of being "with every new object by means of which it is brought into a nearer and fuller acquaintance with its own subjective nature." More generally, he adds, "a new life springs up in the soul with the discovery of every new agency by which the soul is raised to a higher level of wisdom." By way of example, Douglass cites the case of Theodore Parker, who "after mastering more learning, and venturing further into the fathomless depths of truth than most men of his time" was able to see farther into the future than almost everyone.

It remains perfectly possible, of course, that Douglass conceived of these fundamental intuitions about consciousness on his own, well before he met Ottilie Assing. But in his argument concerning the limited nature of all consciousness, Douglass leaves behind direct evidence that his words, if not the ideas, came directly from his reading of Feuerbach. He could have chosen any insect or animal to illustrate the argument, but in his lecture on photography he lands upon precisely the one that Feuerbach uses to make the same point: "The caterpillar knows the leaf on which it feeds, but a higher intelligence must explain the tree."[34]

Perhaps the most consequential aspect of Douglass's Feuerbachian analysis of photography is that he follows his mentor in making an explicitly humanistic turn. In Douglass's version, the "picture-making power" of man "is that which has sometimes caused us, in our moments of enthusiasm, to lose sight of man as a creature, finite and limited, and to invest him with the dignity of a creator." The "picture-making power" supplies "man with his God" and gives "form and body to all that the soul can hope and fear in life and death." For comparison: Feuerbach writes that man's "consciousness of the Infinite" is only "man's consciousness of his own infinite being."[35]

"It is a great mistake to suppose that our Gods are always invisible," Douglass continues. "We find in [man] the qualities we attribute to the Divine being." Feuerbach provides helpful elaboration: "The God of the merciful and just man is merciful and just . . . the God of the selfish and cruel man is a king in wood, stone, iron, or in imagination after his own image." [36] Douglass's conclusions are both scandalously heretical and thoroughly Feuerbachian. "Man everywhere worships man, and in the last analysis worships himself," he writes. "We are all man-worshippers. . . . The church that we build unto the Lord, we build unto ourselves." [37] In brief: "The divine being is nothing else than the human being."

The Feuerbachian language in Douglass's lecture is so direct and emphatic that it raises a question about how the mature Douglass could ever have been represented as anything other than an unapologetic Feuerbachian humanist:[38]

> It matters very little what may be in the text . . . —man
> is sure to be the sermon. He is the incarnate wonder
> of all the ages: and the contemplation of Him is bound-
> less in range and endless in fascination. He is before all
> books . . . —for he is the maker of all books—the essence
> of all books—the text of all books. On earth there is
> nothing higher than the Human Soul.

And again:[39]

> The great philosophical truth now to be learned and
> applied is that man is limited by manhood. He cannot
> get higher than human nature, even in his conceptions.
> Laws, religion, morals, manners, and art are but the
> expression of manhood, and begin and end in man. As
> he is enlightened or ignorant, as he is rude or refined, as
> he is exalted or degraded, so are his laws, religion, mor-
> als, manners—and everything else pertaining to him.

This humanistic vision, Douglass further makes clear, is the actual foundation for all hopes of revolution and reform in society. "The picture-making faculty is flung out into the world like all the others—subject to a wild scramble between contending interests and forces," he explains. "The habit we adopt, the master we obey in making our subjective nature objective . . . is the all important thing to ourselves and our surroundings." We can take our habit of consciousness in a "gloomy religious direction" and become "bigoted and fanatical," he argues. Or we can allow it to lead us toward a more "liberal and enlightened" world. When we pursue the latter course, we use our "picture-making" ability to understand ourselves and one another better. "The process by which man is able to posit his own subjective nature outside of himself . . . so that it becomes the subject of distinct observation and contemplation," Douglass concludes, "is at the bottom of all effort and the germinating principles of all reform and all progress."

All these remarkable reflections on photography, consciousness, humanity, and progress were conceived on the eve of the war and delivered for the first time in public at the moment of greatest desperation in the conflict. The war could not have been far from anyone's mind. As Douglass approaches the end of his first lecture on photography, it becomes clear that it was at the front of his mind after all.

The philosophy of photography explains why slavery is bound to provoke resistance and ultimately bring upon itself its own destruction. "We have attempted to maintain a union in defiance of the moral chemistry of the universe," Douglass announces near the end of his talk.[40] "We have thought to keep one end of the chain on the limbs of the bondman without having the other on our own necks." He boils the case down to a line: "Here is the trouble: slavery and rebellion go hand in hand." Douglass's analysis also points directly toward the solution. Slavery will end when the unrealized power of the enslaved population is at last recognized and thereby realized. It will happen when all see a reflection of themselves in the enslaved.

In the same days and weeks that he delivered his lecture in the Tremont Temple, Douglass was pouring his energy into recruiting Black soldiers into the Union army. Upon bringing in any number, he was keen always to have them photographed in full uniform and to show the photographs wherever possible. His proudest photographs may have been those of his own sons, in uniform, as soldiers in the Massachusetts 54th Infantry.

FEUERBACH'S IDEAS struck Douglass "like a ray of light, and accomplished a complete revolution of his opinions," Ottilie Assing writes to Ludwig Feuerbach himself. This was a reverse conversion experience of world-historical significance, or so she maintains. "I add with great satisfaction that it was German radicalism that worked that revolution, and that to our great, venerated Feuerbach above all others our thanks are due for having pointed out the path to intellectual liberty to that distinguished man, after he had freed himself from the fetters of slavery."[41]

At some point later in life, Douglass acquired a marble bust of Feuerbach. He also picked up a matching sculpture of David Friedrich Strauss. In his home on Cedar Hill in Washington, D.C., he placed the two busts on the mantelpiece overlooking his writing desk, where they might gaze upon him as he composed many of his speeches and books. On the shelves over the desk, one can still find several German grammar books, a few guides for travelers to Germany, and a copy of Feuerbach's *Essence of Christianity*. Douglass's interest in the freethinkers of Germany was no summer fling.

The summer of Feuerbach, on the other hand, could not go on forever. It came to an end in August 1859 with a summons from John Brown. The two men had seen one another as recently as March 1859, at a meeting with Black abolitionists in Detroit. In May, Brown had paid his last visit to the Boston area. In June, he made a last call at the family farm in North Elba, New York. While Douglass and Assing were summering with Feuerbach, Brown was living in a rock quarry in southern Pennsylvania, near Chambersburg, with a multiracial band of twenty-two men, a stash of pikes, and a cache of rifles courtesy of his friends in Boston. Somewhere along the way, he had also picked up a copy of Thomas Paine's *Age of Reason*.[42]

From his rocky hideout, Brown issued a letter requesting Douglass's presence. He wanted cash, too, and a soldier who went variously by the names of "Emperor" and "Shields Green." Douglass knew the man—an escaped slave of broken language and unbreakable will. With some sense of foreboding, Frederick put down his book and said good-bye to Ottilie. He picked up Green and told the world that he was off on another speaking tour. Then he headed south to Chambersburg.

The Terrible, Swift Sword

ON A SUNNY AFTERNOON in late August 1859, Frederick Douglass and Shields "Emperor" Green picked their way through the Chambersburg quarry.[43] They proceeded with extreme caution, for they knew Brown was armed, dangerous, and, perhaps justifiably, paranoid.

In the distance, Douglass caught sight of Brown. He was dressed in his fishing gear, his clothing faded to the color of the sun-dappled rocks. Douglass later recorded his impression that Brown's character seemed to blend with this wild and craggy landscape just as thoroughly as it suffused his spartan cottage in Springfield.

Brown spotted the intruders and primed himself for action. Upon recognizing their faces, his wariness yielded to a warm smile. He embraced Douglass and Green and took them on a tour of his makeshift boot camp, where his grand army of twenty or so men was making last preparations for battle. Then the three men sat down among the rocks, and Brown laid out the operational plan.

No longer was Brown focused on the slow accumulation of fugitives in an Appalachian republic. The idea of harrying the plantations below and funneling slaves to freedom in the

North was just the starting point. The times called for a grand gesture—the kind of exclamation point that might mark the start of a global war. Brown had resolved to place that punctuation mark on an arsenal at Harpers Ferry, Virginia. The plan was to seize the arsenal with his band of two dozen warriors; haul in a trove of weapons; invite the enslaved people of the area to come collect the arms; and then provoke a civil war that would take down the whole infernal system. A swift blow to the South, like a terrible sword from on high, to hack the slave regime to pieces—this was the plan.

Douglass was aghast. He had no objection in principle; he just thought the plan was nuts. Sending in raiding parties from the hills was one thing; trying to hold a huge arsenal against the wishes of the army of Virginia while mobilizing a slave insurrection was something else. He eyed Brown's scraggly band of two dozen heroes and saw so many dead men walking. He warned Brown that he was "going into a perfect steel trap, and that once in he would not get out alive."

For two days among the rocks, Brown argued the pros, and Douglass stuck to the cons. Far from being dissuaded, Brown only worked harder to recruit Douglass to join in the mission. It was soon clear that, money aside, this was the point of his late-summer summons. "When I strike, the bees will begin to swarm, and I shall want you to help hive them," Brown explained. Douglass later debated with himself whether it was cowardice or common sense, or a little of both, that kept him from accepting this metaphorical offer to lead a fantasy republic of liberated honeybees. Later, too, Brown's allies and possibly Brown himself hinted that Douglass had failed to keep a promise—a charge that Douglass denied, arguing (plausibly) that, while he had always supported John Brown's ideals, he had never signed up for John Brown's army.

The differences between the two men on tactics undoubtedly

reflected their very different experiences and conditions in life. Though Brown eagerly befriended and fought alongside Black people, his choice to do so was always just that—a choice. For him, failure in any of his operations, with any luck, might only entail a retreat to white society. Douglass and Black abolitionists in general faced a different calculus of risks. Their experience taught them that in the event of defeat, the retaliation would aim for them first. Black churches and gatherings were at once the most sympathetic and the most skeptical in answering Brown's pleas for support. Like Douglass, their concern with his schemes was not with violence per se but with the consequences that would surely be visited upon them when violence failed.

As the debate bottomed into a stalemate, Douglass at last turned to Shields Green and suggested that they return to New York. But Green had made up his mind. "I b'leve I'll go wid de ole man," he said, in Douglass's recollection. Fairly certain that he was seeing Brown and Green for the last time, Douglass bade them farewell and departed to take up the speaking engagements in Philadelphia that had served as pretext for his visit to Pennsylvania.

ON OCTOBER 16, 1859, John Brown thrust his exclamation point on the course of history. The attack on Harpers Ferry went off far better than anyone had a right to expect and far worse than John Brown had dared to hope. Brown's twenty-two men managed to hold the arsenal for more than a day against overwhelming odds. Surrounded by Robert E. Lee's army, ten were killed in battle and five escaped, among them Osborne Anderson, who lived to write about the tale. Seven men, including Brown, were captured alive. Among them was Shields Green—"the most inexorable of all our party, a very Turco in his hatred of the stealers of men," said Anderson;

"a braver man never lived."[44] There was no mass uprising of slaves in the vicinity.

The impact of the raid on the nation was as psychologically potent as it was militarily useless. The largest part of the American public saw it as an act of terrorism. The southern press and its supporters in the North alternated between tear-your-hair-out hysteria and told-you-so contempt for their antislavery adversaries. Even many of those who supported Brown's aims felt compelled to distance themselves from his violent methods. The line among the abolitionists was that Brown was a saint, but his raid was a sin.

Yet there was a part of the public that saw something more in the news flash of the decade, something that pointed to a brave new future for the republic. In Cincinnati, the fervid 48er and future Union general August Willich organized a meeting in honor of John Brown and invited all the German freethinkers and their fellow travelers in the vicinity.[45] Moncure Conway, a featured speaker at the event, represented Brown as the second coming of Thomas Paine. Peter Clark, a prominent Black freethinker, school headmaster, and abolitionist, told the audience that this was 1776 all over again. He went on to say that the Germans and their friends at the gathering were "the only freedom-loving people of this city." Then Willich set the crowd ablaze, advising them to "whet their sabres" for the day of reckoning to come. Workers of all colors would soon unite and claim their freedom by blood if necessary. To the outrage of conservative newspaper editors, the freethinking crowd of Brown lovers then marched in a procession through Cincinnati.

Over in Illinois, William Herndon, too, found inspiration in the stunning news from Harpers Ferry. In a letter to Parker in Italy, he reports: "John Brown's raid in Virginia . . . has roused us to the greatness and grandeur of America's coming events. You have no idea of the influence of John Brown's acts."[46]

The most enthusiastic—and well-informed—accounts of the terrible swift sword came from the pen of Ottilie Assing. From her reports to her German readership in the days following the raid, it is evident that Assing had inside knowledge of the plot well before the American public did. She knew about Brown's various aliases in the months preceding the operation; she knew about the cache of weapons he had acquired from his friends in Boston; and she knew all about the grand plan for an Appalachian republic. Brown wanted to claim the hills, she explains to her German readers, because he "hoped that the slaves of Virginia would rally to his side in a great mass as soon as they received news of the presence of his force, and the revolt would gradually spread throughout the state."[47] The Brown that emerges from Assing's reporting glows like a once-in-a-century champion of the human spirit. He is the "hero of Kansas" and a "terrible avenger"—even if the tactics at Harpers Ferry were "incomprehensible." The other great hero of the century and the heir to Brown's legacy, at least in Assing's telling, was Frederick Douglass. She perhaps injudiciously decided there was no need to hide the fact from her German audience that Douglass was "one of the secret leaders of the conspiracy."[48]

John Brown was tried but not before putting his accusers on trial and shaking the conscience of the nation. In the month and a half that remained to him, he was resolute, the eye of a national hurricane. "I feel no consciousness of guilt," he told the court—and such was the impression he made that none doubted he was telling the truth. "He will make the gallows glorious like the cross," said Ralph Waldo Emerson in Boston. The crowd at the Tremont Temple loved it; in the South, Emerson's words compounded the outrage.[49]

On December 2, 1859, Brown slipped a note to his guard: "I, John Brown, am now quite certain that the crimes of this guilty land can never be purged away but with blood." Then he was led from his cell and hanged. Two weeks later, Green followed him on the gallows.

IN THE DAYS FOLLOWING the lightning strike at Harpers Ferry, the Secret Six-plus were exposed. John Brown had left behind a satchel of papers in the Virginia farmhouse that had served as base camp, and there the authorities found the incriminating receipts and letters. Samuel Gridley Howe, Franklin Sanborn, and George Luther Stearns fled in haste to Canada. Over in New York, Gerrit Smith decided that the best option was the insanity defense. He worked himself up to a mental breakdown and then checked himself into a sanatorium. (When the threat of arrest cleared, he miraculously recovered his wits.) Thomas Wentworth Higginson remained in Boston. Contemptuous of the other Sixers for failing to stand up for their principles, he hatched a plot to liberate John Brown from his Virginia jail by force of arms. The swiftness of Virginia justice, however, meant that the plot never got past the hot-air phase.

Among the papers seized along with Brown was a note in Frederick Douglass's hand jotted down during Brown's earlier stay in Rochester. The note itself was innocuous in content, and Brown may well have held onto it out of his sentimental attachment to the future president of the Multicolored States of America. But in this moment of national outrage, that was no defense. The governor of Virginia made clear that the one conspirator he wanted above all to get his hands on was the loud Black one. A warrant was issued for Douglass's arrest and sent on to Philadelphia, where the abolitionist was last seen.

Fortunately for Douglass, the telegraph office in the City of Brotherly Love happened to be in the hands of a man named John Hurn—a committed abolitionist and an aspiring photographer who would later take eight photographs of Douglass himself. Hurn pocketed the message and ran to the local

barbershop.[50] The barbers always knew where to find a wanted
Black man. After three suspenseful hours, they latched onto
the right grapevine and transmitted the warning. Douglass
made a dash for the port to board a boat for New York. With
the wanted man hot-footing it out of town, Hurn headed over
to the sheriff's office and pulled the cable out of his pocket in
a leisurely way.

Douglass rushed to Hoboken and into the arms of Ottilie Assing. He spent "an anxious night" at her apartment, he
later wrote with some understatement, while Assing got to
work on the escape plan. She rushed a telegraph to Douglass's
son Lewis in Rochester to destroy the papers Brown had left
behind there. It wouldn't do to have the authorities discover
the Constitution for a multiracial republic in Douglass's desk
drawer. Anticipating that there would be lookouts on trains
leaving New York City, she and one of her German friends
organized for a private carriage to take Frederick with her at
his side out to a train station in New Jersey in the dark hours
of the night. As they parted, Assing begged him not to return
to his home in Rochester.

Douglass went home anyway, determined to see his children one last time. He had to hug his daughter, Annie, not yet
eleven years old, who had recently taken to studying the German language with her father. But the moment he opened the
door, his friends bundled him up and rushed him out, having
been alerted to a kidnapping plot. They ran him to the river
and threw him on a boat bound for Canada.

Even in Canada, Douglass found it necessary to move from
place to place in fear of kidnappers. By the end of the month,
he had found a ship that would take him, for the second time
in his life, to the safety of England. He cannot have known at
the time whether he would ever set foot in the United States
again. Annie would die of an illness before he could return,
stricken with grief, in the year the nation split apart.

OVER IN ITALY, safely ensconced in the knowledge of his own impending death, Theodore Parker alone among the Secret Six-plus enjoyed an opportunity to reflect in calm upon the crisis of the moment.[51] The meaning of Harpers Ferry had to be made clear to the world. "Not once in many ages we get sight of such a spectacle!" Parker exults in letters to the homeland. He swiftly concludes that Brown's action was "just and righteous." More than that, it exposes the fraudulent power of the slaveholding oligarchy: " 'Captain Brown's expedition . . . shows the weakness of the greatest slave State in America . . . and the utter fear which slavery engenders in the bosoms of the masters." From this position of weakness and fear, Parker forecasts, the southern leadership is condemned to overreact to circumstances; and in overreacting, it will start the war that will set the stage for its own demise. In brief: the South will blindly execute the plan that Brown has laid out for them.

A full year before the election of 1860, Parker predicts not just that war between North and South is all but inevitable, but that such a war will not end without emancipation. Once the Republican Party realizes that the future of democracy is at stake, he predicts, it will "go readily enough" into the South and crush the slave regime and end slavery itself. He has no doubt that the process will involve the spilling of great quantities of blood, both white and Black. The fundamental choice the republic faces is the same one Parker articulates in his own "house divided" lecture of 1854, which Lincoln cribbed in his failed 1858 run for Senate, and which Lincoln repeated again in Gettysburg in 1863: "We must give up DEMOCRACY if we keep SLAVERY, or give up SLAVERY if we keep DEMOCRACY."[52]

In his prescient deathbed prophesies, Parker anticipates a sectional conflict between North and South, and yet he conceptualizes the war as something very different from a regional or territorial dispute. He sees the coming war fundamentally as a slave insurrection. He notes that the official shield of Virginia depicts a man standing on a tyrant and chopping his head off with a sword—"only I would paint the sword-holder *black* and the tyrant *white* to show the *immediate application* of the principle." He anticipates "many a possible San Domingo . . . with no white man to help." He explicitly looks forward to a multiracial future for the American idea: "One day it will be thought not less heroic for a Negro to fight for his personal liberty, than for a white man to fight for political independence, and against a tax of three pence on a pound of tea." The deciding power in the conflict between slavery and democracy, he suggests, will be the power of the enslaved population itself: its power under arms and its power to withstand and weaken the oligarchy from within.

Perhaps the most remarkable aspect of Parker's forecast, especially considering his troubled reputation on questions of race, is his prediction that the conflict would help the nation overcome its crippling racial divisions. Parker understood well the racist tendencies of many of the laborers in the North who formed a vital part of the antislavery alliance. The newly formed Republican Party, he acknowledges, "contemplates no direct benefit to the slave, only the defense of the white man in his natural rights."[53] But the party will soon discover that its principles "require much more than what was at first proposed. Republicans will promptly see that *they cannot defend the natural rights of freemen without destroying that slavery which takes away the natural rights of a negro.*" When it at last dawns on the northern workers that none will be free until all are free, they will march to the South and destroy slavery.

Parker's messages on the meaning of Harpers Ferry indeed proved to be his last word. As the winter of 1859–60 closed in, his weight dropped to 130 pounds. He was a gray husk of a man coughing up bloody phlegm in a hotel room in Florence. The end came on May 10, 1860. He was buried in a cemetery in Florence, to be joined in the following year by the body of Elizabeth Barrett Browning and in the years to come by the remains of famous expatriates by the dozen. Twenty-seven summers later, a gray-haired Frederick Douglass visited the tomb and spoke of Parker's "many services" to "the cause of human freedom."

"He died, like Moses, within sight of the Promised Land that he was never to enter, a shadowy figure in the vast drama of national regeneration," his disciple and fellow Secret Sixer Sanborn writes in 1910. Yet he was "the inspirer of Herndon, and through him of Lincoln," Sanborn adds, and consequently "this shadow stands for something substantial." [54]

Fundamental and Astounding: A Theory of the Civil War

ON A WARM AFTERNOON in late May 1863, 20,000 Bostonians lined the streets to cheer as the 54th Massachusetts Volunteer Infantry Regiment received its colors. John Rock, the Black abolitionist who once rebuked Theodore Parker for invoking racial stereotypes, was there, and he paused to remind those present that the late minister "saw this day a little clearer than we saw it, and repeatedly warned us that slavery or this nation itself must go down in blood." "If he was with us now," Rock said, "would he not make our hearts burn while he exposed, in his inimitable way, the duty of the nation?"[55]

Commissioned by the abolitionist state governor John A. Andrew (1818–1867), one-time legal counsel to the members of the Secret Six, the nation's first Black regiment was funded in part by the surviving members of the Six. Its commanding officer was Colonel Robert Gould Shaw, a member of the 28th

Congregational Society, and its staff drew on many other members of the same congregation. It was soon to prove its mettle in the battle of Fort Wagner and become the most famous Black regiment in the Union army.

At a certain point in the afternoon, the loud and colorful procession reached the site of the Boston massacre, where Parker and his fellow abolitionists had hoped to erect a memorial to Crispus Attucks, the first Black hero of the Revolutionary War. As the men of the 54th passed the site, they broke out singing "John Brown's Body." [56]

Frederick Douglass more than any other individual had brought the 54th into being through his indefatigable recruiting efforts. Now two of his sons were marching among its number. [57] But this was for him more than a moment of personal pride. He saw marching before him the validation of his understanding of the meaning of the Civil War.

At the outset, Douglass knew well enough that to frame the conflict as an "abolition war" was futile. Too many northerners would refuse to fight for any cause other than merely preserving the Union, and the border states would join the other side. Yet he believed, with Lincoln and Parker, that slavery was somehow the cause of the war, and he hoped that the war would ultimately turn its guns on that fundamental cause. The arming of Black men, he believed, was the essential step in finding purpose in the conflict. It was the last, best hope for salvaging justice from the brutality of war.

"He who today fights for emancipation, fights for his country and for free institutions, and he who fights for slavery fights against his country and for a slaveholding oligarchy," he told the citizens of Rochester in March 1862. The abolitionists had always known this, he added, but now the truth was visible for all to see. "The negro is the key of the situation" and "the pivot upon which the whole rebellion turns," he declaimed in various forms in dozens of speeches and articles. [58] He meant not just the Black men who would take up arms, but the entire Black population. In the Confederacy, he well knew, Black labor was compelled to supply food and support in the rear of the war effort.

The challenge before the nation, he concludes in his first lecture on the philosophy of photography, is to finish "the work that John Brown nobly began." As the reference to Brown makes clear, his reasoning rests on the bracing theory of the war that Parker had articulated even before it started. The Civil War, Douglass suggests, is really a slave insurrection by proxy. It is a continuation by other means of the prior, ongoing conflict between the slaveholding oligarchy and the enslaved population. The escalating disputes preceding the formal outbreak of hostilities—the fugitive laws, gag rules, the fights over new territories—all derived from the fundamental fact the enslaved people did not wish to be enslaved and could be counted upon to resist their enslavement. Arming the men of the 54th altered the outward form of the conflict, but it did not change the fundamental source.

PRESIDENT LINCOLN EMBRACED the same theory of the Civil War. It is likely that he did so much earlier than is widely believed today. He issued the Emancipation Proclamation in accordance with the logic that Theodore Parker had articulated in his "house divided" lecture of 1854 and then again on the eve of the war. He did not disguise the fact emancipation was a military move intended to unleash the insurrectionary power of the enslaved people. He insisted only that releasing this power was a necessary step in securing the rights of white Americans too. "In giving freedom to the *slave*, we assure freedom to the *free*," he tells Congress in 1862.[59]

Technically, the proclamation of January 1, 1863, did not

end slavery as such; it liberated only those enslaved people in territory that happened to be under rebel control. The border states were exempt, because Lincoln desperately wanted border states to remain in the Union, and he was willing to spare their property in human beings to secure that end. The intent was to weaken the Confederacy militarily and economically. "The colored population is the great *available*, yet *unavailed of*, force for restoring the union," Lincoln tells Andrew Johnson in 1863.[60] W. E. B. Du Bois would later cut the point even shorter: "The Emancipation Proclamation meant the negro soldier, and the negro soldier meant the end of the war."[61] Liberating the enslaved was not an act of charity; it was a bargain with the rising power of the enslaved and free Black population itself. It was the consequence, not the cause, of the growing power and productive value of the enslaved population itself.

That Lincoln acted for tactical purposes does not change the revolutionary nature of emancipation—nor does it alter the fact Lincoln himself was aware of its revolutionary character. Karl Marx explains to his friend Friedrich Engels the course that Lincoln was taking. "The North will, at last, wage the war in earnest," he predicts in 1862, and it will "have recourse to revolutionary methods." "One black regiment would have a remarkable effect on Southern nerves."[62]

DOUGLASS SPENT MUCH of the first two years of the war fuming at the slow pace of the Lincoln administration in mobilizing Black soldiers and taking the war to slavery. The president, he began to suspect, was a weak man doomed to fall well short of the needs of the hour. After the Emancipation Proclamation, however, Douglass issued one of the most famous broadsides of the war: "MEN OF COLOR TO ARMS! TO ARMS! NOW OR NEVER!"[63] The recruitment effort for the 54th Massachusetts was successful enough that, with energetic assistance from John Rock and the Secret Sixers, a 55th Massachusetts soon followed.

Northern racism hobbled the effort from the start. Black soldiers were offered lower wages than their white peers. They served in all-Black regiments, but their commanding officers were nonetheless all white. They were often housed under inferior conditions and consequently suffered higher rates of disease. The gruesome draft riots of July 1863 in New York City, in which mobs of white workers murdered hundreds of Black Americans and attacked an orphanage for colored children, proved that anti-Black racism in the North was as virulent as ever.

On August 10, 1863, his outrage over the treatment of Black soldiers compounded by the horror of the draft riots, Douglass showed up uninvited at the White House. He pushed his way up the stairs past "angry white office seekers," and, somewhat to his own amazement, managed to get in front of the president.[64] It was the first of three occasions on which the two men would meet face to face. As Lincoln well knew, Douglass had been publicly critical of the president for his slow pace on emancipation, for his misguided efforts to placate the colonization lobby, and for his acquiescence in the racist treatment of Black soldiers. Yet the meeting went well, and Douglass came away profoundly impressed and disarmed. Although he was not entirely satisfied with Lincoln's answers on how to correct the unfair treatment of Black soldiers, Douglass sensed that Lincoln was an "honest" man, free of "color prejudice," and that his seeming lethargy on Black recruitment resulted from no ill will but a perceived "concession to necessity."[65] "There are spots on the sun," Douglass tells his own supporters, but "a blind man can see where the President's heart is."[66]

One year later, Lincoln invited Douglass to the White House. Concerned that he would lose the upcoming election,

Lincoln wanted to ensure that as many of the enslaved people as possible claimed their freedom before a new and hostile administration could reverse emancipation. The idea was for Douglass "to go into the rebel states, beyond the lines of our armies, and carry the news of emancipation."[67] It was an astonishing proposal, as Douglass notes, and "somewhat after the original plan of John Brown." The assignment would have involved the national government directly in a biracial project to emancipate the enslaved, and its unambiguous purpose was to secure both the end of slavery and the preservation of the Union in the event that Lincoln should fail to win reelection. Douglass agreed to the plan, and he came away even more impressed with the president, who "showed a deeper moral conviction against slavery than I had ever seen before in . . . him." He did not have the opportunity to take up the assignment, however, as events soon moved in favor of the Union and Lincoln's reelection.

More than 180,000 Black men enlisted in the Union army and navy, accounting for 10 percent of the total of service-members.[68] They made a decisive contribution to the balance of power on the battlefield. They fought alongside as many as 200,000 Germans who served under generals such as Willich and Schurz. In the fall of 1864, with the help of fresh recruits, the Union army under General Ulysses S. Grant delivered the victories that ensured the defeat of the Confederacy and a second term for President Lincoln.

As Parker and Douglass both anticipated, the performative aspect of putting Black men in arms was at least as important in the long run as the immediate military impact. Ottilie Assing drove the point home for her readers. "The black regiments developed a degree of bravery and discipline that would do honor to the best army in the civilized world," she wrote.[69] "Equal citizenship" for all races, she boldly predicts, "will sooner or later be the law of the land, because the spirit of this country, of civilization and progress demand it authoritatively, and because it is the prerequisite for the republic's greatness and permanence."[70] With the benefit of hindsight, the forecast looks optimistic, but the reasoning was surely sound.

Thomas Wentworth Higginson, who saw action in the attack on Fort Wagner in South Carolina and served as an officer in the 33rd United States Colored Troops, drew the same conclusion from his experience with Black soldiers. "We, their officers, did not go there to teach lessons, but to receive them. There were more than a hundred men in the ranks who had voluntarily met more dangers in their escape from slavery than any of my young captains had incurred in all their lives," he records in his 1870 book, *Army Life in a Black Regiment*: "Until the blacks were armed, there was no guarantee of their freedom. It was their demeanor under arms that shamed the nation into recognizing them as men."[71]

The military logic behind emancipation was so compelling that the Confederacy, too, contemplated it.[72] In November 1864, with the tide of war now rushing against the rebellious oligarchy, Jefferson Davis himself called for raising 40,000 soldiers from the enslaved population, with a promise of freedom at the end of the war. But it was too little too late. Davis could not bring himself to offer a general emancipation. What would have been the point of fighting a war to perpetuate a slaveholding oligarchy if slavery itself was lost in the bargain?

IN HIS SECOND INAUGURAL ADDRESS, Lincoln reminds us that at the outset of the war, both sides expected that the conflict would be short and victory sweet. Neither anticipated that slavery would end with, or even before, the war's end. "Each looked for an easier triumph, and a result less fundamental and astounding."

The war, Lincoln means to say, was a revolution. Though

it had its roots in a slave insurrection, it ultimately united the interests of working people of all races against property. It overthrew a political system that failed to represent adequately the sovereignty of the people. Like all successful revolutions, it was in some sense retrospective. It did not create the power of the people; it consolidated a claim to power already established. It answered a certain challenge from the past, but the future would have to be met on its own terms. In the manner of Hegel's "Owl of Minerva," it arose at sunset, as a gloss on the achievements of millions of oppressed people and their 250 years of unrequited toil.

The Civil War was no more inevitable than anything else in the catalog of accidents and omissions we call history. And yet, according to Lincoln's bracing theory, it answered to a certain logic on the ground—a logic as universal and indifferent as the laws of nature. Moral principles and appeals to conscience were irrelevant except insofar as they provided glittering abbreviations for the underlying calculus of the struggle. The ideas of philosophy nonetheless made all the difference, not because they commanded assent through mindless acts of faith, but to the extent that they cleared away the obstacles to understanding. The real story of the war, as Lincoln signals in his Second Inaugural Address, traces the arc of a disenthrallment. It is about the way in which large parts of the American public only gradually came to see the fundamental source of the conflict despite the centuries of religious and cultural conditioning designed to help them avoid seeing it.

In the case of antislavery leaders such as Lincoln, Douglass, and Parker, it was the radical philosophy of the Enlightenment that permitted them to grasp the logic of struggle in which they were engaged. Marked by their youthful rebellions against the orthodoxies in which they were reared as no easy prospects for submission, they turned to the history of ideas to make better sense of their experience. Philosophy converted them not from one creed to another but from the passengers of history into its actors. The American war over slavery is the story—only one such story in human history—of an emancipation of the mind.

AFTERWORD

Let Us Strive On

FREDERICK DOUGLASS UNDERSTOOD the retrospective character of all successful revolutions. He knew that every generation would fight its own fight—power concedes nothing without a demand. It was with this insight in mind that he approached the meeting that William Lloyd Garrison organized for May 1865 following the passage by Congress of the Thirteenth Amendment to the Constitution in January. This was the abolitionists' "mission accomplished" moment, and Garrison was effectively calling for a dissolution of their movement. But Douglass refused to stand down. "Slavery . . . has been called by a great many names, and it will call itself by yet another name; and you and I and all of us had better wait and see what new form this old monster will assume, in what skin this old snake will come forth next," he told the gathered abolitionists, and they voted with him to remain in business.[1]

He did not have long to wait.

Within days of Lincoln's assassination on April 15, the caretakers of the nation's spiritual life set about fabricating a religious persona for the slain president more in keeping with their perceptions of the national interest. Ministers who had met him for an afternoon recorded how he had confessed his faith in the Messiah on the spot. Distant acquaintances mailed in their convictions about his convictions, which were sure to

be high and holy. Biographers rose to the challenge of reimagining Lincoln as an American Jesus. He had been killed on
Good Friday, they pointed out, and he had been carrying out
a mission that, with the benefit of hindsight, could only have
come from the Almighty himself.

Even those who should have known better papered over
his transparent heresies with ineffable pieties. "Lincoln was
unquestionably our most religious President," enthuses historian William Wolf in 1963.[2] According to the mid-twentieth
century theological celebrity Reinhold Niebuhr, "Lincoln's religious convictions were superior in depth and purity to those,
not only of the political leaders, but of the religious leaders of
his era."[3] The evidence mustered in defense of such claims was
mostly Lincoln's promiscuous use of biblical citations. Favorable mention was also made of his upbringing among Baptists
(even though his relations with them were resolutely hostile)
and the fact he opposed slavery (which somehow proved that
he was religious). In historian Allen Guelzo's hands, the belief
system that William Herndon characterizes as "elevated pantheism" gets converted to a "Calvinized deism," as if to suggest
that its origins were orthodox after all, notwithstanding the
vast gap between Calvinistic determinism and the necessitar-
ian naturalism of Lincoln's actual sources.[4]

It was hardly the first time that American history had been
turned into parody. George Washington enjoyed a comparable posthumous ascension to heaven, too, notwithstanding
his lifelong failure to evince any interest in being saved by
the Christian religion. The counterrevolutionary forces that
produced America's first, proslavery iteration of the Christian
nation myth were never going to let the facts about the nation's
secular refounding get in their way.

Lincoln's economic radicalism slipped out of sight almost
as swiftly as his religious infidelity. His insistence on the priority of labor over capital was passed over in silence, as was

his declaration that the rights of the dollar must yield to the rights of man. His debts to the 48ers were canceled, and the fact his analysis of the war over slavery coincided with that of Karl Marx almost to the letter never came up. "Free labor" came to be translated as "free markets," which came to stand for the freedom of the propertied once again to dominate the propertyless. The kind of "liberty" celebrated by John Calhoun and his fellow slaveholders returned, only this time in service of a new oligarchy. The party of Lincoln reinvented itself as the party of the money power and traded away the rights of the freed people of the South along with those of the rest of the working classes to better serve their new masters among the robber barons and their trusts.

The story of how Reconstruction was crushed to make way for Jim Crow and monopoly capitalism is in essence the story of a second counterrevolution triumphant. The revival and reinforcement of a racial system of oppression was the most obvious feature of this second counterrevolution. Less well appreciated, even to the present, is the role of the remnants of the southern oligarchy in the affair. The Black Codes and the anti-Black terrorism that swept the South in the aftermath of the war drew their power from popular racial prejudice, but their fundamental purpose and effect was to secure a cheap labor force for a landed elite. Black labor was the principal target, but white labor suffered a distinct degradation, too. W. E. B. Du Bois was largely correct: "The overthrow of Reconstruction was in essence a revolution inspired by property, not a race war."[5]

The defanging of transcendentalism in the postbellum imagination was equally expeditious and in the end a part of the same process of camouflaging the counterrevolution. William Lloyd Garrison retired, Thomas Wentworth Higginson moved all the way over to the Democratic Party, and Ralph Waldo Emerson found a comfortable seat in the tearooms of the well-to-do. The indefatigable Wendell Phillips almost alone soldiered on in the name of universal reform. By the early twentieth century, the driving intellectual movement of the preceding century had been recast as a bland, quasi-mystical, and apolitical individualism. It was a story about nature-loving hermits and self-reliant spiritualists dedicated to the exaltation of their own literary sensibilities—a tale well suited to enhance the self-regard of America's educated classes, or such was the impression that the nation's chron-iclers conveyed in their surveys. The strident heresies, the daring alliance with labor, the dangerous liaisons with immi-grant radicalism, the violent activism, and above all the blis-tering antislavery politics fell out of view, as Theodore Parker and the members of his 28th Congregational Society retreated into the little-written and less-read chapters of history.

Although Parker has survived in some fine biographies, his most enduring legacy may well be an indirect one. He was the source for one of Martin Luther King Jr.'s most celebrated lines—"the arc of the moral universe is long, but it bends toward justice"[6]—but possibly he was, for King, something more. King spent the formative years of his education at Crozer Theological Seminary and Boston University, both bastions of liberal theology that still bore the traces of Theodore Parker's style of religion. In early writings that his widow released only in the last decade of her life, King identifies himself with the tradition that begins with Friedrich Schleiermacher and that rejects biblical literalism in favor of a creed that seeks jus-tice in this world.[7] Like Parker, King found himself in opposi-tion to adversaries (in his case, the segregationists) who also claimed to have the literal word of scripture on their side. It was a foreseeable stop on the journey that King should have picked up that essay from Parker, "On Justice and the Con-science," from which he borrowed the line about "the arc of the moral universe."

The man that Lincoln named as "the most meritorious" individual in the nation, too, receded from the front pages of the national story. Once among the most famous people in the world, Frederick Douglass fell out of the great post–Civil War surveys of American history[8] and into the backlist, a relic thought to be of interest mainly to Black Americans. For a century, the 180,000 Black soldiers that he helped mobilize for the war, along with the many more individuals whose resistance he inspired, were fenced out of the nation's textbooks. Ottilie Assing's expectation that their service would be received with gratitude and a recognition of equal rights proved drastically premature. When Douglass did begin his comeback in the mid-twentieth century, starting with the work of historian Philip Foner, his fierce humanism was often set aside in the rush to cast him as a precursor of a civil rights movement that was thought to be as religious in its inspirations as it was in its organization.

Meanwhile, the religion that did so much to sustain and promote the slave system has never been held to account. In the immediate aftermath of the war, the southern branches of America's largest Christian denominations, having been relieved of their duties as the bulwark of slavery, retooled themselves into the bulwark of Jim Crow. The northern branches mostly managed to look past their own complicity in the slave system, even as they redoubled their own efforts to entrench segregation and racial prejudice.[9] Enterprising apologists for American religion eventually realized that the best way to deal with the past was to replace it with a more pleasing fiction. They concocted the myth that the same abolitionists whom the churches of the time hounded as infidels and atheists were the heart and soul of early American Christianity, that those evangelists who dedicated themselves to promoting racist colonization schemes were doing something other than carrying water for the slaveholders, and that the vast mass of Christian leaders and followers, who dutifully upheld the slave system in the name of God and country, never existed.

The proslavery theology that supplied the intellectual scaffolding for America's first iteration of fascism never went away; it was the spiritual face of the second counterrevolution, and it is the direct ancestor of Christian nationalism today. Some of its original practitioners, such as Robert Lewis Dabney, continued to peddle the religion of literalism, domination, and race hatred well into Reconstruction. They aimed much of their fire at "the falsehood and deadly tendencies of the Yankee theory of popular state education," which compelled good white people to turn their hard-earned tax dollars over for the education of "the brats of black paupers."[10] A direct line of descent connects James Henley Thornwell and his fellow leaders of the proslavery church to the founding theologians, economic ideologues, and political activists of the religious right of the late twentieth century.[11] The extremist theologian Rousas Rushdoony (1916–2001), in many ways the intellectual godfather of the union between Ronald Reagan and the religious right in 1980, was explicit about his debts to Dabney and the Southern Presbyterians.[12] As proof that history's sense of irony far exceeds that of its actors, some members of the anti-abortion wing of the modern Christian nationalist movement, apparently oblivious to the actual theological origins of their enterprise, have nonetheless attempted to brand themselves as the new abolitionists, apparently unaware that this would also make them infidels.

At the center of most of the revisionism that shrouded America's second revolution lay one of the greatest historiographical frauds of all time. The war over slavery wasn't about slavery after all, the mythologizers asserted; it was all about "states' rights," "self-government," "tariffs," or irreconcilable differences over the meaning of life. It is hard to say which is more remarkable—the audacity of such a falsification of history or the fact it was (and still is in places) entertained as a theory worthy of consideration. "Let us strive on to finish the work we are in; to bind up the nation's wounds," Lincoln had said in his Second Inaugural Address. But the nation often preferred to bind up its eyes rather than to treat the underlying conditions.

IN 1888, FREDERICK DOUGLASS famously denounced "so-called emancipation" as a "stupendous fraud." [13] It was overstatement, of course; but he had a point. When compared with the brutality of the old slavery, the new arrangement counted as progress; when compared with the ideals behind the refounding of the republic and the promise of the early days of radical Reconstruction, the new "new" slavery looked a lot like the old "new" slavery. Why did the second American revolution fall short in this way?

An influential line of interpretation today holds that the revolution failed because it merely yielded to new exercises in white supremacy. Slavery, according to this view, was just one iteration of an ongoing project to establish a permanent racial hierarchy. This line of thought received a first comprehensive statement in the work of political theorist Charles Mills,[14] and it has since been taken up by popular writers such as Ibram X. Kendi,[15] Nikole Hannah-Jones, and Ta-Nehisi Coates.[16] Coming as it does in the context of ongoing denials about the role of racism in the past and present, the renewed attention to race in history is surely a welcome development. For far too long, Americans have minimized the toxic legacies of slavery and racism, and they have systematically underestimated the indispensable contributions of Black Americans to democratic progress.

To represent racial conflict as the sole cause of slavery and its successor systems of oppression, however, is to overlook key aspects of the past and its points of contact with the present. Slavery was not invented to perpetuate racism; racism was promoted to perpetuate slavery. America's planters did not enslave people of African descent because they were Black; they enslaved Black people because it was profitable for them to do so. As Parker and Douglass were at pains to make clear, moreover, slavery did not divide the population only by race; it exploited race to divide the population between rich and poor. It was not a system for transferring wealth from all members of one race to all members of another; it was a system for extracting wealth from the many for the few. Slavery is best understood as a device through which the propertied exploit the entire nation by mobilizing one part of society to enforce the oppression of another at the expense of both. The grand struggle against slavery, which ultimately mobilized millions of Americans, was moreover a multiracial achievement. It united the oppressed classes and their leadership across the color line, if to a very limited and imperfect degree. Some legitimate and valuable resistance to slavery, it should also be noted, arose independently of antiracist ideas and in some cases (not least that of Theodore Parker) despite them. All these complexities of the history are flattened away in narratives that reduce the struggle over slavery to an eternal war of the races.

Racism does not reduce either to a legacy of the past or a fact of nature, even where it draws on history and inclination; it can be and has been reinvented and promoted in the present to serve a new type of master. Reducing the problems of the present to a perpetual struggle with timeless prejudices can sometimes misrepresent the reality to the point of interfering with the struggle for justice. It may be used to suggest, for example, that the solutions are to be found not in a more equitable economic system but in purely personal exercises of moral purification. Self-cleansing is always a more attractive option for those with money and power; it's much less expensive than real change. To the extent that the white supremacist narrative implies that racist ideas are somehow encoded in the DNA of the nation (or perhaps just the DNA of white people), it divides the working population in a permanent race war—a tactic that worked very well for the slaveholding oligarchy and that remains convenient for the oligarchies straddling the modern world.

According to a related line of thought that has gained in popularity in recent years, the second American revolution failed because modern capitalism is just an extension of slavery. All the wealth piled by the enslaved population got invested in the stock market, and we are living off the dividends to the present, or so the story goes. That there are some important parallels between the oppression of slavery and the oppression of the present economic order is an observation worth considering. The claim that the wealth of the modern world rests on the back of slavery, however, crushes the insight beneath simplifications and misrepresentations.

Slavery—just like its successor systems of racism[17]—was a means of concentrating wealth, not creating it. Yes, it converted disguised public subsidies into large quantities of underpriced cotton that fed the oligopolies of northern industrialists; it padded balance sheets for a time with pseudo-capital in the form of licenses to expropriate labor; and it allowed a tiny number of families to build large plantation homes and decorate them with imported finery. But it burdened the future with a far greater bill in the form of schools unbuilt, industries undeveloped, railroad tracks unlaid, and populations of all colors underfed, untreated for disease, and unprotected from violence. Its main bequests were a devastating war, a lethal culture of racism, a virulent strain of authoritarian religion, and a legacy of economic disadvantage that has cycled through the generations to the present. This impoverishing effect of the slave system was glaringly obvious to contemporary observers such as Theodore Parker, and it can be confirmed with a simple glance at the subsequent economic performance of former slave states, which have yet to catch up with their free-state peers in most measures of economic prosperity, education, and health.

The system of wage labor and corporate ownership that we simplistically identify as "capitalism" or "neo-liberalism,"[18] too, is to some extent a means for concentrating rather than creating wealth. In common with the slave system, it elevates the rights of property above the rights of humans. But this does not mean that they do so in the same way, still less that one originated from the other, and still less that they call for the same response. On the contrary, the two codes are distinct and even antagonistic in essential ways. Holding the present system accountable to the rights it traduces means breaking up oligopolies, restoring some balance of power between wage labor and the limited liability corporation, investing in education, recognizing the public good of domestic labor, and stopping the continuing destruction of the environment. Would-be reformers might find some inspiration and enlightenment in the history of the struggle over slavery, but they won't find much in the way of useful policy. We have already tried emancipation, and antiracist training exercises alone won't get the job done.

The ultimate consequence of placing property rights above human rights—and the genuine point of contact between slavery and the economic order of the present—is the extreme degree of inequality in economic power to which both systems give rise. Although the mechanisms that produce this inequality vary considerably, the principal effect is the same. Unreasonable distributions of wealth have always turned their fire on reason.[19] The deep connection between slavery and fundamentalist religion in the early nineteenth century arose from the same dynamic that has brought about the modern alliance between big money and blind faith and the plutocratic funding of misinformation and anti-intellectual prejudice. Political corruption, instability, and conflict are the natural results of the abandonment of reason.

IT IS HARDLY SURPRISING that the second American counter-revolution, like the first, set its sights on the Enlightenment. It is more worthy of attention that in this anti-intellectual project, unfortunately, the reaction has received support from those who present themselves as its critics.

A popular line of argument today goes like this: America's founders invoked the principles of the Enlightenment in establishing the new republic; but some of those founders, along with some of the philosophers who influenced them, were slaveholders, and a larger number held racist views; therefore, the principles of the Enlightenment are racist and proslavery "Light, then, became a metaphor for Europeanness," writes Ibram Kendi. "Enlightenment ideas gave legitimacy to this long-held racist partiality, this connection between lightness and Whiteness and reason, on the one hand, and between darkness, Blackness, and ignorance, on the other."[20]

"Enlightenment," however, is a retrospective English gloss on the French *éclaircissement* and the German *Aufklärung*, both sharing roots with "clear."[21] It has nothing to do with skin color. To suggest that it does is to exclude some of its greatest advocates—not least Frederick Douglass and Toussaint L'Ouverture. The logic of this kind of argument has never been good—the fact Jefferson was a racist doesn't make "all men are created equal" a racist proposition—but the history is generally worse.

The "white Enlightenment" trope belongs to a family of narratives descended from Max Horkheimer and Theodor

Adorno's *Dialectic of Enlightenment* of 1947, which famously argued that "the enlightened world radiates disaster."[22] The "disaster" trope in turn typically reduces to a negative copy of a reactionary myth about the "glories of Western civilization." Though they disagree about the value of the outcome, the partisans of both "disaster" and "glory" routinely suppose not just that some singular culture (variously, "Western civilization," "Western thought," or "Judeo-Christianity") is responsible for the creation of every aspect of the modern world, but also that this culture may be associated with a single ethnic and/or racial group. The latter supposition, however, is racism masquerading as history, and the former supposition is plain bad history, as the case of the "white Enlightenment" trope may illustrate.

The Enlightenment was a scene of intellectual conflict that drew upon utterly foreign cultures in the ancient world and in the New World to destabilize systems of oppression.[23] It was not a unified program but a process of creative intellectual destruction. To be sure, some of the famous names associated with it did indeed participate in racist and slaveholding projects. Even while he was writing the treatises that inspired Jefferson, for example, the English philosopher John Locke was investing in the slave plantations of North Carolina. David Hume and G. W. F. Hegel, too, demonstrably harbored racial prejudices.[24] But no account of the dynamic of the Enlightenment is complete that fails to account for the remarkable cast of thinkers and revolutionaries who opposed slavery or racism or both.

The Enlightenment produced Thomas Paine (whose *Age of Reason* invokes the most common label for the Enlightenment in its time) and Benjamin Franklin (arguably the most famous figure in the age of reason after Voltaire), both of whom participated in the formation of the world's first abolitionist society; the Comte de Volney, who credited the (putatively) Black

Africans of Egypt with founding all civilization on the study of the laws of nature; Alexander von Humboldt, the scientist who explicitly rejected both slavery and racial hierarchies; Denis Diderot, who called for an enlightened Black leader to take down the European colonial empires; the 140 or so members of the *Societe des Amis des Noirs*, a collection of *philosophes* and friends dedicated to ending slavery and advancing the rights of Black people; Thomas Young and his fellow authors of the Pennsylvania Constitution of 1776, which provided for universal manhood suffrage (a right Pennsylvania took away from Black men in 1837); the freethinkers of Vermont, whose Constitution of 1777 offered the first formal emancipation in the history of the modern world; the Massachusetts citizens who tirelessly pushed antislavery cases and achieved emancipation through the state court system well before the end of the War for Independence;[25] and a long line of Left Hegelian thinkers who are typically left out of those narratives that claim to find a straight line between early nineteenth-century German idealism and early twentieth-century German fascism.

The "white Enlightenment" trope does have on its side a long and sorry list of those "pretenders to science," as Douglass called them, who sought confirmation for their racist prejudices in pseudoscience. And it may well be that the pseudoscientific justifications of racism of the nineteenth century are of more interest than the religious ones today, in an age when science has much greater influence, as a useful reminder that the rhetoric of science is easily co-opted for oppressive purposes. But this insight turns to illusion if it distracts from the fact the more sustained and consequential defenses of racism and slavery in the nineteenth century came not from the partisans of the Enlightenment but from its enemies. Defenders of racism and slavery could be found on both sides of the debate about reason, to be sure, but in numbers, vehemence, and influence they were concentrated on the side that stood up for religion against reason. Liberal and heterodox religionists, conversely, were more likely to join with rationalists in abolitionist projects—and on precisely that account found themselves anathematized by conservative religionists. Indeed, church leaders and reactionaries of the time routinely denounced their Enlightenment foes for their reckless antislavery and antiracist views (not to mention their equally obnoxious feminism).

It was mostly about money and power, of course. The radical thinkers of the Enlightenment put forward theories of wealth that exposed the poverty of slavery; they advanced a concept of labor that gave it priority over capital; they provided arguments about human rights that threatened the prerogatives of property; above all, they promoted the dangerous idea of human equality. As far as the defenders of established hierarchies in the nineteenth century were concerned, they were anathema. The leaders of the counterrevolution and their allies today appear to agree.

To be fair, some of the resistance today to narratives drawing on famous names in the history of ideas stems from the reasonable desire to give voice to those who did not have the privilege of seeing their words celebrated in print and on the podium. Lincoln and Douglass were representatives of such an elite—and yet they would surely have approved of the sentiment. According to their theory of the Civil War, after all, the real agents of history were those who had toiled over the preceding two and half centuries and whose dedication in battle decided the course of the war. Emancipation, they understood, wasn't the result of a decree from on high but the sum of millions of lives lived well outside the philosophical salons and political debates of a privileged elite. But Lincoln and Douglass said as much and then acted upon this insight. Giving voice to the voiceless does not require side-lining the philosophical elite.

The tragedy of the white Enlightenment trope is that it undermines an indispensable tool in any quest for social justice and in this way ultimately serves the same interests as anti-intellectualism on the right. This unfortunate convergence is no coincidence. In an unequal world, even those who would fight for justice might absorb the lesson that power accrues to those who appeal not to reason but to its opposite. They, too, advance their own status not by uniting but by dividing and diverting others. It is hard to be reasonable in an unreasonable world. Unreason is always on the side of tyranny.

"WE HAVE TO DO with the past only as we can make it useful to the present and future," Douglass once said.[26] This is an insight worth bearing in mind in any survey of the hopes and disappointments of the American struggle over slavery. The facts of American history have been kind enough at least to give us a choice. We can tell a gloomy tale of unfulfilled promises or we can tell a forward-looking story of a refounding in process. Frederick Douglass, at least, was in no doubt about the better path.

The ideal to which Americans hold the republic accountable today dates not from the year that Thomas Jefferson wrote the Declaration of Independence but from the year that Lincoln delivered his Second Inaugural Address. Only with the defeat of the slaveholding oligarchy did it become plausible to say that America ought to be a place where children are judged by the content of their character not the color of their skin. Only with the subsequent passage of the Fourteenth Amendment to the Constitution did the rights to life, liberty, and the pursuit of happiness become something more than a phrase hurled at a foreign monarch and enter into the formal governing document of the republic. Only with powers accumulated in war and applied for the first time to development of higher education and other matters on a national scale did the federal government at last emerge as the vehicle through which "we the people" might promote the general welfare and secure the blessings of liberty against the quasi-feudal regimes lodged in many state governments. The refounding of America was the work of many remarkable individuals, only some of whose stories are told here.[27] Few of them are well remembered today; by rights, they should be more famous than the founders that still populate most of our origin myths.

The second American revolution, for all its shortcomings, cannot be dismissed as a total loss any more than the first. Douglass was surely right in thinking that the postrevolutionary struggles in both instances confirm something vital about the kind of emancipation they offer. The revolutionary part of the American Revolution holds that human beings are the source of their own authority in the political world; that they achieve self-government not through acts of faith but through acts of understanding; and that should they find themselves beholden to some other imaginary authority, this can only mean that they have constructed the conditions of their own servitude. As Douglass understood very well, the revolutionary aspect of the second American revolution was of precisely the same character. That a second revolution proved necessary does not mean that the first one failed. It shows rather that the revolutionary project of self-government through reason is not a permanent fact but an ongoing struggle. Power concedes nothing without a demand.

ACKNOWLEDGMENTS

THIS BOOK BENEFITED FROM the generous assistance of many individuals. Warm thanks are due to Peter Onuf and Bill Warner for their insightful comments on early drafts. Alane Mason, my editor at Norton for four books now, greatly improved the manuscript. Andrew Stuart, my agent for the past two decades, was indispensable as ever. Versions of the argument were presented at the Boston Athenaeum, the Massachusetts Historical Society, Kenyon College, and the Sekforde. I am grateful to audiences in those places for their responses. I owe more than I can say to Katherine Stewart, Sophia Stewart, and Aaron Stewart.

NOTES

ABBREVIATIONS

CWAL   *The Collected Works of Abraham Lincoln*, ed. Roy P. Basler (Abraham Lincoln Association, 1953)

CWTP   *The Collected Works of Theodore Parker*, ed. Francis Power Cobbe (Tribner, 1864–1875)

FDA   *Frederick Douglass Autobiographies*, ed. Henry Louis Gates (Library of America, 1994)

FDP   *The Frederick Douglass Papers*, ed. John W. Blassingame et al. (Yale University Press, 1973–)

LOC   The Frederick Douglass Papers at the Library of Congress

LWFD   *Life and Writings of Frederick Douglass*, ed. Philip S. Foner (International Publishers, 1950–1975)

MHS   Theodore Parker Papers, Massachusetts Historical Society

RWAL   *The Recollected Words of Abraham Lincoln*, ed. Dan E. Fehrenbacher and Virginia Fehrenbacher (Stanford University Press, 1996)

BIBLIOGRAPHICAL APPENDIX

Frederick Douglass

The best source on Frederick Douglass is Frederick Douglass. Even so, several biographies add perspective and were consulted here. The most recent one is definitive: David W. Blight, *Frederick Douglass: Prophet of Freedom* (Simon & Schuster, 2018).

Douglass delivered at least four versions of his lecture on photography: "Lecture on Pictures," 1861; "Age of Pictures," 1862; and "Pictures and Progress," 1864, 1865. The originals are available in the Frederick Douglass Papers at the Library of Congress. All are published in John Stauffer et al., eds., *Picturing Frederick Douglass: An Illustrated Biography of the Nineteenth Century's Most Photographed Man* (W. W. Norton, 2015). The caterpillar is to be found in "Age of Pictures."

Theodore Parker

This book relies on several excellent biographies and studies of Parker. Works consulted include Dean Grodzins, *American Heretic: Theodore Parker and Transcendentalism* (University of North Carolina Press, 2002); Henry Steele

Commager, *Theodore Parker* (Beacon Press, 1947); Paul E. Teed, *A Revolutionary Conscience: Theodore Parker and Antebellum America* (University Press of America, 2012); and Elisabeth Hurth, *Between Faith and Unbelief: American Transcendentalists and the Challenge of Atheism* (Brill, 2007).

Regarding Parker's sermon, *A Discourse on the Transient and the Permanent in Christianity* (Printed for the Author, May 19, 1841): Parker himself published three editions of the sermon in the aftermath of the controversy, and he printed them himself, as no reputable publisher could be found for such an item. The pamphlets sold out like hotcakes. In the first edition, he made the mistake of editing the text and thus departing from the spoken version, which gave rise to accusations of sneakiness, so in the second he published an appendix charting the (mostly harmless) edits.

The debate over Parker's infidelity took place in a battlefield too complex to trace in detail in these pages. For example: Andrews Norton leveled the charges of infidelity against Parker in 1841 in the context of a pamphlet war with George Ripley in which Parker served as a theological ally of Ripley. Norton penned a *Discourse on the Latest Form of Infidelity*; Ripley hit back with *The Latest Form of Infidelity Examined*, and Norton returned fire with *Remarks on a Pamphlet Entitled "The Latest Form of Infidelity Examined."* It went on, but an interesting feature of the debate is the extent to which both sides, and Norton especially, devote considerable effort to the analysis of Spinoza (and whether he should count as an atheist).

Abraham Lincoln and William Herndon

William Herndon published a description of Lincoln that many readers then did not wish to accept. Consequently, he fell victim to campaigns intended to discredit him, and his reputation has not entirely recovered. Nonetheless, Herndon remains one of the essential sources on Lincoln and especially on the young Lincoln. Sources consulted here include William Herndon and Jesse William Welk, *Herndon's Lincoln: The True Story of a Great Life*, 3 vols. (Belford Clarke, 1889); David Herbert Donald, *Lincoln's Herndon* (Knopf, 1948); Douglas L. Wilson and Rodney O. Davis, eds., *Herndon on Lincoln: Letters* (University of Illinois Press, 2016); Douglas L. Wilson et al., *Herndon's Informants* (University of Illinois Press, 1998); Joseph Fort Newton, *Lincoln and Herndon* (Torch Press, 1910); Douglas L. Wilson, "William Herndon and His Lincoln Informants," *Journal of the Abraham Lincoln Association*, 14, no. 1 (Winter 1993), pp. 15–34; and Michael Burlingame, "Why a New Biography of William Herndon Is Needed," *Journal of the Abraham Lincoln Association*, 35, no. 2 (Summer 2014), pp. 55–66.

The German Connection

On Ottilie Assing, the essential source is Maria Diedrich, *Love across the Color Lines: Ottilie Assing and Frederick Douglass* (Hill & Wang, 1999). Much source material can be found in Tamara Felden, *Frauen Reisen* (Peter Lang, 1993). See also Terry H. Pickett, "The Friendship of Frederick Douglass with the German, Ottilie Assing," *Georgia Historical Quarterly*, 53, no. 1 (Spring 1989), pp. 88–105.

On the revolutions of 1848 and the 48ers in America, important secondary sources include Bruce Levine, *The Spirit of 1848: German Immigrants, Labor Conflict, and the Coming of the Civil War* (University of Illinois Press, 1992); Mischa Honeck, *We Are the Revolutionists: German-Speaking Immigrants and Abolitionists after 1848* (University of Georgia Press, 2011); Carl Wittke, *Refugees of Revolution: The German Forty-Eighters in America* (University of Pennsylvania Press, 2016); William H. Goetzmann, ed., *The American Hegelians: An Intellectual Episode in the History of Western America* (Knopf, 1973); and Jonathan Israel, *The Expanding Blaze: How the American Revolution Ignited the World, 1775–1848* (Princeton University Press, 2017).

A useful compendium of Marx's work on American slavery is Karl Marx and Friedrich Engels, *The Civil War in the United States*, ed. Andrew Zimmerman (1937; repr. International Publishers, 2016).

On the pantheism controversy, see Frederick C. Beiser, *The Fate of Reason: German Philosophy from Kant to Fichte* (Harvard University Press, 2009); Gerard Vallee et al., eds., *The Spinoza Conversations between Lessing and Jacobi* (University Press of America, 1988); for more on Fichte especially, see Allen Wood, *Fichte's Ethical Thought* (Oxford University Press, 2016).

Political Economy of the New Slavery

In the vast literature analyzing the political economy of American slavery, some essential works consulted here include John Ashworth, *Slavery, Capitalism, and Politics in the Antebellum Republic*, Volume I (Cambridge University Press, 1995); Robert William Fogel, *Without Consent or Contract: The Rise and Fall of American Slavery* (W. W. Norton, 1989); James L. Huston, *Calculating the Value of the Union: Slavery, Property Rights, and the Economic Origins of the Civil War* (University of North Carolina Press, 2003); Eric Williams, *Capitalism and Slavery* (University of North Carolina Press, 1944); Sven Beckert and Seth Rockman, eds., *Slavery's Capitalism: A New History of American Economic Development* (University of Pennsylvania Press, 2016); Nicholas Onuf and Peter Onuf, *Nations, Markets, and War* (University of Virginia Press, 2006); James Oakes, *The Scorpion's Sting: Antislavery and the Coming of the Civil War* (W. W. Norton, 2014); James Oakes, *Freedom National: The Destruction of Slavery in the United States, 1861–1865* (W. W. Norton, 2012); James Oakes, *Slavery and Freedom: An Interpretation of the Old South* (Knopf, 1990); Moses I. Finley, *Ancient Slavery and Modern Ideology* (Chatto and Windus, 1980); Keri Leigh Merritt, *Masterless Men: Poor Whites and Slavery in the Antebellum South* (Cambridge University Press, 2017); and a long list of books on slavery by the historian David Brion Davis. On the co-option of the legal system for the enforcement of property rights against human rights, see Hawa Allen, *Insurrection: Rebellion, Civil Rights, and the Paradoxical State of Black Citizenship* (W. W. Norton, 2022); and Katharina Pistor, *The Code of Capital: How the Law Creates Wealth and Inequality* (Princeton University Press, 2019).

Regarding the distributional effects of slavery, the statistical analysis relied upon here combines data from various sources, none of which are entirely satisfactory. Principal sources consulted include James L. Huston, *Calculating the Value of the Union: Slavery, Property Rights, and the Economic Origins of the Civil War* (University of North Carolina Press, 2003), pp. 36ff.; Robert William Fogel, *Without Consent or Contract: The Rise and Fall of American Slavery* (W. W. Norton, 1989), pp. 83–84; Samuel P. Williamson and Louis Cain, "Measuring Slavery in 2020 Dollars" (MeasuringWorth, measuringworth.com, 2022); Fabien Linden, "Economic Democracy in the Slave South," *Journal of Negro History*, 31, no. 2 (April 1946), pp. 140–89; Rodrigo R. Soares, "A Note on Slavery and the Roots of Inequality," *Journal of Comparative Economics*, 40 (2012), p. 578; Charles B. Spahr, *An Essay on the Present Distribution of Wealth in the United States* (Thomas Crowell, 1895), pp. 31, 34. Huston, *Calculating the Value of the Union*, argues that Spahr basically got it right, and that the interpretation of the Civil War ever since has gone backward (p. 64).

In advancing a claim regarding a slavery-driven counterrevolution, I draw on several sources with a variety of related but distinct views on the subject. An essential, original source for any student of counterrevolution is W. E. B. Du Bois, *Black Reconstruction* (1935; repr. Library of America, 2021). For a detailed investigation of this fundamental connection between the New England–centered Federalist counterrevolution and proslavery thought, see Larry E. Tise, *Proslavery: A History of the Defense of Slavery in America, 1701–1840* (University of Georgia Press, 1987). For an acute analysis of the counterrevolution in South Carolina, see Manisha Sinha, *The Counterrevolution of Slavery* (University of North Carolina Press, 2000). Gerald Horne also argues for a "counterrevolution" in several of his many books and draws a connection with W. E. B. Du Bois, though he identifies this counterrevolutionary movement with the first American Revolution, which I do not.

The topic of slave insurrection has benefited from much additional research in recent years. Sources consulted include Hawa Allen, *Insurrection: Rebellion, Civil Rights, and the Paradoxical State of Black Citizenship* (W. W. Norton, 2022); Vincent Brown, *Tacky's Revolt: The Story of an Atlantic Slave War* (Harvard University Press, 2020); and Patrick Breen, *The Land Shall Be Deluged in Blood: A New History of the Nat Turner Revolt* (Oxford University Press, 2015). The extensive literature on the role of fear and insurrections dates from works on Haiti (see below) as well as Lerone Bennett Jr., *Before the Mayflower: A History of the Negro in America, 1619–1962*, originally published as articles in *Ebony* and subsequently available in various editions with the subtitle "A History of Black America."

The analysis of the connection between racism and capitalism arguably begins with W. E. B. Du Bois but has more recently expanded into a lively literature on "racial capitalism" that grew out of the work of Cedric Robinson, *Black Marxism: The Making of the Black Radical Tradition*, 3rd ed. (University of North Carolina Press, 2020). A useful compendium of this school is Destin Jenkins and Justin Leroy, eds., *Histories of Racial Capitalism* (Columbia University Press, 2021). The tradition can also draw on the seminal work of Eric Williams, *Capitalism and Slavery*, 3rd ed. (University of North Carolina Press, 2021) and C. L. R. James, *The Black Jacobins* (Secker and Warburg, 1938).

Theology of Slavery

"The Bible" in this book refers to the Christian Bible, mostly of the Protestant variety. Citations will mostly come from the New International Version for modern intelligibility, though also where appropriate from variants of the King James Version, which was the most common source in antebellum America.

On the structure and content of religion in early nineteenth-century America, sources consulted include Mark Noll, *America's God: From Jonathan Edwards to Abraham Lincoln* (Oxford University Press, 2002); and Nathan O. Hatch, *The Democratization of American Christianity* (Yale University Press, 1989).

On the proslavery church, essential sources include the abolitionists themselves. See especially Frederick Douglass, "The Anti-Slavery Movement," LWFD 2.333–58; William Goodell, *Slavery and Anti-Slavery: A History of the Great Struggle in Both Hemispheres* (William Goodell, 1855); and Stephen S. Foster, *The Brotherhood of Thieves* (William Bolles, 1843).

Some of the more interesting of the dozens of proslavery theology tracts from the antebellum period include James Henley Thornwell, *The Collected Writings of James Henley Thornwell* (Presbyterian Committee, 1873); Richard Fuller and Francis Wayland, *Slavery Considered as a Scriptural Institution*, ed. Nathan A. Finn and Keith Harper (Mercer University Press, 2008); Frederick A. Ross, *Slavery Ordained of God* (J. B. Lippincott, 1857); John Henry Hopkins, *A Scriptural, Ecclesiastical, and Historical View of Slavery* (W. I. Pooley, 1864); and *The Bible View of Slavery* (Saunders, Otley, 1863); see also reference to Hopkins in William Craft, *Running a Thousand Miles for Freedom* (William Tweedie, 1860), pp. 97ff.

Useful collections of assorted primary source documents are Paul Finkelman, *Defending Slavery: Proslavery Thought in the Old South* (Bedford/St. Martin's Press, 2003); Drew Gilpin Faust, ed., *The Ideology of Slavery: Proslavery Thought in the Antebellum South, 1830–60* (Louisiana State University Press, 1981); E. N. Elliott, *Cotton Is King* (Pritchard, Abbott, 1860); see also *Fast Day Sermons; or, The Pulpit on the State of the Country*, published in New York in 1861, which features many of the most prominent clerical voices on the subject of slavery.

Secondary sources useful for the debate on the theology of slavery include Mark Noll, *The Civil War as a Theological Crisis* (University of North Carolina Press, 2006); Larry E. Tise, *Proslavery: A History of the Defense of Slavery in America, 1701–1840* (University of Georgia Press, 1987); Hector Avalos, *Slavery, Abolitionism, and the Ethics of Biblical Scholarship* (Sheffield Phoenix Press, 2013); John R. McKivigan, *The War against Proslavery Religion: Abolitionism and the Northern Churches, 1830–1865* (Cornell University Press, 1984); John R. McKivigan and Michael Snay, *Religion and the Antebellum Debate over Slavery* (University of Georgia Press, 1998); William Sumner Jenkins, *Pro-Slavery Thought in the Old South* (University of North Carolina Press, 1960); Eugene D. Genovese, *The Slaveholders' Dilemma* (University of South Carolina Press, 1992); Eugene D. Genovese, *A Consuming Fire* (University of Georgia Press, 1988); Nathan A. Finn and Keith Harper, *Domestic Slavery Considered as a Scriptural Institution* (Mercer University Press, 2008); Seymour Drescher,

Abolition: A History of Slavery and Antislavery (Cambridge University Press, 2009); Manisha Sinha, *The Counterrevolution of Slavery* (University of North Carolina Press, 2000); Manisha Sinha, *The Slave's Cause* (Yale University Press, 2018); David Torbett, *Theology and Slavery: Charles Hodge and Horace Bushnell* (Mercer University Press, 2006); Charles F. Irons, *The Origins of Proslavery Christianity* (University of North Carolina Press, 2008); Lester B. Scherer, *Slavery and the Churches in Early America* (William B. Eerdmans, 1975); George C. Rable, *God's Almost Chosen People: A Religious History of the American Civil War* (University of North Carolina Press, 2010); and Mitchell Snay, *Gospel of Disunion: Religion and Separatism in the Antebellum South* (University of North Carolina Press, 1993).

On the connections between proslavery theology and modern Christian nationalism, readers may wish to check out R. J. Rushdoony, *Institutes of Biblical Law* (Craig Press, 1973); R. J. Rushdoony, *Systematic Theology* (Ross House Books, 2000); Julie Ingersoll, *Building God's Kingdom* (Oxford University Press, 2015); and Katherine Stewart, *The Power Worshippers* (Bloomsbury, 2020). For more on the connection between racism, proslavery theology, Jim Crow, and Christian nationalism, see also Anthea Butler, *White Evangelical Racism* (University of North Carolina Press, 2021); and Jamar Tisby, *The Color of Compromise: The Truth about the American Church's Complicity in Racism* (Zondervan, 2020).

ABOUT THIS BOOK

1. See the Bibliographical Appendix above for discussion of sources for Douglass's lectures on photography.
2. See in particular Maria Diedrich, *Love across the Color Lines: Ottilie Assing and Frederick Douglass* (Hill & Wang, 1999).
3. Lincoln's Second Inaugural Address may be found in CWAL 8.333–34.
4. FDA 804; LOC mdf.22015, p. 13.
5. For "white man's President," see FDA 917; for a gentler take, see FDA 808–11; for "black man's President," see LOC "Eulogy," 1865; see also LOC "Abraham Lincoln: A Speech," mdf.22015, p. 5. For an overview on the connection between Douglass and Lincoln, see James Oakes, *The Radical and the Republican: Frederick Douglass, Abraham Lincoln, and the Triumph of Antislavery Politics* (W. W. Norton, 2007).
6. FDA 802.
7. LWFD 4.316.
8. LOC mdf.22015, p. 14.
9. Matthew Stewart, *Nature's God: On the Heretical Origins of the American Republic* (W. W. Norton, 2014).
10. LWFD 3.336.
11. FDA 1015.

12. LWFD 4.126.
13. William Herndon and Jesse William Welk, *Herndon's Lincoln* (Belford Clarke, 1889), 3.445.
14. Herndon and Welk, *Herndon's Lincoln*; see also Henry Steele Commager, *Theodore Parker* (Beacon Press, 1947), p. 264.
15. CWAL 5.537.
16. CWAL 5.537.
17. LWFD 3.347.
18. LWFD 1.162.
19. See Mark Noll, *The Civil War as a Theological Crisis* (University of North Carolina Press, 2006); and Theodore Parker, "A Letter to the People of United States Touching the Matter of Slavery" (James Munroe, 1848), p. 71.
20. For more on the argument that inequality begets unreason, see Matthew Stewart, *The 9.9 Percent* (Simon & Schuster, 2021), especially chap. 10.
21. There are some noteworthy recent exceptions, cited further later: Matthew Karp, *This Vast Southern Empire: Slaveholders at the Helm of American Foreign Policy* (Harvard University Press, 2016).

1 / WE MUST DISENTHRALL OURSELVES

1. For the story on Auld's conversion and Henny's death, see FDA 52–53, 254–55, 555–57.
2. LWFD 2.136.
3. FDA 40.
4. FDA 41.
5. FDA 231.
6. FDA 232.
7. The "much worse" appears in the *Narrative of the Life of Frederick Douglass* of 1845 (FDA 52); in the later autobiographies, Douglass tones down the language, no doubt as a result of the blowback from the first publication.
8. Luke 12:47; FDA 53.
9. FDA 68.
10. FDA 360.
11. FDA 362.
12. FDA 96.
13. Louis Menand, *The Metaphysical Club* (Farrar, Straus and Giroux, 2001).
14. See the Bibliographical Appendix for biographies of Theodore Parker, to which this section is greatly indebted.
15. Parker himself published three editions of the sermon; see the Bibliographical Appendix.
16. Commager, *Theodore Parker*, p. 209; Edward Lillie Pierce, *Memoir and Letters of Charles Sumner* (Roberts Bros., 1893), 3.133.

17. See Dean Grodzins, *American Heretic: Theodore Parker and Transcendentalism* (University of North Carolina Press, 2002), for these and other details.
18. James Russell Lowell (anon.), *A Fable for Critics* (G. P. Putnam, 1848).
19. Paul E. Teed, *A Revolutionary Conscience: Theodore Parker and Antebellum America* (University Press of America, 2012), p. 11; Commager, *Theodore Parker*, p. 19.
20. Elisabeth Hurth, *Between Faith and Unbelief: American Transcendentalists and the Challenge of Atheism* (Brill, 2007), p. 19.
21. Frederic Henry Hedge, *Prose Writers of Germany* (Carey and Hart, 1848); Dan McKanan, ed., *A Documentary History of Unitarian Universalism* (Unitarian Universalist Association, 2017), 1.353.
22. Hurth, *Between Faith and Unbelief*, pp. 53–54.
23. *Churchman's Monthly Review* (Wertheim), February 1847, p. 92.
24. Although Strauss's work comes adorned with the sophisticated technologies perfected in Germany's factories of biblical exegesis, the theses are in essence the same ones that the English deists of the previous century put forward, that John Locke defends in his less opaque moments, that Spinoza articulates in detail, and that Giordano Bruno offers in the wild dialogues that led to his inquisition.
25. To add to the ironies—Strauss issued his pamphlet just as he was retreating under fire from orthodox critics for his heresies, and so it is a relatively conservative work within his oeuvre; but Parker's critics hardly stopped to notice, and Parker eventually moved even further in the direction of heresy than did Strauss.
26. Cited in Grodzins, *American Heretic*, p. 165.
27. *Churchmans Monthly Review* (Wertheim), February 1847, p. 92; see Prof. C. Ullman, *The Worship of Genius and the Distinctive Character or Essence of Christianity*, trans. from the German (Chapman, 1847), for a slashing critique of Strauss.
28. Norton leveled the charges in the context of a pamphlet war with George Ripley in which Parker served as theological ally of Ripley; see the Bibliographical Appendix.
29. Commager, *Theodore Parker*, p. 76.
30. Lowell, *A Fable for Critics*.
31. Converse Francis, cited in Teed, *Revolutionary Conscience*, p. 60.
32. Grodzins, *American Heretic*, p. 363; Commager, *Theodore Parker*, p. 88.
33. See Teed, *Revolutionary Conscience*, pp. 207–10.
34. Proceedings of the Anti-Slavery Society of Massachusetts on the Anniversary of the Mob of October 21, 1835 (Boston, 1856), p. 43.
35. Peter Jimack, ed., *A History of the Two Indies: A Translated Selection* (Taylor & Francis, 2017), p. 168.

36. Sudhir Hazareesingh, *Black Spartacus: The Epic Life of Toussaint Louverture* (Picador, 2020), p. 11.
37. Karl Marx and Friedrich Engels, *The Civil War in the United States*, ed. Andrew Zimmerman (1937; repr. International Publishers, 2016), p. 153.
38. Stewart, *Nature's God*.
39. Susan Buck-Morss, *Hegel, Haiti, and Universal History* (University of Pittsburgh Press, 2009).
40. English novelists got in on the act, too. See Harriet Martineau, *The Hour and the Man*, 2 vols. (Harper & Brothers, 1841), which offers a fictionalized account of L'Ouverture.
41. Cited in Diedrich, *Love across the Color Lines*.
42. Diedrich, *Love across the Color Lines*, p. 84.
43. Diedrich, *Love across the Color Lines*, p. 84.
44. Albert Bigelow Paine, *Mark Twain: A Biography* (Harper Brothers, 1912), 3.2.30.
45. On Ottilie Assing, see the Bibliographical Appendix.
46. Tamara Felden, *Frauen Reisen* (Peter Lang, 1993), p. 110.
47. Carl Sandburg quoted from introduction in David Herbert Donald, *Lincoln's Herndon* (Knopf, 1948), p. vii. For further detail on sources for Herndon's life and the Lovejoy episode, see Bibliographical Appendix.
48. Joseph Fort Newton, *Lincoln and Herndon* (Torch Press, 1910), p. 246.
49. Cited in Paul Simon, *Freedom's Champion: Elijah Lovejoy* (Southern Illinois University Press, 1994), p. 168.
50. Simon, *Freedom's Champion*, p. 164.
51. CWAL 1.110.
52. Newton, *Lincoln and Herndon*, pp. 8–9; Donald, *Lincoln's Herndon*, p. 12. The evidence on the Lovejoy event comes from the report of Henry Bascom Ranking, who claims to have heard it from Herndon himself in interviews later in life. Donald attempts to throw cold water on the story, but his objections are mostly tendentious and seemingly motivated by his relentless hostility to his subject and his inability to cast him in any kind of role that might smack of good character.
53. Herndon to Parker, April 28, 1856, MHS.
54. Herndon and Welk, *Herndon's Lincoln*, 2.188.
55. Douglas L. Wilson, "William Herndon and His Lincoln Informants," *Journal of the Abraham Lincoln Association*, 14, no. 1 (Winter 1993), pp. 15–34; Michael Burlingame, "Why a New Biography of William Herndon Is Needed," *Journal of the Abraham Lincoln Association*, 35, no. 2 (Summer 2014), pp. 55–66.
56. See Wilson, "William Herndon and His Lincoln Informants": "Outgoing and exuberant by nature, he was as communicative and unbuttoned as Abraham Lincoln was reserved and self-restrained."
57. Herndon to Parker, December 27, 1856, MHS.

58. CWAL 3.363.
59. Douglas L. Wilson and Rodney O. Davis, eds., *Herndon on Lincoln: Letters* (University of Illinois Press, 2016), pp. 100–102; Herndon and Welk, *Herndon's Lincoln*, 3.439.
60. Constantin François Volney, *Volney's Ruins, or Meditations on the Revolutions of Empires*, trans. Joel Barlow (Charles Gaylord, 1831), 1.21.
61. Volney, *Volney's Ruins*, 1.6.
62. Volney, *Volney's Ruins*, 1.21.
63. Volney, *Volney's Ruins*, 1.4.
64. Herndon and Welk, *Herndon's Lincoln*, 3.349.
65. RWAL 245; Herndon and Welk, *Herndon's Lincoln*, 3.438.
66. Cited in Allen Guelzo, *Abraham Lincoln as a Man of Ideas* (Southern Illinois University Press, 2016), pp. 27–43. Guelzo cleverly attributes the "motive" doctrine to Jeremy Bentham and the utilitarian tradition. He overlooks the fact that the same doctrine is present in Volney and descended through another path from Thomas Hobbes and Spinoza to Bentham.
67. William Herndon to Edward McPherson, February 4, 1866, cited in Wilson and Davis, *Herndon on Lincoln*.
68. Thomas Paine, *The Age of Reason*, in *Thomas Paine: Collected Writings*, ed. Eric Foner (Library of America, 1995), p. 736.
69. CWAL 1.115.
70. Douglas L. Wilson et al., *Herndon's Informants* (University of Illinois Press, 1998), p. 576.
71. Herndon and Welk, *Herndon's Lincoln*, 3.349.
72. Harvey Lee Ross and other historians have questioned the story. Yet there are several sources for the story, and Herndon insists that it is true.
73. All quotations in this paragraph and the next can be found in Herndon and Welk, *Herndon's Lincoln*, 3.440–46.
74. CWAL 1.383.
75. CWAL 1.383.
76. CWAL 1.384.

2 / SOMEHOW THE CAUSE OF THE WAR

1. LWFD 2.193.
2. Joshua D. Rothman, *The Ledger and the Chain: How the Domestic Slave Trade Shaped America* (Basic Books, 2021).
3. On sources regarding counterrevolution, see the Bibliographical Appendix.
4. LWFD 2.473.
5. "The fathers of our republic never meant to perpetuate slavery," in Gordon S. Barker, *Fugitive Slaves and the Unfinished American Revolution: Eight Cases, 1848–1856* (McFarland, 2013), p. 7.

6. CWAL 2.495; Allen Guelzo, *Lincoln and Douglas* (Simon & Schuster, 2010), p. 79.
7. James Madison, "Notes on the Debates in the Federal Convention," August 8, 1787.
8. See Clement Eaton, *The Freedom-of-Thought Struggle in the Old South* (Harper, 1964), p. 15.
9. James Wilson at the Pennsylvania Ratifying Convention, December 3–4, 1787, in Jonathan Elliot, ed., *The Debates in the State Conventions on the Adoption of the Federal Constitution* (Burt Franklin, 1973), 2.451–53, 484–86.
10. Elliot, ed., *Debates in the State Conventions*, 3.
11. Sven Beckert and Seth Rockman, eds., *Slavery's Capitalism: A New History of American Economic Development* (University of Pennsylvania Press, 2016).
12. Friedrich Engels, *Anti-Duhring: Herr Eugen Duhring's Revolution in Science* (Foreign Languages Publishing House, 1962), p. 222.
13. Nancy MacLean, *Democracy in Chains* (Penguin, 2017), p. 9; James L. Huston, *Calculating the Value of the Union: Slavery, Property Rights, and the Economic Origins of the Civil War* (University of North Carolina Press, 2003).
14. Samuel P. Williamson and Louis Cain, "Measuring Slavery in 2020 Dollars" (MeasuringWorth, measuringworth.com, 2022), put the estimate at $3.059 billion; other estimates of the capital value of slaves in current dollars vary somewhat among sources between $2 billion and change up to $4 billion.
15. The case can and has been made that slave labor, by virtue of torture and other forms of managerial discipline, was more productive than non-slave labor, and this difference could in theory account for some of the capital value of slaves. In the "best" case, however, it would account for only a small fraction of the total capital value of slaves. And the best case is actually very bad, as will be explained later.
16. Daniel Lord, *The Effect of Secession upon the Commercial Relations between North and South, and upon Each Section* (Henry Stevens, 1861), p. 61.
17. Moses I. Finley, *Ancient Slavery and Modern Ideology* (Chatto and Windus, 1980); James Oakes, *Slavery and Freedom: An Interpretation of the Old South* (Knopf, 1990); David Brion Davis, *The Problem of Slavery in Western Culture* (Oxford University Press, 1988); David Brion Davis, *The Problem of Slavery in the Age of Revolution, 1770–1823* (Oxford University Press, 1999); and David Brion Davis, *The Problem of Slavery in the Age of Emancipation* (Vintage, 2015).
18. A useful compendium of these and other citations from Marx is Karl Marx and Friedrich Engels, *The Civil War in the United States*, ed. Andrew Zimmerman (1937; repr. International Publishers, 2016).
19. Marx and Engels, *The Civil War in the United States*, p. 2.
20. See Matthew Karp, *This Vast Southern Empire: Slaveholders at the Helm of American Foreign Policy* (Harvard University Press, 2016).

21. John C. Calhoun, *The Political Philosophy of John C. Calhoun* (Liberty Fund, 1811), p. 461.

22. Robert Rutland, ed., *The Papers of George Mason* (University of North Carolina Press, 1970), p. 173.

23. Rutland, *Papers of George Mason*, p. 965.

24. Carl Schurz, *Reminiscences* (J. Murray, 1909), p. 36.

25. Eaton, *Freedom-of-Thought Struggle in the Old South*, p. 20.

26. Huston, *Calculating the Value of the Union* (p. 64), argues that Spahr basically got it right, and that the interpretation of the Civil War ever since has gone backward; Charles B. Spahr, *An Essay on the Present Distribution of Wealth in the United States* (Thomas Crowell, 1895), pp. 31, 34.

27. The statistics here vary somewhat across sources and are probably not certain in the detail, even if they remain accurate as a picture of the skewed distribution of wealth as a whole; see the Bibliographical Appendix. For Du Bois's estimate that 8,000 families ruled the south, see W. E. B. Du Bois, *Black Reconstruction in America* (Oxford University Press, 2007); for Thaddeus Stevens' estimates concerning the distribution of land ownership in the south, see K. Stephen Prince, ed., *Radical Reconstruction: A Brief History with Documents* (Bedford/St. Martin's Press, 2016), p. 47.

28. On "sexual aggression," see James Henry Hammond (1807–1864), governor of South Carolina, who sexually abused four teenage nieces and raped at least two enslaved women, one of whom was likely his 12-year-old daughter. This behavior did not stop him from getting elected to the US Senate, where he delivered proslavery speeches boasting that "Cotton Is King."

29. Marx and Engels, *The Civil War in the United States*, pp. 38ff.

30. Marx and Engels, *The Civil War in the United States*, p. 55.

31. John Stuart Mill, *The Contest in America* (Little, Brown, 1862); see also James Oakes, *The Scorpion's Last Sting: Antislavery and the Coming of the Civil War* (W. W. Norton, 2014).

32. Karp, *This Vast Southern Empire*.

33. For more on the history of fear, insurrection, and the response of the legal system to it, see Hawa Allen, *Insurrection: Rebellion, Civil Rights, and the Paradoxical State of Black Citizenship* (W. W. Norton, 2022); for more nuance on the slave insurrections, see Vincent Brown, *Tacky's Revolt: The Story of an Atlantic Slave War* (Harvard University Press, 2020).

34. Marx and Engels, *The Civil War in the United States*, p. 33.

35. Walter Johnson, *River of Dark Dreams: Slavery and Empire in the Cotton Kingdom* (Harvard University Press, 2013), p. 8.

36. On the co-option of the legal system for the enforcement of property rights against human rights, see Allen, *Insurrection*; and Katharina Pistor, *The*

Code of Capital: How the Law Creates Wealth and Inequality (Princeton University Press, 2019).

37. Manisha Sinha, *The Counterrevolution of Slavery* (University of North Carolina Press, 2000).

38. Cited in Du Bois, *Black Reconstruction*, chap. 10.

39. Marx and Engels, *The Civil War in the United States*, p. 60.

40. Marx and Engels, *The Civil War in the United States*, p. 60.

41. Marx and Engels, *The Civil War in the United States*, p. 153.

42. CWTP 6.120.

3 / BOTH READ THE SAME BIBLE

1. The scene is recounted in David Blight, *Frederick Douglass: Prophet of Freedom* (Simon & Schuster, 2018).

2. J. O. Farmer, *The Metaphysical Confederacy: James Henley Thornwell and the Synthesis of Southern Values* (Mercer University Press, 1986).

3. Essential sources cited on religion in the early republic include Mark Noll, *America's God: From Jonathan Edwards to Abraham Lincoln* (Oxford University Press, 2002); and Nathan O. Hatch, *The Democratization of American Christianity* (Yale University Press, 1989).

4. Data from Noll, *America's God*, pp. 168ff.

5. The South's top three denominations could seat 88 percent of the population, whereas the North's top three had room enough for only 65 percent of the population. Underlying data from Noll, *America's God*, p. 168.

6. Charles F. Irons, *The Origins of Proslavery Christianity* (University of North Carolina Press, 2008).

7. Hatch in *The Democratization of American Christianity* makes the case, and it has been repeated in a variety of ways since. The democratization thesis extends beyond religion and is a notable feature of the historiography in recent decades, especially in the work of Gordon Wood. I contend here that it mistakes the expanding plethora of mechanisms that allowed for the exploitation of popular passions with the growth of actual democracy, that is, of rational self-government by a sovereign people.

8. Jefferson to Dr. Benjamin Waterhouse, June 26, 1822, in Merrill D. Peterson, ed., *Thomas Jefferson* (Routledge, 1997), p. 1458; Paine, *Age of Reason*, p. 667; Ethan Allen, *Reason, the Only Oracle of Man* (Bennington, Vermont: Haswell & Russell, 1784), p. 456.

9. Philip Morin Freneau, "On the Prospect of a Revolution in France," 1790, in *The Poems of Philp Freneau: Poet of the American Revolution*, ed. Fred Lewis Pattree (Princeton University Library, 1903), 2.385.

10. Jefferson to Tench Coxe, January 1, 1795, in Julian P. Boyd, ed., *The Papers of Thomas Jefferson* (Princeton University Press, 2000), 28.373.

11. See Anson Ely Morse, *The Federalist Party in Massachusetts to the Year 1800* (Princeton University Press, 1909), p. 95; in particular letter of November 19, 1795, p. 95.

12. Morse, *Federalist Party in Massachusetts*, pp. 103, 107n60.

13. According to a legend that Lincoln loved to retell, Allen saw that his British captors had hung a portrait of George Washington in their latrine. Old Ethan promptly told them that this was a good idea, because the sight of Washington was bound to scare the crap out of any British soldier.

14. Morse, *Federalist Party in Massachusetts*, p. 101.

15. Alexander Hamilton, "Views on the French Revolution," *The Papers of Alexander Hamilton* (Columbia University Press, 1979), 26.1.738.

16. Timothy Dwight, *Theology Explained and Defended* (Thomas Tegg, 1831), p. 549.

17. Among the many useful sources on the relation between Christianity and slavery in early America, one may include Frederick Douglass himself, "The Anti-Slavery Movement," LWFD 2.333–358; William Goodell, *Slavery and Anti-Slavery: A History of the Great Struggle in Both Hemispheres* (William Goodell, 1855); Lester B. Scherer, *Slavery and the Churches in Early America* (William B. Eerdmans, 1975); and the many titles on proslavery theology cited in the next chapter.

18. Scherer, *Slavery and the Churches in Early America*, p. 76.

19. Manisha Sinha, *The Slave's Cause: A History of Abolition* (Yale University Press, 2016), p. 17.

20. A catalog of these and other early antislavery pronouncements can be found in Goodell, *Slavery and Anti-Slavery*, chap. 5. For more discussion of abolitionism during the revolutionary period, see Robin D. G. Kelley and Earl Lewis, *To Make the World Anew: Volume One: A History of African Americans to 1880* (Oxford University Press, 2005), pp. 103ff.

21. The numbers are uncertain, but it appears that Turner's rebels killed roughly 60 white people; white mobs then killed roughly 120 Black people (most presumably not involved in the rebellion); and then 56 were executed after trial. See Patrick Breen, *The Land Shall Be Deluged in Blood: A New History of the Nat Turner Revolt* (Oxford University Press, 2015).

22. Charles F. Irons, *The Origins of Proslavery Christianity* (University of North Carolina Press, 2008).

23. David Walker, *Appeal . . . to the Coloured Citizens of the World* (David Walker, 1829).

24. John R. McKivigan, *The War against Proslavery Religion: Abolitionism and the Northern Churches, 1830–1865* (Cornell University Press, 1984), p. 20.

25. Paul Finkelman, *Defending Slavery: Proslavery Thought in the Old South* (Bedford/St. Martin's Press, 2003), p. 125.

26. Genesis 16:9.

27. Exodus 21:20.
28. Deuteronomy 5:14–15.
29. Deuteronomy 5:21; Exodus 20:17.
30. Exodus 21:8.
31. Leviticus 25:44–46.
32. Frederick A. Ross, *Slavery Ordained of God* (J. B. Lippincott, 1857), p. 152.
33. The poem appears in *Frederick Douglass' Paper*, January 16, 1857; it is reproduced by William Glasson in Robert S. Levine and Samuel Otter, *Frederick Douglass and Herman Melville* (University of North Carolina Press, 2008), p. 126.
34. David Walker, in his 1829 *Appeal*, for example, argues that some standout slaves in Egypt, notably Joseph of the amazing coat, were given high military commands and allowed to take high-status wives.
35. Ross, *Slavery Ordained of God*, pp. 145–46.
36. Richard Fuller and Francis Wayland, *Slavery Considered as a Scriptural Institution*, ed. Nathan A. Finn and Keith Harper (Mercer University Press, 2008), p. 135.
37. 1 Corinthians 7:21. There is a long history of efforts to reinterpret or simply rewrite this passage in order to make it seem less slavery friendly, as Hector Avalos, *Slavery, Abolitionism, and the Ethics of Biblical Scholarship* (Sheffield Phoenix Press, 2013), details.
38. Galatians 3:28.
39. Ephesians 6:5–6.
40. Colossians 3:22.
41. Walker, *Appeal*, p. 43.
42. John Henry Hopkins, *A Scriptural, Ecclesiastical, and Historical View of Slavery* (W. I. Pooley, 1864), p. 209.
43. Letter from Moses Stuart to Wilbur Fisk, April 10, 1837, cited in Stephen S. Foster, *The Brotherhood of Thieves* (William Bolles, 1843), p. 47.
44. James Henley Thornwell, *Collected Writings of James Henley Thornwell* (Presbyterian Publications, 1873), 4.456.
45. John Rankin, cited in McKivigan, *The War against Proslavery Religion*, p. 31.
46. Matthew 7:12.
47. James Henley Thornwell, *National Sins*, November 21, 1860 (Southern Guardian Steam Power Press, 1860) p. 39; Hopkins, *Scriptural, Ecclesiastical, and Historical View of Slavery*, pp. 223ff.
48. Cited in Foster, *The Brotherhood of Thieves*, p. 38.
49. FDP 1.4.249.
50. Acts 17:26.
51. There is no evidence in the Bible to support the claim that Ham and Canaan were Black. But that spurious interpolation of unadulterated anti-Black racism was in reality a metaphorical superfluity, neither adding to

nor subtracting from the underlying message that enslavement of groups descended from a common ancestor could and did receive divine sanction. A number of more sophisticated proslavery theologians either rejected or downplayed the "mark of Ham" argument as crowd-pleasing theology.

52. Jefferson Davis, speech from 1859; cited in Joseph Fornieri, *Abraham Lincoln: Philosopher Statesman* (Southern Illinois University Press, 2014), p. 41.

53. Jefferson Davis, *The Essential Writings* (Random House, 2004), p. 160.

54. James Henley Thornwell, *The Collected Writings of James Henley Thornwell*, ed. John B. Adger (Presbyterian Committee of Publication, 1873), 4.460.

55. LWFD 2.295.

56. Thornwell, *National Sins*, p. 37; Noll, *America's God*, p. 399; Eugene D. Genovese, *A Consuming Fire* (University of Georgia Press, 1988), pp. 80ff.; see also Thornwell, *The Collected Writings*, 4.403: "It is a public testimony to our faith, that the Negro is of one blood with us, that he has sinned with us, and that he has an equal interest in the great redemption."

57. Leviticus 25:55.

58. Philippians 1:1; 1 Corinthians 6:20; Ephesians 6:6; Colossians 3:24.

59. Matthew 24:50.

60. Romans 13:1.

61. Thornwell, *The Collected Writings*, 4.461.

62. Mark A. Noll, *The Civil War as a Theological Crisis* (University of North Carolina Press, 2006).

63. Noll, *The Civil War as a Theological Crisis*, appears to agree: "proslavery advocates had largely succeeded in winning the battle for the Bible."

64. James Henley Thornwell, "The Relation of the State to Christ," in Adger and Girardeau, eds., *Collected Writings of James Henley Thornwell*, 4.549–56; and "Sermon on National Sins" in ibid., pp. 510–48.

65. Cited in Manisha Sinha, *The Counterrevolution of Slavery Politics* (University of North Carolina Press, 2000), p. 247.

66. Sinha, *The Counterrevolution of Slavery Politics*, p. 242.

67. August Baldwin Longstreet, the president of four of the South's most distinguished universities in succession, joined the chorus of denunciations and ensured that southern students would be raised free from such evil philosophical influences.

68. James Warley Miles. For more, see: George C. Rable, *God's Almost Chosen People: A Religious History of the American Civil War* (University of North Carolina Press, 2010); Mitchell Snay, *Gospel of Disunion: Religion and Separatism in the Antebellum South* (University of North Carolina Press, 1993); *Christian Standard* (Charleston, SC), June 21, 1854; CWTP 6.135; *Richmond Examiner*, June 30, 1854; CWTP 6.134.

69. *Macon Telegraph*, February 7, 1861.

70. *Central Presbyterian*, March 22, 1856; John R. McKivigan and Michael Snay, *Religion and the Antebellum Debate over Slavery* (University of Georgia Press, 1998), p. 18.
71. "Narrative on the State of Religion," in *Minutes of the General Assembly of the Presbyterian Church of the Confederate States of America* (Presbyterian Board of Publication, 1862); see also Randall Miller, Harry Stout, and Charles Wilson, eds., *Religion and the American Civil War* (Oxford University Press, 1998), esp. the essay by Eugene Genovese.
72. Larry E. Tise, *Proslavery: A History of the Defense of Slavery in America, 1701–1840* (University of Georgia Press, 1987), p. 143.
73. LWFD 3.329.
74. "The popular religion of New England teaches that it is Christian to buy Slaves, sell Slaves, and make Slaves," in CWTP 6.9.
75. "Christianity not only permits, but in supposable circumstances enjoins the continuance of a master's authority"; see Foster, *The Brotherhood of Thieves*, p. 37.
76. "The precepts of the New Testament . . . beyond all question, recognize the existence of slavery." See also Moses Stuart, *Conscience and the Constitution, with Remarks on the Recent Speech of the Honorable Daniel Webster* (Crocker & Brewster, 1850).
77. Any criticism of slavery is "dishonorable to God, and subversive of his government," cited in McKivigan, *The War against Proslavery Religion*, p. 30.
78. The Fugitive Slave Act is in no way "contrary to the Law of God." This information is available on the Yale Slavery and Abolition website, yaleslavery.org.
79. Hopkins, *Scriptural, Ecclesiastical, and Historical View of Slavery*, p. 5; and John Henry Hopkins, *The Bible View of Slavery* (Saunders, Otley, 1863), p. 6; see also reference to Hopkins in William Craft, *Running a Thousand Miles for Freedom* (William Tweedie, 1860), pp. 97ff.
80. See McKivigan, *The War against Proslavery Religion*.
81. CWTP 6.128.
82. "Letters to Forsyth," in Timothy Byrnes, *Catholic Bishops in American Politics* (Princeton Legacy Library, 1991).
83. Cited in Noll, *The Civil War as a Theological Crisis*.
84. LWFD 3.330.
85. With regard to a representative abolitionist petition, Parker adds, "No minister of any *famous* church signed the Anti-Slavery Protest" (CWTP 6.74). Parker observes that slavery "has long found its most effectual support in the American church." The American Tract Society of Boston, he scathingly notes, distributed 3,334,920 tracts—"not a word against Slavery in them all"; the New York Society disbursed $406,707 for the same purpose—"and it did not

print one single line or whisper a single word" against slavery. The Methodists of New York issued 2,000 bound volumes every day, and 2,000 pamphlets— "there is not a single line in them all against Slavery." See CWTP 6.144.

86. FDP 3.2.238.
87. *North Star*, April 7, 1848.
88. LWFD 3.499.

4 / WELCOME INFIDELITY!

1. Holly Jackson, *American Radicals: How Protest Shaped the Nineteenth Century* (Crown, 2019), p. 93.
2. Lawrence B. Goodheart, *Abolitionist, Actuary, Atheist: Elizur Wright and the Reform Impulse* (Kent State University Press, 1990), p. 80.
3. Samuel Brooke, *Slavery, and the Slaveholder's Religion* (Cincinnati, 1845), p. 30; "Anti-slavery will triumph, but only on the ruins of the American Church," predicted Henry C. Wright (*The Liberator*, June 20, 1851); "The American church is the mighty bulwark of American slavery, the haughty, corrupt, implacable, and impious foe of the Anti-Slavery movement," Garrison said (New England Anti-Slavery Convention, May 1852); these and other anti-church sentiments were bundled together as evidence for the belligerence, malignancy, and destructiveness of abolitionism in Joseph C. Stiles, *Modern Reform Examined, or The Union of North and South on the Subject of Slavery* (Lippincott, 1857), p. 276.
4. LWFD 2.197.
5. FDA 97.
6. LWFD 2.60.
7. Henry Steele Commager, *Theodore Parker* (Beacon Press, 1947).
8. CWTP 12.191.
9. Elizabeth Cady Stanton, "Theodore Parker," *The Index: A Weekly Paper*, August 5, 1886, 7.6.65.
10. Mark W. Harris, "Caroline Dall," *Dictionary of Unitarian and Universalist Biography* (Rowman, Littlefield, 2018), p. 161; Dean Grodzins, *American Heretic: Theodore Parker and Transcendentalism* (University of North Carolina Press, 2002).
11. LWFD 4.454; FDA 1015.
12. CWTP 8.449.
13. CWTP 9.11.
14. CWTP 6.43.
15. CWTP 6.17. And also this: "I have known some men who take the ghastly and dreadful name of Atheists; but they said, 'there is a law higher than the slaveholder's statute.' But do you know a Catholic priest that is opposed to slavery? I wish I did."

16. Letter to M. A. H. Niles, March 4, 1845, MHS; CWTP 4.282.
17. Letter to S. P. Chase, 1854, MHS; CWTP 2.226.
18. *The Liberator*, November 14, 1851.
19. Henry C. Wright, *The Errors of the Bible, Demonstrated by the Truths of Nature* (Bela Marsh, 1858).
20. *The Liberator*, May 11, 1848.
21. Garrison at Fifth National Convention of women's suffrage, October 14, 1854, cited in Elizabeth Cady Stanton et al., eds., *History of Woman Suffrage* (Susan B. Anthony, 1889) 1.383.
22. Mary Elizabeth Burtis, *Moncure Conway, 1832–1907* (Rutgers University Press, 1952).
23. Mischa Honeck, *We Are the Revolutionists: German-Speaking Immigrants and Abolitionists after 1848* (University of Georgia Press, 2011), p. 91.
24. Gerrit Smith, *Three Discourses on the Religion of Reason* (Ross & Toussey, 1859). In a debate with a Congregationalist minister, the indefatigable Smith echoes Parker when he declares that his opponent "sees no hope for freedom, if the Bible shall be given to the side of slavery. But I see no hope for the Bible if it shall be proved to be for slavery." In a typical bid to recover the sheen of orthodoxy, he adds that "the religion which Jesus so perfectly illustrated . . . was no other than the religion of reason—that one and only true religion which is adapted to all ages and to all peoples." This, of course, was the gesture passed down from Spinoza and Locke through the philosophers of Germany to Parker, and it cut no ice with the defenders of the faith.
25. *The Presbyterian Magazine* (Joseph M. Wilson, 1859), 9.9.397, 407.
26. Honeck, *We Are the Revolutionists*, p. 145.
27. John R. McKivigan and Michael Snay, *Religion and the Antebellum Debate over Slavery* (University of Georgia Press, 1998), p. 254.
28. G. Frederick Wright, *A Biography of Charles Grandison Finney* (Oberlin, 1891), chap. 6.
29. Paul E. Teed, *A Revolutionary Conscience: Theodore Parker and Antebellum America* (University Press of America, 2012), p. 202; CWTP 3.243, 211, 231 ("The Revival We Need"; "A False and True Revival of Religion").
30. For more detail on Finney, see McKivigan and Snay, *Religion and the Antebellum Debate over Slavery*.
31. John Rock, "Address to the Massachusetts Anti-Slavery Society," January 23, 1862, reprinted in *The Liberator*, February 14, 1862.
32. Gilbert Hobbe Barnes, *The Antislavery Impulse: 1830–1844* (Peter Smith Publishing, 1964).
33. Kerri Greenridge, *The Grimkes: The Legacy of Slavery in an American Family* (W. W. Norton, 2022).
34. LWFD 2.524.

35. Thornton Stringfellow, *Scriptural and Statistical Views in Favor of Slavery* (Randolph, 1856), p. 31.

36. Thornwell, *Collected Writings of James Henley Thornwell*, 4.405.

37. Cited in Larry E. Tise, *Proslavery: A History of the Defense of Slavery in America, 1701–1840* (University of Georgia Press, 1987), pp. 258, 259.

38. Mark A. Noll, *The Civil War as a Theological Crisis* (University of North Carolina Press, 2006), p. 32.

39. Kimberly Nichols, "The Red Harlot of Infidelity: The Rise and Fall of Frances Wright," *Newtopia Magazine*, May 15, 2013.

40. LWFD 1.162.

41. Alexis de Tocqueville, *Democracy in America* (Sounders & Otley, 1835), 1.59–60.

42. Jon Butler, *Becoming America: The Revolution before 1776* (Harvard University Press, 2000); Jon Butler, *Religion in American Life: A Short History* (Oxford University Press, 2011); and Nathan O. Hatch, *The Democratization of American Christianity* (Yale University Press, 1989).

43. Clement Eaton, *The Freedom-of-Thought Struggle in the Old South* (Harper, 1964), p. 376.

44. Tocqueville, *Democracy in America*, 2.1.7.417ff.

45. Eaton, *Freedom-of-Thought Struggle in the Old South*, p. 226.

46. David Blight, *Frederick Douglass: Prophet of Freedom* (Simon & Schuster, 2018), p. 329.

47. LWFD 2.538–40.

48. LWFD 3.328.

49. CWTP 6.302.

50. Theodore Parker, "A Letter to the People of the United States Touching the Matter of Slavery" (James Munroe, 1848), p. 71.

51. CWAL 3.204.

52. CWAL 3.205.

53. RWAL, p. 25.

5 / WITH ALL NATIONS

1. Maria Diedrich, *Love across the Color Lines: Ottilie Assing and Frederick Douglass* (Hill & Wang, 1999).

2. Jonathan Israel, *The Expanding Blaze: How the American Revolution Ignited the World, 1775–1848* (Princeton University Press, 2017), p. 586.

3. Israel, *The Expanding Blaze*, p. 550.

4. CWTP 5.89.

5. *North Star*, April 28, 1848; and August 4, 1848.

6. LWFD 3.497.

7. There is a continuing discussion about whether Fuller married her lover Giovanni Ossoli in secret or simply had a baby with him, and it starts

with the biography written by her admiring friend, Thomas Wentworth Higginson, *Margaret Fuller Ossoli* (Houghton Mifflin, 1884).

8. Margaret Fuller, *Memoirs of Margaret Fuller* (Philips, Samson, 1852), 2.172.

9. Theodore Parker himself cites the line from Webster in a scathing anti-eulogy, *A Discourse Occasioned by the Death of Daniel Webster* (John Robertson, 1853), p. 17.

10. *The Pro-Slavery Argument, as Maintained by the Most Distinguished Writers of the Southern States* (Lippincott, Grambo, 1853), pp. 149, 172.

11. Matthew Stewart, *Monturiol's Dream: The Extraordinary Story of the Submarine Inventor Who Wanted to Save the World* (Pantheon, 2003).

12. Elisabeth Hurth, *Between Faith and Unbelief: American Transcendentalists and the Challenge of Atheism* (Brill, 2007), p. 115.

13. Friedrich Kapp, *Die Sklavenfrage in den Vereinigten Staaten* (Goettingen, 1854).

14. Mischa Honeck, *We Are the Revolutionists: German-Speaking Immigrants and Abolitionists after 1848* (University of Georgia Press, 2011), p. 22.

15. Kapp to Becker, 1857, in Honeck, *We Are the Revolutionists*, p. 196.

16. *Cincinnati Republikaner*, December 6, 1858; Honeck, *We Are the Revolutionists*, p. 84.

17. *Cincinnati Republikaner*, January 5, 1860.

18. Honeck, *We Are the Revolutionists*.

19. Eleanor Jones Harvey, *Alexander von Humboldt and the United States* (Princeton University Press, 2020).

20. *Morgenblatt für gebildete Leser*, June 24, 1860, 26.619.

21. *The Liberator*, July 9, 1858.

22. G. W. F. Hegel, *The Philosophy of History* (Cosimo, 2007), p. 88.

23. Walt Whitman, *Notebooks* (New York University Press, 2007), 6.2011.

24. Honeck, *We Are the Revolutionists*, p. 156.

25. Honeck, *We Are the Revolutionists*, pp. 86–90.

26. FDP 1.3.256; LWFD 4.254.

27. Tamara Felden, *Frauen Reisen* (Peter Lang, 1993), p. 118.

28. Felden, *Frauen Reisen*, p. 120.

29. For more on the material in this chapter, see Diedrich, *Love across the Color Lines*.

30. Diedrich, *Love across the Color Lines*, pp. 138ff.; David Blight, *Frederick Douglass: Prophet of Freedom* (Simon & Schuster, 2018), pp. 290ff.; *Sclaverei und Freiheit: Autobiographie von Frederick Douglass aus dem Englischen uebertragen von Ottilie Assing* (Hoffman, 1860).

31. Maria Diedrich imagines the encounter for us with a fictionalized dialogue of the first encounter between Assing and Douglass; Diedrich, *Love across the Color Lines*, pp. 130–36.

32. Terry H. Pickett, "The Friendship of Frederick Douglass with the German,

Ottilie Assing," *Georgia Historical Quarterly*, 53, no. 1 (Spring 1989), p. 100; Felden, *Frauen Reisen*, p. 123.

33. Felden, *Frauen Reisen*, p. 124; *Morgenblatt für gebildete Leser*, July 19, 1857, 29.696.
34. Pickett, "The Friendship of Frederick Douglass with the German, Ottilie Assing," p. 102.
35. Felden, *Frauen Reisen*, p. 113, *Morgenblatt für gebildete Leser*, January 11, 1857, 2.47.
36. Sudhir Hazareesingh, *Black Spartacus: The Epic Life of Toussaint Louverture* (Picador, 2020), p. 67.

6 / EVERY DROP OF BLOOD

1. FDA 60–66, 258–87, 563–92; the growing page counts in the three autobiographies provide a rough indication of the growing importance of the parable of Covey for Douglass.
2. Daniel Victor, "Bill O'Reilly Defends Comments about 'Well-Fed' Slaves," *New York Times*, July 27, 2016.
3. Thornton Stringfellow, *Scriptural and Statistical Views in Favor of Slavery* (Randolph, 1856).
4. Richard Fuller and Francis Wayland, *Domestic Slavery Considered as a Scriptural Institution* (Mercer University Press, 2008), p. 8.
5. FDA 321.
6. James W. C. Pennington makes the same point: "The cart whip, starvation, nakedness" are direct "consequences" of "the chattel principle. Talk not then about kind and Christian masters. They are not masters of the system. The system is the master of them." James Pennington, *The Fugitive Blacksmith* (Charles Gilpin, 1849), p. iv.
7. CWTP 5.31.
8. LWFD 4.381.
9. Douglass dates it 1847 in FDA 719, though his biographers and the chronology indicate that it was probably 1848. The Douglass quotes in this chapter are from FDA 714–20.
10. See Thomas Wentworth Higginson, *The Magnificent Activist: The Writings of Thomas Wentworth Higginson* (Little, Brown, 2000), p. 119.
11. Cited in Stephen S. Foster, *The Brotherhood of Thieves* (William Bolles, 1843), p. 15.
12. FDA 719.
13. *North Star*, May 26, 1848; LWFD 2.546, 1.359.
14. *The Liberator*, June 8, 1849.
15. LWFD 2.286.
16. FDA 286.

17. Frederick Douglass: *A Critical Reader* (Wiley-Blackwell, 1998), p. 280.

18. For more on the Craft affair and the fugitive crisis in Boston, see Theodore Parker, *Memoranda of the Troubles Occasioned by the Infamous Fugitive Slave Law from March 15, 1851, to February 19, 1856*, Boston Public Library Special Collections; Peter Wirzbicki, *Fighting for the Higher Law: Black and White Transcendentalists against Slavery* (University of Pennsylvania Press, 2021); Gordon S. Barker, *Fugitive Slaves and the Unfinished American Revolution: Eight Cases, 1848–1856* (McFarland, 2013); *North Star*, October 31, 1850, and December 5, 1850; *The Liberator*, November 1, 1850; R. J. M. Blackett, *Beating against the Barriers* (Cornell University Press, 1986), pp. 87–137; James Oliver Horton and Lois Horton, *Hard Road to Freedom* (Rutgers University Press, 2001), p. 154.

19. FDP 3.1.434.

20. William and Ellen Craft, *Running a Thousand Miles for Freedom* (University of Georgia Press, 1999).

21. CWTP 6.194, 6.193; the Boston Public Library contains a valuable collection of materials from the Vigilance Committee of Boston, collected by Parker himself and turned over by his wife in 1873.

22. Frederic May Holland, *Frederick Douglass: The Colored Orator* (Funk & Wagnalls, 1895), p. 187.

23. CWTP 6.148.

24. Barker, *Fugitive Slaves and the Unfinished American Revolution*, pp. 98–99; Harriet Beecher Stowe, *A Key to Uncle Tom's Cabin* (Clarke, Beeton, 1853), 1.378.

25. CWTP 6.148.

26. Paul E. Teed, A *Revolutionary Conscience: Theodore Parker and Antebellum America* (University Press of America, 2012), p. 136.

27. CWTP 2.97.

28. Theodore Parker, *Discourse Occasioned by the Death of Daniel Webster* (John Robertson, 1853), p. 17.

29. Theodore Parker, *The Trial of Theodore Parker* (Boston: Published for the Author, 1855), p. 187.

30. Barker, *Fugitive Slaves and the Unfinished American Revolution*.

31. Ralph Waldo Emerson, "Lecture on the Times," in *Works of Ralph Waldo Emerson* (Houghton Mifflin, 2019), 5.227.

32. Ralph Waldo Emerson, *Emerson's Antislavery Writings*, ed. Leo Gourgeon (Yale University Press, 1995), p. 85.

33. Ralph Waldo Emerson, *The Prose Works* (Houghton, Osgood, 1880), 3.148.

34. Parker, *Trial of Theodore Parker*, p. 188.

35. Wirzbicki, *Fighting for the Higher Law*; Barker, *Fugitive Slaves and the Unfinished American Revolution*.

36. CWTP 6.289f.

37. Letter to Wasson, December 12, 1857, MHS.
38. John Weiss, ed., *Life and Correspondence of Theodore Parker* (D. Appleton, 1864), 1.397.
39. *The Liberator*, May 23, 1856.
40. Wirzbicki, *Fighting for the Higher Law*, pp. 194ff.
41. *The Liberator*, June 6, 1856.
42. Parker to George Bancroft, March 16, 1858, MHS.
43. Jonathan Katz, *Resistance at Christiana* (Crowell, 1974), p. 336.
44. FDA 1016.
45. FDA 756f.
46. Tamara Felden, *Frauen Reisen* (Peter Lang, 1993).
47. On the relation between Brown and Parker (and the rest of the Secret Six; discussed in Part 10), see Jeffrey Rossbach, *Ambivalent Conspirators: John Brown, the Secret Six, and a Theory of Slave Violence* (University of Pennsylvania Press, 1982).
48. Teed, *Revolutionary Conscience*, p. 207.
49. Parker to Herndon, November 17, 1856, MHS.
50. Teed, *Revolutionary Conscience*, pp. 207–11.
51. Wendell Phillips Garrison and Francis Jackson Garrison, *William Lloyd Garrison: The Story of His Life Told by His Children* (Century, 1889), 3.188.
52. Barker, *Fugitive Slaves and the Unfinished American Revolution*, p. 18.
53. Parker, *Trial of Theodore Parker*, p. 201.

7 / ALL THE WEALTH . . .

1. FDA 355.
2. W. E. B. Du Bois, *Black Reconstruction in America* (Taylor & Francis, 2017), p. 24.
3. Philip S. Foner and Yuval Taylor, *Frederick Douglass: Selected Writings* (Chicago Review, 2000), p. 522.
4. John Henry Hammond, in Paul Finkelman, *Defending Slavery: Proslavery Thought in the Old South* (Bedford/St. Martin's Press, 2003), pp. 86–87.
5. Hammond, in Finkelman, *Defending Slavery*: "The man who lives by daily labor . . . your whole hireling class of manual laborers . . . are essentially slaves."
6. William Harper, *Memoir of Slavery*, in Drew Gilpin Faust, ed., *The Ideology of Slavery: Proslavery Thought in the Antebellum South, 1830–60* (Louisiana State University Press, 1981), p. 95.
7. Foner and Taylor, *Frederick Douglass*, p. 522.
8. CWTP 13.349.
9. Paul E. Teed, *A Revolutionary Conscience: Theodore Parker and Antebellum America* (University Press of America, 2012), p. 148.

10. CWTP 6.292.

11. Frederick Law Olmsted, *The Cotton Kingdom* (Mason Brothers, 1862), 1.13.

12. William Goodell, *Slavery and Anti-Slavery* (William Harned, 1852), 2.134.

13. See Keri Leigh Merritt, *Masterless Men: Poor Whites and Slavery in the Antebellum South* (Cambridge University Press, 2017).

14. Hinton Rowan Helper, *The Impending Crisis of the South and How to Meet It* (A. A. Burdick, 1859).

15. CWTP 5.312; Theodore Parker, *The Liberator*, December 12, 1854.

16. Edward Baptist, *The Half Has Never Been Told: Slavery and the Making of American Capitalism* (Basic Books, 2014).

17. CWTP 5.312, 6.73. Among forward-thinking abolitionists, the reliance of southern slavery on northern military investment was a constant source of outrage. In his harangue against the proslavery churches, Stephen S. Foster sarcastically observed that the slaveholding states "are indebted for a permanent safeguard against insurrection" to the free states; see Stephen S. Foster, *The Brotherhood of Thieves* (William Bolles, 1843).

18. *The Liberator*, April 21, 1848.

19. Theodore Parker, *Saint Bernard and Other Papers* (American Unitarian Association, 1911), p. 347.

20. CWTP 6.110.

21. Gordon S. Barker, *Fugitive Slaves and the Unfinished American Revolution: Eight Cases, 1848–1856* (McFarland, 2013), p. 46.

22. Speech of John Rock, January 23, 1862, *The Liberator*, February 14, 1862.

23. CWTP 14.189.

24. CWTP 9.120.

25. Paul E. Teed, *A Revolutionary Conscience: Theodore Parker and Antebellum America* (University Press of America, 2012), p. 79.

26. CWTP 5.296.

27. The correspondence may be found in MHS.

28. Herndon to Parker, July 29, 1857.

29. Parker to Herndon, January 1855, MHS.

30. William Herndon and Jesse William Welk, *Herndon's Lincoln* (Belford Clarke, 1889), 2.21.

31. Herndon and Welk, *Herndon's Lincoln*, 2.363.

8 / THE JUDGMENTS OF THE LORD

1. Douglass explained more about the incident in a letter of March 24, 1885, to Elizabeth Chace Wyman later published in the *New England Magazine*. Alex Schwartz, "'Is God Dead?': Frederick Douglass's Recollection of a Contentious Moment in Antislavery History," *New North Star*, 3 (2021), pp. 64–66.

2. FDA 719.

3. Matthew Stewart, *The 9.9 Percent* (Simon & Schuster, 2021); and Stewart, *Nature's God.*

4. On the pantheism controversy, see Frederick C. Beiser, *The Fate of Reason: German Philosophy from Kant to Fichte* (Harvard University Press, 2009); Gerard Vallee et al., eds., *The Spinoza Conversations between Lessing and Jacobi* (University Press of America, 1988).

5. Alexander Pope, *Essay on Man*, 1.267–68.

6. J. G. Fichte, *Addresses to the German Nation*, ed. Gregory Moore (Cambridge University Press, 2008). For more, see Allen Wood, *Fichte's Ethical Thought* (Oxford University Press, 2016).

7. Frederick Beiser, *German Idealism* (Harvard University Press, 2009), p. 472.

8. Georg Wilhelm Friedrich Hegel, *Lectures on the Philosophy of World History* (Cambridge University Press, 1980), p. 44.

9. Hegel, *Lectures on the Philosophy of World History*, p. 95.

10. Heinrich Heine, "Germany," in *The Works of Heinrich Heine* (Heinemann, 1892), 5.97.

11. *Frederick Douglass' Paper*, June 26, 1851.

12. Cited in Ludwig Feuerbach, *The Fiery Brook: Selected Writings*, ed. Zawar Hanfi (Verso, 2015).

13. Feuerbach, *The Fiery Brook.*

14. Feuerbach, *The Fiery Brook.*

15. "Geschichte der neuern Philosophie," *Gesammelte Werke* (Akademie Verlag, 1967), 2.264–66.

16. Ludwig Feuerbach, "Principles of the Philosophy of the Future," in *The Fiery Brook*, p. 15; Ludwig Feuerbach, "Zur Beurteilung der Schrift Das Wesen des Christentums," *Gesammelte Werke* (Akademie Verlag, 1967), 9.230.

17. Ludwig Feuerbach, *The Essence of Christianity* (Prometheus Books, 1989), p. 11: "God is pure, unlimited, free feeling."

18. Pope, *Essay on Man*, 1.331.

19. *The Liberator*, June 7, 1850.

20. CWTP 11.27.

21. CWTP 11.123.

22. CWTP 12.199.

23. CWTP 11.114.

24. CWTP 11.123.

25. Megan Marshall, *Margaret Fuller: A New American Life* (Houghton Mifflin Harcourt, 2013), p. 65.

26. Constantin François Volney, *Volney's Ruins, or Meditations on the Revolutions of Empires*, trans. Joel Barlow (Charles Gaylord, 1831), 2.11.

27. " 'God has given each man a back to be clothed, a mouth to be filled, and a pair of hands to work with.' And since wherever a mouth and a back are

created, a pair of hands is also provided, the inference is unavoidable, that the hands are to be used to supply the needs of the mouth and the back" (CWTP 9.119).

28. Parker to S. J. May, September 25, 1852, MHS.

29. Elisabeth Hurth, *Between Faith and Unbelief: American Transcendentalists and the Challenge of Atheism* (Brill, 2007), p. 131.

30. Feuerbach, "Zur Beurteilung der Schrift Das Wesen des Christentums," 9.230.

31. CWTP 11.83.

32. CWTP 11.4.

33. CWTP 11.103.

34. FDP 4.42.

35. LWFD 4.232.

36. LWFD 4.237.

37. LWFD 2.437.

38. FDA 189.

39. LWFD 3.336.

40. FDA 913.

41. LOC, "Abraham Lincoln, a Speech," p. 14.

42. Herndon to Parker, February 1857, MHS.

43. George Tuthill Borrett, *Letters from Canada and the United States* (J. E. Adlard, 1865), pp. 250–55.

44. CWAL 4.3.

45. Psalm 19:9.

46. William Herndon to Edward McPherson, February 4, 1866, cited in Douglas L. Wilson and Rodney O. Davis, eds., *Herndon on Lincoln: Letters* (University of Illinois Press, 2016).

47. Volney, *Volney's Ruins*, 1.21.

9 / THE SWEAT OF OTHER MEN'S FACES

1. Keri Leigh Merritt, *Masterless Men: Poor Whites and Slavery in the Antebellum South* (Cambridge University Press, 2017), p. 73. Merritt cites average wages of $7 to $8 per month for farmhands in the southern states (as against $13 per month in the northern states). Frederick appears to have earned as much as $9 per week. Even half that amount would put him at double the southern average wage and above the northern average wage.

2. FDA 341.

3. FDA 83.

4. FDA 553.

5. FDA 337.

6. G. W. F. Hegel, *Phaenomenologie des Geistes*, IV.A. "Selbstaendigkeit und

Unselbstaendigkeit des Selbstbewusstseyns; Herrschaft und Knechtschaft," in *G. W. F. Hegel: Gesammelte Werke* (Felix Meiner, 1968–), 9.109–15.

7. J. G. Fichte, *Sammtliche Werke* (de Gruyter, 1970), 3.39; "If there are to be human beings at all, there must be more than one"; Fichte, *Sammtliche Werke*, 1.440.

8. Fichte, *Sammtliche Werke*, 3.39.

9. Fichte, *Sammtliche Werke*, 1.189.

10. Hegel, *Phaenomenologie des Geistes*, 9.103.

11. Hegel, *Phaenomenologie des Geistes*, 9.108.

12. Ludwig Feuerbach, *The Essence of Christianity* (Prometheus, 1989), esp. chap. I.

13. "The great thing in Hegel's *Phenomenology* and its final result . . . is that Hegel conceives the self-creation of man as a process, objectification as loss of object, as alienation, and as sublation of this alienation; that therefore he grasps the nature of labor and conceives objective man as the result of his own labor"; Karl Marx, "Critique of Hegel's Philosophy in General," *Economic and Philosophic Manuscripts of 1844*, XXIII. And also this: Consciousness benefits from labor first in enjoying the "individual manifestation of my life during the activity." It benefits again when, in contemplating the fruit of its labor, it has "the individual pleasure of knowing my personality to be objective." It benefits third and above all when another consciousness puts its product to use, for now it is "conscious of having satisfied a human need, that is, of having objectified man's essential nature, and having thus created an object corresponding to the need of another man's essential nature"; Karl Marx, "Comment on James Mill, *Elements of Political Economy*," 1844, available in Karl Marx and Friedrich Engels, *Gesamtasugabe* (Berlin, 1932), 1.3.

14. Ludwig Feuerbach, "Towards a Critique of Hegel's Philosophy," in *The Fiery Brook: Selected Writings*, ed. Zawar Hanfi (Verso, 2015).

15. Feuerbach, *Essence of Christianity*, chap. VIII, "The Mystery of the Cosmological Principle," p. 81.

16. Ludwig Feuerbach, *Gesammelte Werke* (Akademie Verlag, 1967), 1.18.

17. G. W. F. Hegel, "Encyclopedie: Philosophie des Geistes," in *G. W. F. Hegel: Gesammelte Werke* (Felix Meiner, 1968–), 13.199.

18. The long history of Hegel as avatar of German nationalism begins with the First World War and receives a definitive statement in Karl Popper, *The Open Society and Its Enemies* (Routledge, 2003).

19. See, for example, Charles Taylor, *Philosophical Papers* (Cambridge University Press, 1985); and Charles Taylor, *A Secular Age* (Harvard University Press, 2007).

20. G. W. F. Hegel, *Philosophie des Rechts*, in *G. W. F. Hegel: Gesammelte Werke* (Felix Meiner, 1968–), 14.1.71.

21. G. W. F. Hegel, "Jena Lectures 1805–6," in *G. W. F. Hegel: Gesammelte Werke* (Felix Meiner, 1968–), 8.223.

22. FDA 144–45.

23. FDA 192.

24. FDA 169.

25. LWFD 4.345.

26. FDA 374; LWFD 518–21.

27. FDA 805.

28. LWFD 4.117.

29. Philip Foner, ed., *Frederick Douglass: Selected Speeches and Writings* (Lawrence Hill, 1999), p. 722.

30. LWFD 4.492.

31. "Pictures and Progress," p. 5; see Bibliographical Appendix.

32. "Pictures and Progress," vol. 4, p. 519.

33. Raoul Peck, *I Am Not Your Negro* (film), 2017.

34. W. E. B. Du Bois, *The Souls of Black Folk* (Dover Publications, 2016), p. 2.

35. There is an interesting parallel here with Eric Williams, *Capitalism and Slavery* (1944; repr. Penguin, 2022).

36. Dean Grodzins, *American Heretic: Theodore Parker and Transcendentalism* (University of North Carolina Press, 2002).

37. Charles A. Sheffield, ed., *The History of Florence, Massachusetts, Including a Complete Account of the Northampton Association of Education and Industry* (Published by the Editor, 1895), p. 126; Andrew Zimmerman, "From the Rhine to Mississippi: Property, Democracy and Socialism in the American Civil War," *Journal of the Civil War Era*, 5, no. 1 (March 2015), 3–37.

38. Betty Fladeland, "Our Cause Being One and the Same: Abolitionists and Chartism," in *Slavery and British Society 1776–1846*, ed. James Walvin (Louisiana State University Press, 1982), pp. 69–99.

39. Peter Wirzbicki, *Fighting for the Higher Law: Black and White Transcendentalists against Slavery* (University of Pennsylvania Press, 2021).

40. Barker, *Fugitive Slaves and the Unfinished American Revolution*, p. 33.

41. CWTP 5.89.

42. Speech of John Rock, January 23, 1862, *The Liberator*, February 14, 1862.

43. "Political Economy," *National Era*, October 6, 1859; "The Poor Whites of the South," *North Star*, March 1, 1850.

44. J. G. Palfrey, *North Star*, 1848, cited in Keri Leigh Merritt, *Masterless Men* (Cambridge University Press, 2017), p. 36; LWFD 4.289.

45. Jefferson Davis, *The Essential Writings*, ed. William J. Cooper (Random House, 2004), p. 160.

46. Karl Marx, *Capital: A Critique of Political Economy* (Modern Library, 1906), 1.329. Du Bois makes the same point and extends it into the Jim Crow

period: "So long as the southern white laborers could be induced to prefer poverty to equality with the Negro, just so long was a labor movement in the South made impossible."

47. One source in the secondary literature that identifies this theory and helpfully expounds upon it is Jeffrey Rossbach, *Ambivalent Conspirators: John Brown, the Secret Six, and a Theory of Slave Violence* (University of Pennsylvania Press, 1982).
48. Henry Steele Commager, *Theodore Parker* (Beacon Press, 1947), p. 250.
49. Theodore Parker, *The Trial of Theodore Parker* (Boston: Published for the Author, 1855), p. 184.
50. Thomas Wentworth Higginson, speech at New York Anti-Slavery Society, May 12, 1858, cited in Rossbach, *Ambivalent Conspirators*, p. 168.
51. Rossbach, *Ambivalent Conspirators*, p. 154.
52. Sidney Blumenthal, *A Self-Made Man: The Political Life of Abraham Lincoln, Volume 1: 1809–1849* (Simon & Schuster, 2016), p. 3.
53. LWFD 4.317.
54. FDA 923.
55. CWAL 3.480.
56. CWAL 3.478–80.
57. CWAL 3.463.
58. CWAL 5.52.
59. Marx and Engels, *The Civil War in the United States*, p. 154.
60. Marx and Engels, *The Civil War in the United States*, p. 61.
61. Marx and Engels, *The Civil War in the United States*, p. 133.
62. Marx and Engels, *The Civil War in the United States*, p. 154.
63. CWAL 3.374–76.
64. CWTP 7.101.
65. CWAL 3.315.

10 / AND THE WAR CAME

1. Parker to May, October 26, 1856, MHS.
2. Paul E. Teed, *A Revolutionary Conscience: Theodore Parker and Antebellum America* (University Press of America, 2012), p. 209.
3. FDA 757.
4. Joseph Fort Newton, *Lincoln and Herndon* (Torch Press, 1910), p. 154.
5. William Herndon and Jesse William Welk, *Herndon's Lincoln* (Belford Clarke, 1889), 2.396.
6. CWTP 8.132.
7. CWTP 7.292.
8. Herndon and Welk, *Herndon's Lincoln*, 2.396; CWTP 6.245.
9. Parker uses essentially the same words in his letter to Herndon that he

uses in published texts. See Parker to Herndon, September 4, 1858, MHS; Theodore Parker, *The Trial of Theodore Parker* (Boston: Published for the Author, 1855), p. 10.

10. In a letter to Herndon, Parker puts the matter before the nation this way: "Shall we admit Slavery as a Principle and found a Despotism, or Freedom as a Principle and found a Democracy." See Parker to Herndon, September 4, 1858, MHS.
11. CWTP 6.132.
12. CWAL 2.461–69; 2.452 for draft of speech.
13. Sidney Blumenthal, *All the Powers of the Earth: The Political Life of Abraham Lincoln, 1856–60* (Simon & Schuster, 2019), p. 414.
14. CWTP 6.115.
15. Herndon and Welk, *Herndon's Lincoln*, 2.399f.
16. CWAL 2.501.
17. Blumenthal, *All the Powers of the Earth*, p. 429.
18. William Jennings Bryan, ed., *The World's Famous Orations, Volume IX* (Funk & Wagnalls, 1906).
19. CWTP 3.275.
20. Teed, *Revolutionary Conscience*, p. 225.
21. Teed, *Revolutionary Conscience*, p. 222.
22. Teed, *Revolutionary Conscience*, p. 229.
23. CWTP 12.271.
24. CWTP 12.150ff.
25. Teed, *Revolutionary Conscience*, p. 227.
26. Maria Diedrich, *Love across the Color Lines: Ottilie Assing and Frederick Douglass* (Hill & Wang, 1999), p. 227.
27. Diedrich, *Love across the Color Lines*, p. 104.
28. Tamara Felden, *Frauen Reisen* (Peter Lang, 1993), p. 125; *Morgenblatt für gebildete Leser*, December 18, 1859, 51.1223.
29. "Pictures and Progress," LOC mfd.28009, p. 1; text also available in John Stauffer et al., eds., *Picturing Frederick Douglass: An Illustrated Biography of the Nineteenth Century's Most Photographed American* (Liveright, 2015).
30. "Pictures and Progress," LOC mfd.28009, p. 11.
31. "Lecture on Pictures" and "Pictures and Progress," in Stauffer et al., *Picturing Frederick Douglass*.
32. FDP 1.3.255.
33. This and subsequent taken from "Age of Pictures" in Stauffer et al., *Picturing Frederick Douglass*.
34. "Age of Pictures," in Stauffer et al., *Picturing Frederick Douglass*.
35. Ludwig Feuerbach, *The Essence of Christianity* (Prometheus Books, 1989), chap. I.
36. "Age of Pictures," in Stauffer et al., *Picturing Frederick Douglass*.

37. Compare Feuerbach, *Essence of Christianity*, Second Preface, p. xvi: "religion itself, not indeed on the surface, but fundamentally . . . believes in nothing else than the truth and divinity of human nature."
38. "Pictures and Progress," LOC mfd.28009, p. 4.
39. "Pictures and Progress," LOC mfd.28009, p. 22.
40. "Lecture on Pictures," in Stauffer et al., *Picturing Frederick Douglass*.
41. Diedrich, *Love across the Color Lines*, p. 229.
42. Harvey Kaye, *Thomas Paine and the Promise of America* (Hill & Wang, 2005), p. 155; Stephen B. Oates, *To Purge This Land with Blood: A Biography of John Brown* (University of Massachusetts Press, 1984), p. 280; Thomas Wentworth Higginson, *The Magnificent Activist: The Writings of Thomas Wentworth Higginson*, ed. Howard N. Meyer (Da Capo, 2000).
43. FDA 758–80.
44. Osborne P. Anderson, "A Voice from Harpers Ferry" (Boston, 1861).
45. Mischa Honeck, *We Are the Revolutionists: German-Speaking Immigrants and Abolitionists after 1848* (University of Georgia Press, 2011), pp. 94, 114.
46. Herndon to Parker, December 15, 1859, MHS.
47. Diedrich, *Love across the Color Lines*, p. 219.
48. Diedrich, *Love across the Color Lines*, p. 221; also Felden, *Frauen Reisen*.
49. George Willis Cooke, *Ralph Waldo Emerson: His Life, Writings, and Philosophy* (James B. Osgood, 1882), p. 140.
50. See David Blight, *Frederick Douglass: Prophet of Freedom* (Simon & Schuster, 2018), p. 306.
51. CWTP, 12.164–77.
52. Autobiographical Writings in CWTP, 12.165; letter on John Brown, from Rome, November 24, 1859.
53. CWTP 12.174.
54. Franklin Sanborn, "Introduction," in Newton, *Lincoln and Herndon*.
55. Teed, *Revolutionary Conscience*, p. 239.
56. "John Brown's Body" was a popular ballad created two years earlier by a Boston garrison of their fellow Massachusetts soldiers.
57. LWFD 3.186; FDP 1.3.520, "The War and How to End It," March 25, 1862; see Blight, *Frederick Douglass*.
58. FDA 780; LWFD 3.186.
59. CWAL 5.537.
60. CWAL 6.150, March 26, 1863.
61. W. E. B. Du Bois, *Black Reconstruction in America* (Taylor & Francis, 2017), p. 82.
62. Marx and Engels, *The Civil War in the United States*, p. 121.
63. FDA 778.
64. FDA 780.
65. FDA 780.

66. FDP 1.3.520.
67. FDA 796.
68. Some sources estimate 180,000 Black troops, others estimate 200,000.
69. *Morgenblatt für gebildete Leser*, April 2, 1863, 14.332; Felden, *Frauen Reisen*.
70. *Morgenblatt für gebildete Leser*, September 24, 1865, 39.924; Felden, *Frauen Reisen*.
71. Thomas Wentworth Higginson, *Army Life in a Black Regiment* (Fields, 1870), p. 267.
72. Philip Klinkner and Rogers Smith, *The Unsteady March: The Rise and Decline of Racial Inequality in America* (University of Chicago Press, 1998), p. 69.

Afterword / LET US STRIVE ON

1. Frederick Douglass, *The Life and Writings of Frederick Douglass*, ed. Philip S. Foner (International Publishers, 1955), 4.169.
2. William Wolf, *The Religion of Abraham Lincoln* (Seabury Press, 1963), p. 192.
3. Reinhold Niebuhr, "The Religion of Abraham Lincoln," in *Lincoln and the Gettysburg Address*, ed. Allan Nevins (University of Illinois Press, 1964), p. 77.
4. Allen Guelzo, *Abraham Lincoln: Redeemer President* (Eerdmans, 1999), p. 18. On the other hand, Guelzo appears to recognize that attributing Lincoln's necessitarianism to the fact he was brought up around backcountry Calvinists is a rather thin claim; see Allen Guelzo, *Abraham Lincoln as a Man of Ideas* (Southern Illinois University Press, 2016).
5. W. E. B. Du Bois, *Black Reconstruction in America* (Taylor & Francis, 2017).
6. CWTP 2.48.
7. See in particular Martin Luther King Jr., "The Sources of Fundamentalism and Liberalism Considered Historically and Psychologically," and "The Weakness of Liberal Theology," in *The Papers of Martin Luther King, Jr., Volume I*, ed. Clayborn Carson et al. (Stanford University Press, 2007).
8. Douglass receives little notice in late nineteenth-century histories such as John B. McMasters, *History of the People of the United States* (Blackwells, 2018) and James Ford Rhodes, *History of the United States* (Macmillan, 1892).
9. For more on the connection between racism, proslavery theology, Jim Crow, and Christian nationalism, see also Anthea Butler, *White Evangelical Racism* (University of North Carolina Press, 2021); Jamar Tisby, *The Color of Compromise: The Truth about the American Church's Complicity in Racism* (Zondervan, 2020).
10. Robert Lewis Dabney, *Discussions*, ed. C. H. Vaugh (Sprinkle Publications, 1994), 4.177.
11. Although the genealogy is too involved to detail here, it is worth mentioning that a central figure who connects proslavery theologians such as Robert

Lewis Dabney with modern Christian nationalist activists such as Gary North and David Barton is the highly influential Rousas John Rushdoony. See R. J. Rushdoony, *Institutes of Biblical Law* (Craig Press, 1973); and R. J. Rushdoony, *Systematic Theology* (Ross House Books, 2000); Julie Ingersoll, *Building God's Kingdom* (Oxford University Press, 2015); Katherine Stewart, *The Power Worshippers* (Bloomsbury, 2020).

12. Katherine Stewart, "A Founder of American Religious Nationalism," *History News Network*, March 3, 2020.

13. LWFD 4.109.

14. Charles Mills, *The Racial Contract* (Cornell University Press, 1997).

15. Ibram X. Kendi, *Stamped from the Beginning: The Definitive History of Racist Ideas in America* (Penguin, 2016).

16. Ta-Nehisi Coates, *Between the World and Me* (Spiegel and Grau, 2015).

17. The point is made well in Heather MacGhee, *The Sum of Us* (Penguin, 2021).

18. See Matthew Stewart, *The 9.9 Percent*, chap. 7 (Simon & Schuster, 2021).

19. See Stewart, *The 9.9 Percent*, chap. 10.

20. Ibram X. Kendi, *Stamped from the Beginning: The Definitive History of Racist Ideas in America* (Bold Type, 2016), p. 80.

21. In their spirited and often insightful critiques of the 1619 Project, writers for some socialist websites made this and other points; I have lost the citation.

22. Theodor Adorno and Max Horkheimer, *The Dialectic of Enlightenment* (Seabury, 1944, 1972), p. 3.

23. I argue in *Nature's God* that the Epicurean philosophy in particular acted as an alien force in early modern Europe, and that the encounter with native peoples and the experience of life in the New World served to amplify this intellectual shock from outside.

24. Hegel, for example, wrote: "The negro exhibits the natural man in his completely wild and untamed state"; and "Africa is no part of world history."

25. See Sean Wilentz, *No Property in Man* (Harvard University Press, 2018).

26. Melvin Rogers uses this quote and makes a similar point. "Democracy Is a Habit," *Boston Review*, July 15, 2018.

27. Refounders not covered in this book but deserving of inclusion are the leaders of Radical Reconstruction such as Thaddeus Stevens and Charles Sumner; leaders of the women's rights struggle such as Elizabeth Cady Stanton; and the many Black political leaders who emerged for a moment at the start of Reconstruction.

INDEX

abolitionism
American Revolution and, 74, 165,
175–76
Black abolitionists, 98–99, 166,
169–70, 248, 252
Bleeding Kansas and, 171, 172–73,
174
colonization movement, 115, 116
disenthrallment and, xix, 302–3
Frederick Douglass's discovery of,
7–8
economic critique of slavery,
180–81, 182–84, 185–88
1850s comprehensive movement,
174–75, 192
Enlightenment and, 316–17
European radical immigrants and,
138, 139, 142, 143–44, 149
European revolutions of 1848 and,
132–33
evangelical wing of, 113–17
as failed revolution, 45, 311, 313
Fugitive Slave Act and, 162, 167–68,
169, 172, 185
Garrisonian moral-suasion school,
111, 142, 160, 173, 197,
252
global nature of, 74–75
Harpers Ferry Raid and, 289
Herndon's discovery of, 28–29,
331n52
labor and, 113, 247–50
lecture circuit and, 181–82

Lincoln senatorial campaign (1858)
and, 270
Lincoln's support for, 28, 194, 218
Lovejoy murder, 26–28, 331n52
middle-class nature of, 248
new wave of (1830s), 76–78
Theodore Parker's impact on,
106–8, 109, 110, 295
racism and, 168–70, 312
schisms within, 110, 111–12,
113–14, 173, 197, 251, 252
as second founding, xx–xxi, 319–20
Thirteenth Amendment and, 305
vigilantism against slavecatchers
and, 162–66, 169
violent protests against, 17, 103, 122
See also abolitionist freethinking;
antislavery ideologies; Brown,
John; violent resistance
abolitionist freethinking
John Brown and, 159
concentration of wealth and, xix
counterrevolutionary attacks on,
111, 118–19, 122
Frederick Douglass and, 104–5, 112
postwar reimagining of, 307–8
as rejection of Christianity, 104–5,
108–9, 113, 341n24
Gerrit Smith and, 110–11, 341n24
transcendentalism and, 105–6
28th Congregational Society and,
105–6, 163, 174, 248, 265, 275
See also Parker, Theodore

proslavery ideologies and, xx,
42–43, 54–55, 58–60
southern Christian unity and, 94–95
See also proslavery ideologies
Cousins, Victor, 12, 30
Covey, Edward, 153–55, 156–57, 197,
218, 344n1
Craft, William and Ellen, 162–66, 172,
185, 248, 273
Cuba, 46

Dabney, Robert Lewis, 78, 310,
356n11
Dall, Caroline Healey, 107
Davis, David, 35
Davis, Jefferson, 65, 88, 249, 302
Declaration of Independence, xx, 44,
199, 256
deism, 15, 33, 49, 69, 207, 219,
330n24
democracy
counterrevolution and, 120–21
evangelical surge and, 68, 69, 120,
121, 335n7
Lincoln's House Divided speech on,
265–69, 270, 293
Theodore Parker on, 189–90,
266–67, 353n10
d'Holbach, Baron (Paul Henri Thiry),
19, 32–33
Dialectic of Enlightenment (Horkheimer
and Adorno), 315–16
Diderot, Denis, 18, 19, 317
*Discourse of Matters Pertaining to Reli-
gion* (Parker), 16
Domschke, Bernhard, 140
Donald, David Herbert, 331n52
double consciousness, 246
Douglas, Stephen, 140, 216, 257, 269,
270
Douglass, Frederick
abolitionist schisms and, 111–12

American Revolution and, 175–76
anti-abolitionist violence and, 122
on antislavery theology, 98, 119
Ottilie Assing and, 145, 146–49,
153, 276–77, 284, 292
on biblical arguments, 82, 86–87,
88–89
Black soldiers and, 284, 297,
299–300, 309
childhood of, 241–42
on Christian enslavers, xvii, 5, 6
on Civil War as slave insurrection,
297–98
on counterrevolution, 55
Covey story and, 153–55, 156–57,
161, 197, 218, 344n1
William and Ellen Craft and, 162,
163
discovery of abolitionism, 7–8
on domestic slave trade, 41
on education, 254
Emancipation Proclamation and,
301, 311
enslavers of, 3–4, 5–6, 153–54,
344n1
European radical immigrants and,
144
European revolutions of 1848 and,
132
on evangelical abolitionism, 117
on false consciousness, 225–26, 245
Feuerbach and, ix–xi, 208, 276–77,
278, 279–80, 281, 284
on founders, 43
on freedom of speech, 122–23
freethinking and, xx, 104–5, 112
Haitian Revolution and, 148
hiring out and, 223–24, 225–26,
349n1
historical inattention to, 309, 355n8
humanism and, 281–83, 309
on Alexander von Humboldt, 141